THE OPTIMIST

Laurence Shorter worked in the business world for a decade before making the move into writing and comedy in 2001. Since then he has done a one-man show at the Edinburgh Festival, written for the BBC, Channel 4, the *Independent*, *Observer* and opendemocracy.net, and toured some of the capital's finest pubs as a comedy dancer. With his focus on the world of therapy and spiritual development he is taken seriously by a growing number of cultural commentators, including his father, his father's girlfriend and their brain damaged cat. Laurence was born in New York and raised in Edinburgh. Today he lives in South London, though he was recently seen trying to escape on a small bicycle.

THE OPTIMIST

One Man's Search for the
Brighter Side of Life

Laurence Shorter

Doubleday Canada

Doubleday Canada and colophon are trademarks

Library and Archives of Canada Cataloguing in Publication has been applied for

ISBN: 978-0-385-66452-3

For permissions acknowledgements please see p. 329.

Printed and bound in the USA

Published in Canada by Doubleday Canada,
a division of Random House of Canada Limited

Visit Random House of Canada Limited's website: www.randomhouse.ca

10 9 8 7 6 5 4 3 2 1

'I mean,' said Don Quixote, 'that if thou returnest with all speed imaginable from the place wither I design to send thee, my pain will soon be at an end, and my glory begin.'

Cervantes, *Don Quixote*

Preface

Summer, 2006.

I was still in bed.

Sunlight beamed through the curtains, flickering as a neighbour's car pulled out of the drive. I looked at the humps of my arms under the covers. They felt lethargic and heavy. A car revved up outside. I pictured the BMWs and Mercs along the street, beaded with dew, ready to be driven to their places of work by people who leapt out of bed every morning. How did they do it? I stared hopelessly at the ceiling.

What was wrong with me?

I switched the radio on, let my head sink to the pillow, and waited for the reassuring voices on the morning news. There was a scientist talking about avian flu and how it was going to kill a hundred million people. An activist came on to explain that the polar ice cap was melting and was now so thin that in places you could use it quite effectively as a substitute for tracing paper.

I levered myself up and glared at the stereo. For years the calm and measured voices on the BBC had been my daily comfort. But this was quite the opposite of reassuring. What was happening?

A minister of the government started talking about terrorism. I leant over. For the first time in my life, mid-sentence, I switched off the *Today* programme. Good God, I thought, is this why I'm still in bed? Something was moving in the toils of my brain.

I put on my dressing gown and walked to the kitchen. My father was eating toast, his face a mask of concentration.

'Dad!' I said.

'Shh . . .' He nodded at the radio. I pivoted and left the room. On the sofa there were recent copies of the *Independent*. The headlines jumped out at me – like a short, aggressive man with panicky arms:

NO ONE IS IMMUNE FROM THE EFFECTS OF GLOBAL WARMING . . . AFRICA IS FACING THE GREATEST CATASTROPHE IN HUMAN HISTORY . . . A SPECTRE IS HAUNTING EUROPE – THE SPECTRE OF AN ACUTE, CIVILISATION-CHANGING ENERGY CRISIS . . .

Underneath was a picture of a wildly burning rainforest. I felt my eyes retreating fearfully into their sockets. On the dresser was a pile of newspapers going back for months. I was drawn towards it, as if by gravity.

DRAMATICALLY SPIRALLING COSTS . . .
THREAT TO MILLIONS . . .
THE SPIRALLING COST OF OIL . . .
THE SPIRALLING COST OF BASIC FOODS . . .

The papers slipped from my hands. Lord have mercy, I mumbled. What's a spiralling cost? Is it worse than a rising cost? I felt a weakness in my knees, a reflex of guilt and fear I recognised from the last hundred times I had read the papers. Why hadn't I noticed it before? The papers, the BBC . . .

I stumbled away.

Was that the cause of my lethargy? This strange cloud of apathy hanging over me? What kind of horror story were they peddling to us? I turned to look at the sun shining on our terrace. This air of gloom, this lack of motivation: *it was nothing to do with me.*

It was the news!

The BBC – which we invited into our house every morning like an honoured guest – was piping depression and anxiety straight into my bedroom. The bulletins, the interviews, the tone of grim urgency: their voice was pervasive, enslaving. I felt as if I had stuck my head in a motorcycle helmet twenty years ago and I had forgotten to take it off. No wonder I couldn't find the right career. What was the point of getting up at all, when the future looked so bad? I might be annihilated at any moment.

I lay back down on my bed, my mind racing.

Up until now the bad news had left me unscathed. I was an optimist, and I was proud of my ability to ignore events and carry on as if everything were fine. That was the privilege of optimism. Deep down, if you're an optimist, you know that everything is going to be OK. You don't know why – you just know. It's like your little secret.

But recently something had started to shift, and I was beginning to lose my nerve. It had started gradually. First there was Hurricane Katrina and the Asian tsunami. Then suicide bombers struck London. Within months a new type of flu with 70 per cent mortality rates had crossed over from chickens to human beings. Oil prices went through the roof. Food became scarce. Images of African poverty were punctuated by depressing stories from Iraq and Palestine, while everyone lived in unspoken fear that terrorists might one day unleash nuclear bombs they'd bought in car parks from Russians in macs.

It was starting to get under my skin. Even if these things were wildly exaggerated by the media, I was beginning to realise that – optimistic as I was – the background noise of gloom and catastrophe was slowly wearing me down, like the sound of an extractor fan that you don't notice until it gets switched off, and then you wonder how you survived all that time without going mad.

Of course, I should have seen it coming. Ever since the outbreak of war in Iraq I had noticed optimism coming under attack. Any time I got too cheerful at a party or a dinner I would find myself ambushed and humiliated by some clever pessimist – usually in front of beautiful women. Whenever I claimed that everything was going to be OK, one of these miseries would come up with some reason why it wasn't. What's more, they had always read more books than me, and they had volumes of facts and statistics about World Bank lending, Third World exploitation or anything else that supported their self-righteous belief that everything was terrible. And if you claimed that it wasn't so bad they would always ask you why? – as if we need *reasons* to feel OK. And then they would give you that sardonic look that only pessimists can – as if to say, do you know how *uncool* it is to be cheerful?

Yes, in a way that I found deeply disturbing, it was widely considered *silly* to be an optimist and *cool* to be a pessimist. Pessimists are cynical about everything and, for reasons I still hadn't fathomed, that was considered a very attractive quality in a person. Pessimists had all the great role models – Leonard Cohen and Woody Allen, Humphrey

Bogart and Marlon Brando. The only optimist icon I could think of was Pollyanna – a thirteen-year-old girl with freckles and a ponytail. Who would want to identify with Pollyanna, outside a certain very specific demographic group?

Not only was I losing the debate, I was beginning to feel like a very dull person.

Yet somehow, I knew there was another way. I knew that, somewhere out there, there were optimists who could back me up – optimists with more experience than me, and a lot more facts. Optimists who were suave and impressive, and didn't have freckles. I knew these people existed. I had seen them on TV, I had heard them on the radio – if only I could remember when. They were tucked away, unnoticed, content to get on with their lives. These optimists were happy – happy and full of energy. That's what I liked about them. They jumped straight out of bed every morning and did world-changing things. Or just surfed and climbed mountains and base-jumped off Hawaiian clifftops and left it at that. They didn't care about the news. They had nothing to prove. They were ideal human beings.

As I lay there that summer morning, my face planted deep in the pillow, I suddenly realised what was wrong with my life. It wasn't just the news. It was me. I needed some of that *je ne sais quoi*, that optimist energy. Sure, I was an optimist – but I was a limp, unconvinced version of the species. I lived in comfort, surrounded by friends and family in one of the great cities of the world, and yet there was something amiss, something not yet . . . as it should be. I didn't have faith; I didn't have the *Jump out of Bed Factor*.

And if there was one thing I needed, it was the *JBF*. Other people had it, why not me? After all, I was in my thirties and still living with my father. I hadn't had a job in five years, and my entire life revolved around my Samsung laptop – a laptop with a broken lid. True, I had done a few interesting things – raising millions for a website that didn't work, closing it down it and relaunching myself as a comedy dancer in an underground pub – but that didn't change the basic facts: I had no real career, my life was a mess, and the world was falling apart before I even had a chance to buy a car – not to mention getting married, having kids, and all those other things you want to get done, as a bare minimum, before the world ends.

But now I was starting to understand *why*. As I lay there, drifting past 9.30 a.m. like a boat cut loose from its mooring, I watched the clouds parting and joining in the sky. Sunlight filled my room, and I felt the rush of a premonition. Soon I would be leaving this place.

I sat up. These optimists – I needed to meet them. I needed to track down these elusive people and speak to them, reveal their secrets to the world. I'd write a book. It would be enormous. The editor of the *Independent* would resign in shame. And the world would fall at my feet. After all, optimism wasn't exactly a minority interest. My audience was a natural one – the entire human race.

I pulled my laptop into bed and typed the word 'pessimism' into Google. My intuition had been correct. Pessimism was a global affliction. I found an NBC poll which showed that 79 per cent of Americans thought they were heading for a crisis:

And among those who believe that the nation is headed on the wrong track, a whopping 81 per cent believe it's part of a longer-term decline and that things won't get better for some time.

Good, I thought. It was a problem that spanned the solar system. And in Britain . . .

> A YouGov survey found world events left people feeling powerless (56 per cent), angry (50 per cent), anxious (35 per cent) and depressed (26 per cent).

Life had finally given me a mission. I had to help these people. I had to change the way they thought about the world.

The task began to take shape in my mind: I would track down the world's optimists and ask them the truth. I would print the interviews in a book. Together we would defeat the spectre of pessimism once and for all, and prove that everything was OK.

I threw off my bedclothes. I would never have to lose another argument in my life – starting right here at home.

My father was such a committed pessimist he listened to four different news programmes every morning, in three different languages, to make sure he didn't accidentally slip into feeling good. As long as he listened to all those bulletins, I realised, he was sure to have something to feel worried about. 'History is an endless cycle of human idiocy,' he once told me. 'Human beings are horrendously unsuited to the modern world they've created. I don't see how we can survive. We'll be lucky to make it to the end of the century.'

Dad was the perfect foil, the ultimate challenge. If I could convert him, I could convert anyone. Maybe then the world would listen, instead of just sniggering rudely behind its hand.

I skipped into the living room. The *Today* programme was over, leaving my dad with no further bad news until one o'clock. He stared morosely into the garden.

'Dad!' I said. 'I'm going to write a book. I'm going to interview the world's leading optimists.'

'Optimists,' said my father. 'Well.' He mused for a moment. 'What about Bill Clinton?'

My father had been talking about Clinton ever since they stood next to each other in a gents' toilet in Tokyo, 1993 – alongside John Major and the German Premier Helmut Kohl. The President hadn't even bothered to say hello. Yet, for me, that was the moment that Clinton became a household god.

'I saw him speak that afternoon,' reminisced Dad, 'and I was dazzled by his fluency, his grasp of everything. He didn't miss a beat. He was able to deal with world leaders one minute and then turn his attention to minor domestic issues the next. It was his mastery that did it. I was dazzled. He was just brilliant. And personable too.' He smiled and shook his head. 'One very, very smart guy.'

I listened silently. I would do anything for a report card like that.

'I'll meet him,' I resolved.

'Oh yes?' said my dad. 'Good luck to you!'

Yes, I thought, if I pulled that off, my mission would be complete. Life would be perfect. I would no longer need to meet optimists, I would actually become one, the ultimate one perhaps. Soon I would be giving lectures at international conferences. Soon I would take my place among the great and the good. Soon, all the things I had been waiting for, the girl, the career, the life that had been eluding me . . . it would all click into place.

I sat down, propped my laptop against a stack of books and sketched out my first graph. If I succeeded in these outlandish goals, I would actually prove the first Law of Optimism: that optimism works.

FIRST LAW OF OPTIMISM

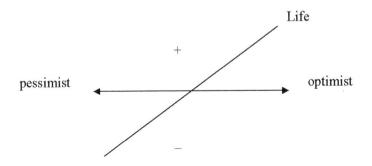

The more optimistic you are, the better life gets.

True, it was a bit simplistic, but it was a start. If I was going to change the world I would have to have some theories. The people would want some theories.

It was midday by the time I walked out of the house. I didn't know where I was going, but I was ready. I was glad and, for the first time in weeks, I felt full of optimism.

Hero

1

*Confidence is the feeling you have
before you understand the situation.*

Anonymous

The girl put a hand on her cheek. 'What does that mean?'
'It means *optimism*,' I said. 'It's as simple as that.'
She gazed at me thoughtfully.
'People have had enough. They've had enough of this
cloud of pessimism. It's a basic human right to feel positive about the future, to jump out of bed feeling good. We
want to be optimistic. We need it!' I banged the table with
my palm.

I now had the attention of the entire table. It had been
two weeks since I had started work on the project. Since
then I had been testing my idea out on every person I met,
to assess whether it was really a viable notion for the launch
of my literary career. Here I was, at a dinner party in
Islington, home of London's left-wing intelligentsia, and
to my amazement, it was judged to be a thoroughly
wonderful idea. *Open Sesame!* I had faced my first audience of potential pessimists, and the field had been won
without a fight.

'I think you might be onto something,' said my host,
pouring me a drink.

I smiled modestly. 'I'm going to write a book and start a website. I'm going to speak to experts, politicians, world leaders. I'm going to make optimism respectable again. Everything is going to be OK.'

The girl looked at me gratefully. I pictured myself at the plenary of the United Nations in New York, addressing the assembled leaders of the world. 'Optimism!' I would declare. 'We need more optimism!'

'But . . . how?' she asked. 'How is it going to be OK?' Suddenly her eyes welled with tears. The pessimists had obviously shaken her up – pessimists who were masquerading as 'realists'. I hesitated. No one had asked me for *reasons* before. 'What about the Shropshire hill farmers?' she sobbed. 'They're being destroyed by climate change. And the swallows! Are you going to write about them?'

The room went quiet. I coughed and looked down at my drink. I wasn't even sure what a swallow looked like. I gave her a meaningful look. 'Don't worry,' I said. 'Everything's going to be all right.'

The girl nodded and the conversation moved on, but I fell silent. The pessimists were a terrible and inscrutable enemy. Even though we lived in the most wonderful and fortunate period of human history, there were still people out there addicted to negativity, who made it their task to spread fear and anxiety. Angry, stupid people. People with fewer A levels than me. There was more to this than I had thought: it wasn't enough just to track down role models of optimism. Soon the whole world would be coming to me for answers. I couldn't just brush them off with vague, positive anecdotes. I had to find *answers*.

And so it was, one unnaturally warm afternoon in October, that I walked down to the British Library and started reading about freak weather, carbon dioxide emissions and the heat-death of the universe. Of course, I could have chosen from any number of pessimistic subjects – swallows, premature balding or the fundamental meaninglessness of life, a topic which had been bothering me ever since I saw the film *Bambi*. But climate change seemed like a natural place to start. After all, this was the hottest year since 1632. Everyone seemed to be worried about it.

'The entire capitalist system is going to collapse,' my father had said that morning. 'We're going to run out of water, and drown, at the same time.'

'My nail varnish keeps melting,' added Annie, our lodger.

Soon I was at a desk, surrounded by pillars of books. Somewhere in this place, I told myself, there must be *someone* who feels good about the future. I could feel the sweat forming on my temples. It was vital that I prove these people wrong before the pessimists claimed any more victims.

I trawled through pages of Greenpeace documents. I stared at transcripts from the World Economic Forum. I lost myself in bulletin boards on which maniacs – apparently Americans – exchanged messages of such demented panic that I wondered if the world had gone mad. Shockingly, even the 'experts' seemed to agree. Climate change was causing a slow but inevitable catastrophe. The polar ice caps were melting and we had reached the point of no return. Fifty species of beetle were extinct.

I clutched my side and slipped out of the reading room.

'I don't know if I can do this,' I confided in my father. 'I'm afraid the pessimists might be right.'

He snorted. 'Of course they're right!'

I went back to the library. Spread out on my desk were two sheets of paper – the first draft of my plans for the book that would save the world. At the bottom I had written a list:

THINGS WE FEEL REALLY DEPRESSED ABOUT

global warming
species death
ice caps
oil running out
cancer
the decline of society into fragmentary sub-cultures
    without any common sense of community
crackheads
criminals
the limits of economic expansion
call centres
supermarkets
plastic bags
the war on terror
Guantanamo Bay
Iraq
food poisoning
the death of infants
poverty
running out of stuff
shopping malls
bling
Victoria Beckham
most other people
genetic engineering
clones
the falling standard of education
overpopulation
China
the oppression of the free people of Tibet
Robert Mugabe
journalists

Russians
nuclear proliferation
the absence of any sort of tangible, interventionist
    deity
Africa
food prices
religious fundamentalists
natural disasters
- hurricanes
- earthquakes
- tsunamis
- super-volcanoes
- super-viruses
aliens
the basic unfairness of life
public transport
the decline of English grammar
illness
old age
war

I surveyed the list, anxiously. It was meant to be disappearing. After a week in the British Library, though, it was actually getting longer. Much longer. It had all seemed so simple at the start: remind people to be positive, and find impressive optimists who agreed with me. But ever since that fateful conversation in Islington – with the girl who wanted *reasons* – I had also taken on the task of finding answers for all of the world's problems. Because she was right: it was these 'problems', I realised, that stood between the world and full-blown optimism.

I watched a stray hair detach itself from my cranium and float earthwards towards the desk. The stress was starting to take its toll.

Seeking refuge in the library café I bumped into a friend. 'What are you doing here?' he asked. 'I thought you were starting a school for mime artists.'

'That was last year,' I said.

I told him about my project and a religious light shone in his eyes. 'You should meet my aunt. She's been disabled for thirty years but she still goes mountain climbing and teaches at a day-care centre for homeless mothers. She'd be a great person to meet!'

'Sure,' I said, politely. 'Give me her email and I'll get in touch.'

Jasper frowned. 'She doesn't have email. She's eighty-five years old.'

The truth is I wasn't interested in Jasper's aunt, and I wasn't interested in other tales of human achievement either. By this time I was only interested in one thing – finding answers for my list of THINGS WE FEEL REALLY DEPRESSED ABOUT.

And now that I understood the scale of the global warming problem I was beginning to panic. How does it help me if a single mother works sixteen hours a day to support a family, then trains to win the triathlon every night? It doesn't. Call me a coward, but I want to know that someone is looking after the melting ice cap.

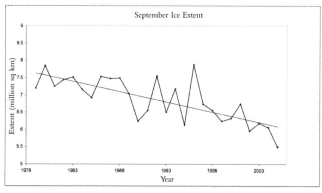

Source: National Snow and Ice Data Center

Call me naïve, but when I read that

> Scientists calculate the current rate of shrinkage at 8
> per cent per decade; at this rate there may be no ice
> at all during the summer of 2060. (BBC News Online)

I want someone to tell me that everything is going to be OK.

Sure, maybe these statistics were lies and exaggerations, but if so I needed someone to prove it to me. That's why I fell under the influence of the 'global warming deniers'.

It was day four when I finally stumbled on a reference to this tiny group of optimists. As I read the internet article about these so-called enemies of the environment I felt a slow dawning of relief. Bjorn Lomborg was a Danish statistics professor who claimed, ambitiously, that things weren't as bad as everyone thought. He was the leader of a group of scientists – notorious and vilified – who dared to offer a minority report against the consensus that the world was going to end. His 2001 book *The Skeptical Environmentalist* ignited an international controversy which had been raging ever since. In it, he claimed, quite simply, that the scientific community had got its statistics wrong. In fact, there wasn't any problem after all – or rather, it was a completely different problem from the one we thought we had.

This got me hooked. So far, all the other climate change experts I had come across were running around panicking – in public. They weren't doing anything to make me feel better. But these guys were different.

> We take a far more optimistic view of Mankind's
> ability to learn, adapt and find solutions to the
> problem. (*The Copenhagen Consensus*, 2004)

The deniers, as they were known to their enemies, the environmentalists, claimed that the problem of global warming was exaggerated – like almost all world problems.

> Overall, the benefits of global warming are likely to outweigh the damage until the rise is greater than 2.5°C, and even then the net damage would be far smaller than originally thought.

According to these sceptics, the main aim of most environmental groups was to terrify us into slowing down economic growth. And, in their view, slowing down economic growth would be the ultimate disaster. Instead, these sober academics argued, we should use 'cost-benefit' analysis to figure out the best solution, instead of getting emotional and worrying about trees and other silly things.

> The highly expensive, social engineering approach to reducing emissions is not justified!

Their views were clearly controversial. But what a relief it was to learn that there was hope; that the men in coats hadn't yet agreed that we were going to fry to death. On balance, I'd be happy to give them the benefit of the doubt. Especially Bjorn Lomborg.

The best thing about Lomborg was his contradictory personality: his youth, his looks, his blow-dried hair. It was impossible for the pessimists simply to pigeon-hole him as a fan of George Bush or a stooge of the military-industrial complex. He was openly gay. He drank herbal tea. He's not the sort of person you would expect to ignore the environment. It was all so clever. With his cunning semiotic camouflage, Lomborg managed to confuse everyone, even his own supporters. Thus he pulled off the feat of sounding impressively rational and absurdly positive at the same time. Like me, he couldn't bear unexamined pessimism. Like me, he was on a crusade against negativity. He kept saying things like

> The world is not without problems, but on almost all accounts things are going better and they are likely to continue to do so in the future.

It wasn't only global warming. Bjorn's reassuring statements covered everything from deforestation to seagulls.

> Though the Exxon Valdez oil spill killed 250,000 birds, this is roughly equivalent to the number of birds that die in one day from colliding with plate glass in the USA or two days' death toll from domestic cats in Britain.

He was clearly a sensible man. But when I wrote to Lomborg he answered within hours:

> Dear Laurence,
>
> Unfortunately, I am very busy and would have to decline on that account alone. Moreover, I don't see myself as an optimist, but rather as a realist.

I read the email with a sinking heart. What did he mean, he was a *realist*? Was optimism something to be ashamed of, like voting Tory or being a communist? What to do now? I had been rejected by the world's leading statistically educated optimist, and I still didn't have anything convincing to say about swallows. Not only that, but my hero wouldn't even admit that he was one of us.

Maybe Lomborg was the wrong person after all. The professor had made no effort whatsoever to recognise the importance of my work. Besides, he was becoming less and less fashionable. The daily flow of bad news about the environment had not slowed down; in fact, quite the opposite. Lomborg wrote his book back in 2001. Surely his views were out of date now? Hurricane Katrina had since destroyed New Orleans and the melting ice caps were dominating the headlines. The Dane's bland reassurances were beginning to seem like yesterday's news. I sent him another email.

What do you make of the recent hurricanes?

He didn't reply.

It looked like the end between me and the professor, and I didn't know what to do. If I screwed up the environment piece, the project was dead – and Lomborg was the only global warming optimist worth knowing. My room darkened. I gazed at the fading twilight on my desk. Maybe I wouldn't be able to persuade *anyone* to meet me. Maybe it was time to give up. For the first time in a fortnight I asked myself whether my task wasn't bigger than I had originally expected. Maybe it wasn't too late to change the subject of the book altogether.

The telephone rang.

'Feeling optimistic?' asked Xanthe.

'Who told you?'

'You told me, Laurence. Yesterday.'

Xanthe was a friend of mine. But then, I had a lot of friends. I couldn't be expected to remember every conversation I had with all of them.

'I want everyone to feel included,' I explained.

'Then tell me,' said Xanthe, 'what are we going to do about climate change?'

I scanned the pile of papers in front of me.

'Listen,' I replied firmly, 'everything is going to be OK.'

'How do you know?'

'I *know*,' I said, 'I just know.'

I glanced down at my list of THINGS WE FEEL REALLY DEPRESSED ABOUT.

'Have you heard of Tim Smit?' she asked.

'Nope.'

'He built the Eden Project.'

The Eden Project.

'It's one of the wonders of the world,' she explained. 'It's a huge dome in Cornwall with a tropical jungle and its own weather system. It's an educational centre, and an experiment in sustainability.'

'Sustainability!' I felt a flash of irritation. 'I'm looking for visionaries. Businessmen. World leaders. Not *environmentalists*.' I delivered the word carefully, like a piece of litter you don't want to touch.

'Tim's a revolutionary. He's trying to change the way we think. There's something very special about this guy,' she added. 'Believe me.'

'Does he know Bill Clinton?' I asked.

'I don't know,' she said. 'Just switch on the radio. He's about to give an interview.'

I sighed and turned on the radio. Glancing at my desk, which was wedged in a corner of my father's spare room, I lay on my bed and closed my eyes.

The programme had already begun.

Tim Smit was talking about his career. How he quit the music industry and ran away to Cornwall. How he stumbled on a walled garden and made it into a famous tourist attraction. How he conceived a lunatic plan to build a hi-tech 'biome' in an abandoned mine, to change the way that people think about the environment. I listened carefully. His voice was dry, crisp, a little tense. It was an interesting voice, a voice I liked. Xanthe was right. Tim was no pansy, no dolphin-loving fool – he was an optimist, a cool optimist. 'I make no apology for being optimistic about the future,' he said. 'I am.' He laughed contemptuously. 'I can't think of *any problem* that humans can't deal with. Not one. The world may be scary but we can deal with it. The future is a very hopeful place.'

I felt the hairs on my neck standing up. Tim qualified. He definitely qualified. The man was a visionary. And he smoked Cohibas. He was the Che Guevara of shrubbery.

We had a lot to talk about.

It was a cold autumn morning when I finally checked in for my flight to Newquay, clutching my dictaphone and a bundle of printouts. All I had was a sports jacket and a briefcase. I felt a thrill of excitement. The mental health of five billion people depended on the success of my mission. It was unnaturally early, but I was on my way to meet one of the country's leading optimists.

I sat in the departure lounge, chuckling as I read a *Daily Mail* feature on Martin Rees, the 'Astronomer Royal'.

Martin Rees gives no better than 50/50 odds that humanity will survive until New Year's Day, 2100, citing nuclear war, terrorism, environmental catastrophe and nanomachines. He also offers a £1,000 bet that a bioterrorism incident will kill at least a million people by 2020.

Hah! I would deal with Rees next week. For the moment, nothing was going to get me down. I was still buoyed up by Che's ultra-positive response:

Dear Laurence

An admirable quest. Get in touch when you are ready.

Warmest regards

Tim

I pictured the two of us talking late into the night, drinking whisky and scheming how to make my idea a reality. Maybe he would offer to join the project. Or maybe he would give me a cigar and invite me to come and work for him. I would have to consider it seriously. Men like Tim and I weren't born every day.

Standing in the foyer of the Eden Project, I gazed around and asked a red-jacket for directions. Far below, through a plate-glass window, I made out the shapes of three giant domes, like the eggs of a high-tech Godzilla. The guide smiled and waved me on as if her job of punching tickets were the most fulfilling career that could be dreamed up by mankind.

Che was obviously doing something right.

I walked amongst the tourists, blending in. The 'Tropical Zone' was a full-size jungle surrounded by a monumental plastic dome, built from hundreds of hexagons. Waves of warm dew smothered my face as I gazed up at the distant, mist-shrouded ceiling. On my way out I passed a group of staff. They were gossiping about Smit. My ears perked up. Apparently Tim was so well-respected, politicians of every party came down here to pay homage and get their Green credentials. David Cameron, the Tory leader, had visited him that very morning for his blessing. Prince Charles had been a couple of weeks before.

I felt light-headed, weightless. Compared to all this I was nothing. All I had was an idea, an unformed piece of fluff. I clutched my briefcase in my hand.

Four hours passed, then five. Dusk came. Our meeting had been put back to the end of the day, at six o'clock – but I had left myself some extra time, just to be safe. Finally the secretary called. It was dark. I walked up to the office – a secret location at the top of the quarry. No doubt, I told myself, Tim had put me at the end of his schedule so we could relax and kick back over a long, well-earned drink. Then we could chew things over, man to man. But now I was starting to wonder. There was a desolate feeling in the reception area. Where had everyone gone? I sat in the abandoned office canteen, fiddling with my dictaphone. Would anyone notice if I simply vanished? The secretary appeared and led me into his office.

'Hey!' said Tim. 'What's up?'

I beamed at him and offered my hand. My first optimist! All was forgiven. With his wild hair and pin-stripe suit Tim looked like a castaway from the 1970s.

He smiled and scratched his head. 'So . . . what can I do for you?'

I hesitated. 'I'm Laurence Shorter, the optimist.'

'The optimist! Of course.' He stared at me blankly. 'It's been a long day.' He waved me to a seat near the door. Geometrically, it was probably the lowest point in the room.

'I have to sit here,' he said, 'for my back.' Tim returned to his desk – fifteen feet away – and relaxed into his swivel chair. I nodded mutely as he produced a Havana. 'You don't mind . . .' he muttered.

I waited for him to offer me one but he just sat there staring at me, lighting up, waiting for my pitch. 'Optimism is important,' I started. 'It's . . .'

'Hmm . . . ?' he said absently.

'These are difficult times,' I said, reading from my notes. 'We're flooded by bad news every day and it affects us in a very negative way. It's making us all into pessimists.' I looked at him. My throat had dried up. I felt like a villager who had come to ask the chief for a favour. My sofa, though apparently relaxed, was pinning me against the wall in a low-rank slouch.

'That's why I'm writing this book,' I said, trying to sound intelligent and impressive. 'That's why I'm talking to you. It's time for us to feel better about the future.'

Tim thought for a moment and chewed slowly on his Robusto.

'I think that's bullshit,' he said, looking calmly at his fingers. 'People aren't really pessimistic. Most people couldn't give a damn about global warming. They're more worried about David Beckham's haircut, or . . . who's shagging who.'

He gazed appreciatively at his cigar. 'I mean, I'm not saying your idea is pointless, Laurence. I think it's . . .' He tailed off. 'Who else are you meeting?'

I thought quickly. 'The Pope . . . Bill Clinton. That sort of thing.'

'Nelson Mandela's an optimist,' he said. 'What about Desmond Tutu?'

I shook my head. 'You can't say people aren't pessimistic, Tim. Last week the Arctic Climate Commission reported that the ice cap is thinner than ever. If it melts any more we're going to reach a "point of no return", and then . . .'

I left an ominous silence. A plume of smoke obscured Tim's warlike face.

'You misunderstand me, Laurence. I'm not saying there's nothing to worry about. I'm saying that most people can't see further than their noses, that's all. People aren't good at thinking long-term.'

' . . . If you're saying that we should just let it melt . . .'

'It's not so clear-cut. For example, some people say that if we slow down air travel, global warming might actually get *worse* because of the mirroring effect of the particulates in the air.'

'But wait a second . . .' I wasn't here to defend a pessimistic outlook, quite the opposite, but at least we had to agree that there was something to be pessimistic about. I pulled a printout from my bag. 'Look . . .'

The science is now unequivocal! We need a 90 per cent cut in carbon emissions by 2030!

'What about that?' I said. 'That was written by a *journalist*.'

By 2030 . . . carbon emissions in the atmosphere reach 430 parts per million, and that is the point at which most of the world's major ecosystems go into positive feedback. The biosphere becomes a net source of carbon dioxide, and then the game is out of our hands.

'Positive feedback!' I repeated.

'Yeah,' said Tim, shaking his head. 'You see, that doesn't worry me. Global warming is just a side issue. It's a distraction. The real battle is for our *souls*.' He released a giant cloud of smoke. 'The real battle is about *meaning*.'

I listened, baffled. 'Everyone is searching for meaning, Laurence, whether they realise it or not. You've got to understand that the biggest problems are in our heads. Look at all the disasters that were supposed to wipe us out! SARS, mad cow disease, bird flu. None of them was as bad as they expected. If you think about the tsunami last year . . . yes, it killed a lot of people. But it was only four times the *number of children who die every day* because of poverty.' He leant forward. 'Ask yourself, Laurence, who really benefits from these "crises". Who *wants* you to be frightened?'

'Friends of the Earth?'

'Don't be silly!' he said, cradling his cheroot. 'The media. It's the media who have the greatest interest in scaring you. So they exaggerate all these problems.'

'Right,' I said, grabbing the arm of the sofa. 'So these "problems" aren't real?'

'Oh, they're real all right,' said Tim, shaking me off again. 'We have all sorts of problems. But they can't be separated. They're all just symptoms of the larger predicament – our *alienation*. You have to solve that first.' He gazed into the bottom of his ashtray. 'Listen, science has become our religion. It has abolished all the stories and myths that used to make life meaningful, but we haven't replaced them with anything else. You see? It's totally empty.'

'I see,' I said. 'I see.' My eyebrows were beginning to hurt. 'And what's the connection with climate change?'

He pushed a hand through his scruffy hair. 'We're entering a new age, an age of *meaning*. People are refusing to be defined by the commodities they buy. They've had enough. Take organic food. It's finally reached a tipping point. It's about to go massive.'

I nodded meaningfully. As long as Tim thought I was

following him, I was in with a chance. I was scribbling as fast as I could. There was something Churchillian about the man. I could imagine families crowding around their transistors listening to his words, then going out to buy recycled juice.

'People are finally demanding change,' he said. 'And it's not just consumers. It's the people who work in business, too. Most of them are children of the 1960s. They're *good guys*. That's why I'm so optimistic.' He puffed on his Havana. 'Because people are basically good. They are basically decent. So there's nothing we can't figure out!'

That's nice, I thought, *I like that*. I could feel the blood working its way around my head. My arms were tingling. Maybe this was all the pessimists needed. It was beautifully vague. But there was something missing. I felt as if I had lost my footing completely and I was swimming in a sea of vagueness – Tim's vagueness, Tim's sea, Tim's total lack of interest in agreeing with me. 'But what about all the other problems?' I asked. 'What about overpopulation and water shortage and . . . and China?'

'China?' Tim interrupted. 'I'm very optimistic about China. When it comes to environmental action, they're leapfrogging us. They're extremely worried about their environment. They have to be.'

I scratched my forehead. 'Are you saying there's nothing to be afraid of?'

'Listen – *people are at their best in a crisis*. Take Eden. When we built this place we had to shift 1.8 million tonnes of soil in six months. Do you know how much earth that is?'

I shrugged.

'It's the equivalent of *8 million* workers working a full day with shovels and wheelbarrows!' He relit his cigar and stared at the burning embers. 'It's the stuff of pyramid

building! My point is this, Laurence, if human beings have
to solve a problem we can . . . and we will. That's why I'm
optimistic. Because there's nothing – and I mean *nothing* –
that we can't solve if we decide to.'

'Yes!' I cried. 'But no one realises that. We have to change
their minds!'

Tim rocked forward in his seat. 'You know what I'm
going to do next? I'm going to bring together people from
the world of business and ideas and science and arts and
I'm going to throw them in a room until they come up
with some solutions for the planet. And I'm not going to
let them out until they agree. I want Eden to be like a
United Nations for the Environment, a Foundation for
Possible Futures, a . . . a . . .' He made great shapes with his
hands. 'I'm going to construct the most important museum
on earth – it's going to be built underground and lit by
fire!'

I sank back in my chair, whole paragraphs of enthusiasm stuck somewhere in my throat. All he could talk
about was himself. *And me?* I thought. *What about me?* 'We
need to get this message out there,' I said. 'People are
afraid.'

Tim made a Napoleonic gesture with his cigar. 'People
are too afraid of death. They need a bit of fear!'

A trickle of blood found its way into my mouth. Hadn't
he just contradicted himself? It was impossible to tell. Logic
didn't seem to count for anything in Tim's world. Just pride
and manliness. He gazed down at his hand. 'A funny thing
happens,' he said, 'when you find the right work. It's as if
the energy comes out of your fingertips.'

I frowned and stared at mine. They were turning prune-
like from the effort of taking notes. If I were in Tim's shoes
things would be different – sitting at a large desk, with a
secretary and hundreds of employees, doing something

worthy and widely reported in the press. My hands would be glowing then. Things would shoot out of them, like emails and money. Life would be effortless. It would feel wonderful.

Tim's PA appeared. 'You're late,' she said.

Late?

'I'm afraid I've got to go to a party,' explained Tim, smiling apologetically.

I looked at my watch. We had been talking for twenty minutes. 'Right!' I said, trying to hide a flush of disappointment.

'Did you get what you need?' he asked, bluntly.

I looked down at my notes. To show weakness now would be fatal. 'Sure, that was absolutely perfect.' I snapped my notebook shut.

'Really, Laurence? Great!'

He jumped up, and pulled on his jacket, a kid who had just been let out of class. I sat and gazed nostalgically at his desk. Tim would need time to digest everything, that was all. And I would come back in a blaze of glory with a book deal and a Channel 4 series and a proper dictaphone. Then I would demand forty-five minutes of his time. At least.

I had one final question. 'What's your message for the little people, Tim?'

He looked down at me through his misty, wartime eyes.

'You're not little,' he murmured. 'Link up with other little people . . . then others . . . Think big. Make it happen. Anything is possible.'

When I woke the next morning I felt unsure of my success. I had a sneaking feeling Tim had given me short shrift. But he had done it so gallantly I couldn't be sure. In my tummy I had the uncertain sensation you get after being ripped off by a very expert salesman. Tim hadn't exactly endorsed my plan, but he had sent me away with a certain vague feeling of positivity.

Someone knocked on my door and dropped a newspaper on the floor. I suddenly felt very alone.

By the time I got to the airport it was late morning. Tourists sat in the departure lounge warming themselves in the autumn sun. Planes taxied slowly outside. I watched their white hulls with approval, bouncing heat onto the tarmac. Tim was wrong to dismiss the problems of the world. There really were serious crises facing us, and if people weren't pessimistic now then they would be soon. But my visit hadn't been a total waste of time. Tim had said nothing specific about the icecaps or the CO_2 quotient in the atmosphere, but his confidence had left its impression on me. Cheap flights might cause a global crisis, but it would be a crisis that we could solve together. I imagined the anarchy that would descend over South England, and the position of authority I would no doubt be forced to accept.

There's no problem we can't solve, I said to myself.

When I got back home my father was in the kitchen, pacing up and down. He was listening to the radio.

'Have you heard the news?' he said. 'Iran just pulled out of negotiations with the UN.' He turned up the volume and stared into the garden. I felt the darkness seeping into the corners of the room. *No,* I thought. I was bigger than this. I imagined Tim's hair, his shoulders. I gestured towards the cloud-streaked sky.

'There's no problem we can't solve, Dad, not if we decide to. That's . . . that's what Tim Smit says.'

'Oh, yes,' he said.

'Yes, and people are too afraid of death. They need a bit of fear!'

Dad rolled his eyes ominously. 'Is that right?'

He turned around to strain his tea.

2

*Sir, As I am only 12 years old I don't normally speak
my mind. But I have always wondered why everyone is suddenly
saying that we will all die in less than 50 years. Frankly it
worries me that everyone is so scared . . . I think that everyone
should stop worrying.*

MATHILDA SMITH, Poole, Dorset

The Times

'I'm very interested in your book,' said the writer suddenly.
My fingers stiffened around my wine glass.
'Are you . . . are you an optimist?' I asked. The whole party
was watching us now, although they were pretending not to.
Pinter leant back on his walking stick, his dark glasses mirroring
the field. 'I'm optimistic about wine!' he wheezed. I quickly
filled his glass. A wave of relief passed through the tent.

I was sitting at the birthday lunch of Pinter's wife, Lady
Antonia Fraser, in the middle of a cow field on the Dorset
coast. In front of me was a picnic table covered with sandwiches and expensive crisps. A dozen people sat around it,
drinking wine and munching prawns: children and grandchildren; cousins and step-cousins; friends and neighbours.
And me.

I had been invited to this gathering by Alastair, a local

landowner who had recently adopted his own stately home. 'Have you met my neighbour Harold Pinter?' he had asked me.

'The *writer?*'

'No,' he said. 'The car mechanic.'

I didn't know anything about Harold Pinter except that he wrote menacing plays, disliked the government, and had his own adjective, as in 'Pinteresque'. Once you have your own adjective, it's generally accepted that winning the Nobel Prize is a matter of mere formality. Whatever his views were, I figured, Harold Pinter would be an adornment to my quest, an appropriate flood mark of the rising tide in the life of Laurence.

'He's famous for his robust views,' said my friend. 'I warn you though, it can be an intimidating experience. People have been known to burst into tears.'

I winked. 'I think I can handle it.'

I found myself a place next to the famous writer, eating crabmeat sandwiches from a paper plate. Lady Antonia sat behind her sunglasses, peering over them from time to time to observe her guests and the cows which were circling our canopy. A spirit of raw nerves jangled just below the surface of the happy scene. Cousins and step-sons glanced nervously over at Pinter, as if the great writer might suddenly wave his stick and cast them into the outer darkness.

'Lovely cake,' he muttered, with a grandfatherly smile. With the manor house behind us and the dancing sea in front, Pinter looked perfectly out of place in his black clothes and smoky glasses, like an ageing gangster who has been brought to die in inappropriately pleasant surroundings. This particular mobster, I thought to myself, had renounced violence and moved away from the city only to find he still terrified the living shit out of everyone he came into contact with. When he murmured, I noticed, everybody listened – his voice was as gravelly as an estuary beach.

'I must say, this is a lovely occasion,' he rasped. I squinted for a hint of menace in his words, but whatever threat there was was hidden behind his shades. He waved an arm to indicate the meadow and the English Channel – a rural, perfectly English scene.

'And who are you?' asked Antonia, watching me from under the brim of her straw hat. I looked around. Who *was* I? I had spent most of the morning trying to convince myself that there was no difference between me and the cluster of landed gentry gathered around me. We were all human beings, after all, despite various cultural differences. What did it matter if I had never stalked deer, or run a steeple-chase, or slept with my dogs? As long as no one brought it up in conversation, or asked me where I lived.

'Are you a friend of Alastair's?' she asked.

'I'm an optimist,' I replied. 'And I'm writing a book. My argument is that we don't have enough of it in this country.'

I glanced hopefully at the playwright. I desperately wanted to interview Pinter but I was even more desperate not to be unmasked by the other guests as a townie journalist or – fate worse than death! – some kind of *Guardian*-reading liberal who agreed with his left-wing views.

My neighbour leant over: 'Whatever you do, *don't mention America.*'

Pinter looked around, as if alerted to the presence of dissent. 'Who's in this book?' he demanded hoarsely.

'Well,' I said, delighted, 'Tim Smit? He's a very interesting man, a horticulturalist and . . .' Pinter glanced away. 'I'm going to meet Bill Clinton,' I said, decisively.

'Clinton's a prick!'

I blushed and took a mouthful of crisps. Someone

tittered behind their hand. What was this – some evil spectator sport? I was considering making a break for the trees when Harold leant over and whispered loudly: 'No, really, I am very interested in your book.'

'Right . . .' I said.

'Yes, because the *spirit* remains.' He gestured at the field. 'You see it here, you see it everywhere. Life is beautiful!'

'It is,' I said.

' . . . But the world is HELL.'

'Hell?'

'The world created by men!' he exclaimed. 'Do you know how many nuclear weapons they have pointed at us right now? The so-called powers of the world?'

I bit my lip.

'It's only a matter of time,' he croaked. 'It's all unravelling!'

I took a hefty swig of wine. I had been temporarily blinded by Pinter's fame and our charming, rustic surroundings. But now that the playwright had drunk a few glasses he was starting to reveal his true colours. He was starting to remind me of my father: same age, same generation, same over-the-top pessimism. Men of the 1960s, gloomy, anti-establishment – they took genuine pleasure in predicting the doom of the human race. Not enough to declare that the ruling classes are evil, the Americans are criminals, and the whole world is ruled by a secret cabal of evil capitalists. No. The entire human project is flawed; we're awful people and we're all screwed. I groaned inwardly as Pinter started talking about the Americans. I had heard it all before.

'Mr Pinter,' I said, a flush rising to my face. 'Do you not think we're lucky to live in a country where we can say whatever we please and do whatever we want, and you can write whatever you like – without fear of persecution? . . .

Shouldn't we be grateful to the Americans for securing this
. . . this unprecedented level of freedom and security?'
   A shiver of delighted tension passed through the tent.
Pinter looked at me and smiled. 'Do you want to hear
a poem I wrote?' He nodded at my notebook. 'It's called
"Democracy".' The whole party had now turned, discreetly,
to listen in.
   'Write this down!' he ordered, pointing at my pen. I
looked around, embarrassed. The playwright lifted his big
chin.
   '*There's no escape . . .*' he barked. '*The big pricks are out . . .
They'll fuck everything in sight . . . Watch your back!*'
   He stared me in the eyes until I flinched. Then chuckled
quietly to himself.
   'Well,' I smiled, 'that's certainly optimistic.'
   'I am optimistic!' he wheezed, putting a hand on my
arm. 'I really believe that this country – even though we're
under huge pressure from the government – even here in
this lovely field – the surveillance, the censorship . . .
Nevertheless we are able to talk, you're right! But it's pre-
carious! And I think it must be finally a European force
that says to the United States . . . go and fuck yourself!'

I spent the rest of that week thinking about the challenges
of dating Scarlett Johansson. Why not? I'd already met
Harold Pinter. Despite our frank exchange of views, it was
quite possible that the writer would invite me to one of
his garden parties, and Scarlett Johansson might be there
too. It's not that I especially wanted to be around famous
people. It just felt inevitable. For example, I had no special
desire to be publicly recognised, but once I had completed

my quest to restore optimism to the world, fame might be unavoidable. I would just have to deal with it. One obvious benefit would be going to parties where I would meet Scarlett Johansson and we would have a joke over the drinks table, and I would say something witty, and we would end up going out with each other. Obviously Scarlett and I came from very different backgrounds – she was a Hollywood film star and I was an intellectual visionary – but didn't all great love affairs start like that? There was something unusual about the woman, something insightful and special. I could tell that just by looking at her. She was the sort of girl I could get along with. And when we ran into each other, Scarlett would surely fall for me, and before long I would be appearing in photos at award ceremonies, smiling in the background while she posed for the cameras – like Arthur Miller and Marilyn Monroe. Of course there would be problems to overcome. Scarlett was a professional actress. She'd be on the road all the time doing films and premiers, while I'd be having nights in with Dad or writing in my bedroom all day. We would just have to be practical about it.

I lay on my bed and stared at the cobwebs in the corner of the ceiling. Until then, I had a lot of work to do. Not only were there the forty-two remaining problems on my list to deal with (after the eight, I calculated, that Tim had sorted out) I also had to assemble my team of top optimists. In other words, like-minded men and women who were willing to stand with me against the pessimists and the threat they represented to my happiness. It wasn't just Harold Pinter and my father I was concerned about. Pinter was merely the symbol of a whole era – a reflex pessimism, a weak and pathetic response to world events – that I had resolved to rid from my generation.

But just to be sure, and to remind myself that the plague of pessimism really existed and wasn't just in my imagination, I walked into a newsagent's in Euston Station, a place I usually avoided for health reasons. That morning a massive bomb plot had been uncovered at Heathrow airport – an outrage intended to bring multiple planes out of the sky. As expected, the papers were covered with photos of the incident. Avoiding direct line of sight with the newspapers, I watched the commuters as they browsed the headlines, their faces creased with gloom and anxiety. I smiled at a woman as she purchased a copy of *The Times*. So much for Tim's view that 'people aren't really pessimistic'! *Yes*, I thought, *these are my people, and my mission is to help them.* They are innocent Londoners and their lives are being destroyed by pessimism.

As if to supply me with immediate encouragement the BBC website popped up the following article:

> Wars around the world are both less frequent and less deadly since the end of the Cold War, a new report claims.
>
> The Human Security Report found a decline in every form of political violence except terrorism since 1992 . . . the number of armed conflicts had fallen by more than 40 per cent in the past 13 years, while the number of very deadly wars had fallen by 80 per cent.

I felt my heart working faster. This information wasn't reaching the world. Had we seen this report on the TV or in the newspapers? Did it feature on the headlines the unhappy commuters were reading? Of course not. Yet war was one of the biggest items on my list of THINGS WE FEEL REALLY DEPRESSED ABOUT.

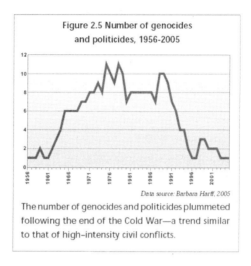

Figure 2.5 Number of genocides and politicides, 1956-2005

Data source: Barbara Harff, 2005

The number of genocides and politicides plummeted following the end of the Cold War—a trend similar to that of high–intensity civil conflicts.

If only I could show this to Pinter. I'd like to see him getting out of that one.

'Dad!' I said, strolling into the kitchen. 'Look.'

My father stooped over the printout and tilted his specs. I read out the data on battle deaths per state-based armed conflict, 1950–2005. 'No one knows about this,' I said. 'It's been buried in a sub-directory of the BBC news site.'

'Well,' he said, 'that is surprising. However, there are other wars looming, *major* wars – over resources, water and energy in particular – which will dwarf anything we've seen before.' He was getting that look in his eyes. 'There will be pandemics too,' he added, hitting his stride. 'Diseases and famines. They'll kill millions.'

'Let me get this straight,' I said. 'I just read you a respectable international report about the improving prospects for peace, and now you feel even worse? I'm writing this down,' I warned him, wagging my notebook.

He laughed heartily.

'Dad,' I said, 'why are you so pessimistic?'

'I'm optimistic,' said Dad, 'about the continuation of

the solar system.' His eyebrows compressed suddenly. 'I don't think there's any way we could fuck that up!'

I watched his face closely. Something in my father's brain had just been triggered – some dormant routine of inner irritation which had been passed down from generation to generation – a programmed reflex which delivered, each time it was activated, exactly the same catastrophic thoughts about the world.

How could I make him see without being disrespectful?

By hitting the project with renewed determination. It took me half an hour to clear my inbox of emails and chain letters from friends who were campaigning to save the rainforest or raising awareness of the vanishing honey bees. No gloomy, pessimistic liberal worries would be tolerated. It was time to go fundamentalist.

'There's no problem we can't solve,' I reminded myself, thinking of Tim's uncompromising positivity. I decided to take up his recommendation to contact another optimist: John Elkington, director of a think tank called SustainAbility. The name didn't bode well, but it was all I had to go on.

'I want people to see that things are getting better,' I told John, as we sat down in the lobby of his London office, 'that, on the whole, the world is improving.'

'Well,' said Elkington calmly, 'I'm not sure it is so smooth and untroubled as you suggest. For example, I think it's almost inescapable that we'll have another world war in the twenty-first century.'

'What?' The lamp in the foyer cast a sinister light across his face.

'If you look back at the historic record,' he replied,

'our species seems best able to develop to a new level by going through major discontinuities like a slump and then a world war.'

'But wars are declining,' I said, raising my voice.

John smiled wryly. 'By mid-century we face the prospect of a world of 9 billion people: a world increasingly linked by air travel, so the issue of pandemics becomes much more critical; the privatisation of weapons of mass destruction, where people can build germ warfare in their bedrooms; the number of nuclear devices which have gone missing from Russia . . .' He paused, registering the look on my face.

'How many?'

'There are a lot of them out there. What happened in Heathrow is just the precursor of someone letting off a subway-wide germ warfare attack or coordinated small nuclear bomb attacks. Those are going to happen, I don't think there's any way to avoid it.'

He shrugged apologetically and it was only then I realised: I had wandered into the headquarters of a fully paid-up pessimist, possibly even a Marxist. Why hadn't I guessed? I recalled Tim's sly smile as he handed me John's email address. I had walked right into a trap.

'In the next fifty years,' said the academic, 'we're going to have to destroy the bulk of the global economy and rebuild something completely different. And at the moment it isn't remotely clear what that is going to involve.'

I nodded to myself. All the signs of the pathology were present: the wild conspiracy theories, the dire warnings, the secret enjoyment of it all.

'And yet you call yourself an optimist,' I said.

John smiled lugubriously, as if he'd noticed the tone of sadness in my voice. 'Yes. People can't believe it when I say that. But my optimism comes from a sense that all this is possible. That there are enough people out there, enough institutions and technologies; we could actually do this if we finally believed it was necessary.'

'There's no problem that we can't solve,' I bounced back, bitterly.

'Yes, I really believe that. But experience has shown that we need major global dysfunction before we pull our socks up. That's why I say the next big disaster will catalyse the next stage of our evolution.'

'But we have evolved already,' I told him. 'We have the internet and satellite communications and twenty-four-hour news. How could there be a world war?'

I thought about using my favourite argument: the 'paradigm shift'. The words 'paradigm' and 'shift' usually left my combatants disorientated and confused, unable to think of an adequate response. As far as I was concerned, history was a straight line, going diagonally upwards. If you believed life was directionless or cyclical or, even worse, slightly triangular, it made everything pointless.

No wonder Elkington looked depressed. This delusion was highly developed. Best not to provoke such a person. Best just to leave.

I stood up.

'History makes you a bit more realistic,' said the intellectual, holding out his hand. 'Unless you're determined to be romantic about it. There are up waves and down waves, and I think we're moving into a period where things will get quite rough.'

I smiled quickly and ran down the stairs. There was limited time for me to bring light into these miserable people's lives. Right now I needed to find men who thought the same way I did, people who could actually help me turn the tide.

Luckily, John Bolton – an American diplomat and one

of the masterminds of the war in Iraq – was in town. I had been wanting to see a neocon for years. They, like me, had been misunderstood; they, like me, saw history as a steady progress towards democracy and freedom rather than a wobbly, disorganised circle. They were not afraid of power – they knew its value. And Bolton was the ultimate neocon. For fifteen tumultuous months John had been George Bush's ambassador to the United Nations, a man determined to stamp America's vision and authority on a wavering, woolly-thinking planet. He was a man I could talk to.

I closed my bedroom door. I didn't want my father knowing about this meeting, not because I was ashamed but because I wanted to avoid unnecessary trouble. Not everyone has the subtlety of thought necessary to appreciate the American right, especially not liberals frozen in an attitude of impotent resentment against the ruling classes. I, of course, was born to be one who rules, not one who complains. And so it was that I found myself extending the hand of friendship and solidarity to one of our staunchest allies. Soon the world would know that I was one of them. No one would dare to call me naïve again.

Ambassador Bolton was only in town for a few days so I hired a suite at the Hilton and made arrangements with his security personnel to meet him at fifteen hundred hours in the York Room. They phoned me several times to change the time – presumably for security reasons – to outwit any activists who might have tapped my dad's phone.

At last, we shook hands over the mahogany sheen of a boardroom table. John's personnel left us alone together and locked the door behind them.

'Your Excellency,' I said. He smiled briefly, under his white handlebar moustache. A busy man, he was here in England to meet with his counterparts in the Conservative party – neocons and straight talkers like him – and to raise awareness about the imminent threat from Iran.

'I trust the security is up to your standards.' I waved towards the meeting room, decked like a battleship with neat rows of paper and pencils.

'I'm sure,' he coughed, checking his watch.

'I believe the USA has been terribly misunderstood,' I told him, pushing my hair back across my head. 'Just because things didn't work out in Iraq, everyone assumes that the Americans are villains, criminals . . . that they did it for selfish reasons.' I waved my pen. 'When in fact they are extremely idealistic and doing it for the good of the world!'

Bolton tucked his chin into his neck. What was everyone so afraid of? Bolton was just an ordinary, well-meaning diplomat, not some thug or 'war criminal'. He was drinking fizzy water, for heaven's sake, just like me.

'My aim, Ambassador, is to remind the world that there is still cause for optimism, that things are in hand, and everything is going according to plan. I believe the American right has a message of hope that is completely drowned out by pessimistic news coverage. I want to return optimism to the world!'

He laughed uncomfortably. 'Well, let's see how it goes.'

I leant forward. 'What's the good news? Where is the vision now?'

Bolton fixed his eyes halfway up the table. 'You have to view the present day in its current context,' he said, speaking quickly, 'which is the end of the Cold War and victory over communism, the collapse of the Soviet Union and the end of the threat of nuclear annihilation.'

I breathed a sigh of relief. To find someone at last who shared my views!

'Proliferation of WMD in the hands of terrorists or rogue

states remains a very grave threat but it's a different kind of threat than living under mutual assured destruction.'

'That's what I've been saying!'

'The fact is, having come through these challenges may mean that we can finally get about our business and not have to worry about these overarching threats. That is not to say that the entire world will be filled with McDonald's hamburger stands but . . .' Bolton fell silent, his eyes blanking out like television monitors.

'What about terrorism?' I asked.

'We've made considerable progress against terrorism,' he said amiably. 'There have been no attacks on American territory since 9/11.'

'But Heathrow, Mr Ambassador, I don't know if you heard . . .'

His eyes softened. He knew what I was talking about. We were in this together. 'Whenever you face a long battle against this kind of threat,' he said, 'you can't expect overnight results. Just as four decades went by in the Cold War when we remained optimistic that our system would beat the communist system and we proved ultimately victorious.'

'They say . . .' I dropped my voice. 'They say that twelve suitcase bombs have gone missing.'

Bolton paused. 'I don't think it's underestimating the level of threat to say continuation of the struggle is important to make sure that threat is minimal.'

I quickly wrote down his words. 'That's . . . that's very reassuring.'

'Iran is also a problem,' he continued. 'In the case of Iran – thanks to four years of bungled diplomacy by the Europeans – I think our options are now limited to regime change or the use of force.'

'Regime change!'

The neocon stared at the table. 'Diplomacy with Iran is a mistake. I think many in Europe believe they've passed beyond history and there are no external challenges, and when challenge does arise they can all be handled by diplomacy. Force is sometimes necessary.' His cheeks reddened. 'You have to understand, the UN is often flawed and ineffective. I worked there for sixteen months, so I know the organisation pretty well.'

'What is it like?' I asked.

'It was a target-rich environment.' He looked up. 'That is, there were a lot of things that needed to be corrected.'

I paused. 'Ambassador, do you not think . . . wouldn't we be better off spending all this money on education and development? I mean, couldn't we have a kind of Marshall Plan for the Middle East? I think that would make people feel a lot more optimistic.'

'No, I don't,' said Bolton, a metallic edge to his voice. 'Weakness does not contribute to peace. Weakness encourages aggression and contributes to instability and war. Defence is not aggression. Defence is defence.'

'Right.' I nodded rapidly.

'And that's hard for many people to understand.'

'What you're saying is, behind all the military power, America is actually a very idealistic country. The neocons are optimists. And no one understands that.'

He weighed up my words. 'I think the Americans are by and large a pretty hard-headed people.'

'And you?'

The ambassador's eyes flicked up for a second. 'I think Americans are idealistic but they don't necessarily see that there's a direct conversion into practical effects from it.'

Quite right, I thought. He was a modest man and I didn't want to push him. I could imagine sharing a beer with John on the porch of the White House, or perhaps in some discreet clapboard hideaway in New England. He had a reputation for being a bully, but here he was, just an ordinary guy – a kind-hearted academic with a Kwik-Fit moustache.

'Are you still in touch with Mr Bush?' I asked him. Even George Bush, eventually, would have to take a hand in spreading optimism around the world. He was never going to take the place of Bill Clinton, but I was willing to be open-minded. Even George Bush, underneath everything, had to be a decent person.

Bolton hesitated. 'I have spoken to others in the administration but not to him.'

'Do you think it's worth me trying to meet him?'

'You could take a shot at it.'

'Would you give me a hand?'

'I'll be happy to say, um, you know, he . . . it can't hurt you to ask.' Bolton consented bashfully.

'Thanks,' I said, glancing at his autobiography, which I had brought for him to sign. It was called *Surrender is not an Option*.

'That's an excellent title,' I said.

The ambassador smiled. 'Surrender is not an option.'

'Surrender is not an option.' I agreed.

I wished Scarlett Johansson could see me in my suit.

3

*Judging by history, the current turbulence will eventually
yield to an era of relative stability, an era when global political,
economic and social structures have largely tamed the new forms of
chaos. The world will reach a new equilibrium, at a level of
organisation higher than at any past equilibrium.*

Robert Wright, *Nonzero*

After my meeting with Bolton I was impatient to get ahead.
Meeting someone at such a high level who grasped the
value of my mission was just a taste of things to come. Time
was now of the essence.

By this stage I had realised that pessimism was more
widespread than even I had realised. It wasn't a conspiracy
so much as a massive, undiagnosed sickness, a set of assumptions that even relatively normal people suffered from. These
assumptions had become so rampant that people of all ages
and backgrounds now accepted them as reality. I started a
new page in my notebook.

WHAT PESSIMISTS BELIEVE

- The world is a mess and it always will be
- History is circular, one disaster after another

- People can't be trusted, they will always mess things up
- There is no light without dark, no happiness without suffering
- There will always be war and poverty
- Injustice and corruption are facts of life

These negative assumptions about life, I saw now, were the root cause of all our unhappiness. They crossed all boundaries of politics, nationality and age. I realised now that it wasn't just manic-depressive socialists with an inferiority complex who were pessimistic, as I had previously thought. It was anyone who believed these untrue, deeply cynical things about the world.

It was overwhelming to reflect on how pervasive these beliefs really were, but I was buoyed up by the knowledge that the world was secretly longing to be cured. In fact, it wasn't out of the question that I would win the Nobel Peace Prize for this piece of work. Pessimism was like a virus, I concluded. The assumptions of pessimism – which were so addictive and convincing, so tempting for people to adopt – hopped from person to person, taking over their bodies and making them believe everything they read in the *Daily Mail*. The trouble was, most people had absorbed these beliefs without even questioning them. In other words, they were so used to feeling terrible about everything that *they didn't even notice it any more*.

Which led to the classic symptoms of pessimism:

WHAT PESSIMISTS FEAR

- Soon we will run out of everything
- The environment will collapse
- Society, culture and education are falling apart

- Crime will increase every year, forever
- We will be wiped out by bio-terrorists
- Nuclear destruction is inevitable
- Capitalism will eat itself, then collapse
- Technology will enslave us all

and all the other things on my list. No wonder we didn't want to get out of bed in the morning.

I stood on the terrace of the British Library and let the sun warm my face. By now my list had evolved into a two-by-three matrix cross-referenced with assumptions and different 'types' of optimist. To cover everything on the matrix – taking into account the rate at which new problems were adding themselves – I calculated that it would take me more than six years to finish. By which time I would be forty. Or possibly dead.

Maybe I was trying to do too many things at once.

What if I changed my approach? What if – instead of a complicated matrix of cross-referenced problems and experts – I simply interviewed people who were famous? Wouldn't that be easier? They didn't have to be massively well-known, just interesting enough so that the public would pay attention. Sure, these people might not be the ideal optimists I was originally planning to meet, but then neither was Tim Smit. Now that I was officially writing a book, I had a perfectly good excuse to approach anyone I wanted to.

Anyone.

The first thing I did was send an email to the President of Iran, Mr Ahmadinejad. I'd heard he had his own blog and sometimes replied to emails. Deep down, he was obviously a nice guy. If I could get the firebrand of Tehran to say a few words about the clash of civilisations it would be a massive coup. And if he wasn't an optimist, I would convince him to be one. Maybe I could bring the rabble-rousing President and the hardline neocons together. Maybe I could personally broker an end to the stand-off.

I wrote:

Dear Sir

I am making a book about the world's leading optimists. I would like to interview you, as I believe you have been greatly misunderstood in the Western media. We have some important things to talk about – and we can do this entirely by telephone.

Yours sincerely

Laurence Shorter

I also sent a letter to Prince Charles. He, too, had been badly misrepresented by the media and would make an important contribution to the restoration of optimism. With our mutual interest in organic yoghurt and upper-class women I imagined the prince and I becoming close friends.

Finally, I decided, it was time for a bit of glamour.

That night I met a friend who worked for a charity raising awareness of AIDS and sexually transmitted diseases. I listened patiently as he described the challenges of preventing illness in Third World countries – a fundamentally dismal subject. Then I asked him the question that I had come here for. 'Dave, did you not tell me once that you had a Hollywood actress working for PSI?'

'Do you mean Ashley Judd?' he said. 'She's one of our global ambassadors.'

'Ashley Judd!' I said. 'That was it.' I could feel my eyes glittering. I didn't know who Ashley was exactly, but the name sounded familiar. There was something shining about it, something personally significant.

'Do you think I could . . . ?'

'Sure,' he said. 'Why not?'

I looked up Ashley on the internet. Sure enough, she was a Hollywood actress, sure enough she worked for PSI. She was about my age, and she was a major star. I felt an immediate connection. Ashley had the same air of serenity and intelligence as Scarlett. My brain flashed forward to a possible future: the two of us eating breakfast, going for long walks in the Scottish Highlands, having all-night conversations about Hegel and Kierkegaard.

Ashley was *bound* to be inspired by the concept of optimism. And she would be flattered, I was convinced, by the opportunity to help me save the world from pessimism.

Dave gave me the number of her agent in Los Angeles.

'Do you have endorsement?' asked the agent. 'A publisher, a sponsor of any kind?'

'Oh, right,' I said. 'Absolutely. I'm developing this with the BBC. And I have a friend in Channel 4.'

This was a small exaggeration, I knew. But I was now employing a concept I had learned from Tim Smit's autobiography – the 'future truth': something which isn't true yet but *will be soon*. If I could get Ashley involved in the book then I felt sure the BBC and Channel 4 *would* be interested. And who knows what else might happen? It would snowball uncontrollably. One famous optimist would lead to another. Ashley would invite me to meet her friends in LA and the whole thing would take off.

The agent agreed to set up a telephone interview. She gave me a time and a date. I sat and watched my phone.

Eventually it rang.

'Ashley!' I cried. There were dogs barking in the background.

I imagined her sitting near some open windows, looking out over the twilight. 'What time is it there?'

Ashley's tone was calm and polite. 'It's early,' she said, 'but that's fine. I'm always happy to talk about my work. Besides, I'm jet-lagged. I've just come back from India.'

'Wow!' I said. 'Were you on holiday?'

Her voice came back hard and serious. 'I was there to visit sex workers.'

'OK . . .'

'I spent three days in brothels with teenage girls enslaved for sex work.'

I gulped. 'I hear dogs in the background,' I said, hoping to change the subject. 'Are you a dog lover?'

'Yes,' she said. There was an uncomfortable pause. 'So . . . you're writing a book about optimism?'

'I want to change the way people think . . . That's why I wanted to talk to you, so we could . . . maybe . . .' There was silence on the other end of the line. 'So, are you optimistic?'

'Oh, yes,' said Ashley, 'otherwise I couldn't do what I do.'

'Which is what exactly?'

'What we do in these places,' she said, 'is reach out to poor people with upbeat, effective behavior-change messages focused on medically accurate sex education.'

'Nice . . .' I paused. 'So, you're optimistic?'

'The very fact we're doing this work is cause for hope – twenty years ago these problems were brushed under the carpet. On the other hand,' she sighed, 'prostitution is the third largest industry in the world. And it is getting more and more brutal as organised crime gets involved, hand-in-hand with extreme physical violence.'

'Right.'

'And AIDS is a serious problem there: India has more HIV sufferers than anywhere else in the world.'

I faltered. 'But it's looking OK?'

Ashley's voice crackled down the handset. 'I met children living in stinking rooms where their mothers make one or two dollars for sex with drunk men. I met married couples from West Bengal who come to Mumbai to enroll the wife in sex work. I spent time in a brothel where the girls are literally slaves. This is a million-person slum we're talking about. Our workers go in there and doctor to the girls, do their best to educate them.'

'I'm writing a book about optimism,' I reminded her.

'Put it this way,' said Ashley, 'the day I went to those slums was the best day of my life. I just spent three consecutive days in brothels with women who have recently been sequestered for sex work, pee in a corner in a bucket or a drain, and it was the best day in my life.'

'It was?'

'When I'm in that situation I feel like: where's the dirtiest, the sickest, most repugnant person? That's the person I want to hug. The more unlovely and unlovable, the better it is, the greater I feel.'

I shivered. 'Can you say . . . why?'

'Well . . . although my circumstances are not comparable in any way with the plight of these women I *have* suffered and I *can* identify with them. And I can really say, these people are no different than I am. The best exists inside of me as well as the worst.'

I felt a chill creep up my spine.

'I completely own my darkness,' she continued, 'because I lived in it a long time before I started my recovery. I had a lot of rage, and it was eating me alive. When I finally started to accept my anger and deal with it I found it could be transformed into these empowering gifts. On the other hand, I feel a presence greater than myself when I do this work, a grace and a light and I know I have some sort of protection around me . . . It's a key part of why I'm an optimist. Today I truly embrace that everything happens for my greater good.'

I shuddered. I felt like rushing out into the street and finding someone normal to talk to – a policeman maybe, or a woman with a pram.

'Of course I would never deign to say that to a sex slave. It's abusive enough to be in the problem they're in but to point out what can seem like a blithe spiritual formula can be the height of insensitivity.'

'But we can alleviate this suffering,' I said. 'We can find *solutions*.'

'Personally, I believe that suffering will always exist. I've learned to accept that.'

I put down my pen. 'I think we have different definitions of optimism,' I said.

'Maybe, but what I've learned is this: accept yourself and accept the negative. God is love, so if we do loving things, be loving, love ourselves and let the love for ourselves emanate out, that will set us on the path to finding the peace and serenity that is possible in this lifetime.'

There was a long pause.

'Thank you, Ashley. I should probably go now.'

'I hope that was helpful?'

'Very,' I said.

I put down the phone and walked out into the street. Why did I have the feeling that Ashley had just invalidated my whole project? Instead of us hitting it off, as I had hoped, the conversation had become difficult and edgy almost from the start. What is more, the actress had added new problems to my list – prostitution and sex slavery – which I hadn't even thought of before.

I paced up and down outside. Ashley talked as if it were somehow naïve to be an optimist, as if suffering and darkness and negativity were *good things* that we should *accept* as part of life.

But that was the whole point. I don't *have* to accept them.

Mid-morning. I sat down in the cool and understated lobby of McKinsey & Co., and waited as the receptionist checked me in. What a relief! McKinsey was a management consultancy firm with offices all over the world. Their analysts were known for their cool heads and professionalism. I stretched my legs and inhaled the comforting smell of expensive paper and brushed-metal light fixtures. The atmosphere felt monastic and peaceful, far away from the chaos and stupidity of the outside world. Just one look at the font and texture of their brochure reminded me why I had come.

After my call with Ashley I had decided to change tack, to go to the very opposite end of the spectrum. What need did I have for fame and celebrity? Here at the highest level of business – where politics, society and ideas met, and the fate of the world was decided in quiet rooms by well-mannered and intelligent people – here I would find someone who understood.

The receptionist handed me a badge. I watched her neat heels crossing the floor. This was the world of business: happy, psychologically balanced people providing high-quality service. No room for darkness and ambiguity here. No room for misery and suffering!

I was an optimist, for God's sake. I was looking for the *bright side.*

I travelled up in the elevator, admiring the glass walls of the building. If anyone was going to get it – that there was something missing in this world, something eminently obvious and simple – it would be Ian Davis.

Ian was the CEO of McKinsey. I had discovered him after reading a paper he had published about the 'social contract' between business and society. In it, he argued that companies needed to start viewing themselves as guardians of society and the environment – not just because it was right but for their own economic good. Ian was living proof that business was evolving in the right direction, that multinationals had the best interests of humanity at their heart, despite the suspicions of most Europeans. I remembered what Tim Smit had said: the people running the world's companies were good guys, just like us. That was the whole point. But no one saw it.

Ian greeted me with a smile. 'I'm fascinated by your question. I'd like to give it some proper thought.' He sat down across from me. 'The best way to influence this debate is by sheer historical example. The overwhelming evidence is that on many dimensions the human lot has improved dramatically. When you look, there's still poverty and depression and horrendous problems, but you would happily, happily be in this century than any other.'

'Right!' I had finally found an optimist who was totally on board. Maybe we could start a collaboration. Maybe Ian would invite me to join him as guest speaker on his next panel at the World Economic Forum.

'Why has the human lot improved so dramatically?' pondered the CEO. 'Science and technology have played a key role, the transfer and availability of knowledge has played a role, the media has played a role. What drove all of that? It was basically people who believed that things could be made better.'

'I couldn't agree more.' I felt overjoyed to be back in the company of intelligent beings – people who didn't think

I was weird for using long sentences with embedded sub-clauses and frequent references to Moore's Law of Microprocessor Efficiency. 'But no one seems to get it,' I said. 'There's this negative assumption that people have – that nothing good can happen without something bad, that progress is always harmful, that there is no *dark* without *light*. I was talking to a woman earlier this week . . .' I paused for breath. I felt slightly tearful, as if I'd finally found my home after years of wandering in the desert. 'It's like two completely different worldviews. And people don't realise! Yet history shows us that society is a steady evolution of greater and greater pools of cooperation, driven by the ineluctable advantages of cooperation. The current global system of free trade is just the most advanced expression of that!'

'Yes,' said Ian. 'Yes. I take your point. But you could also argue that technology and business are evolving *too* quickly. The human state isn't moving so fast – one of the sources of tension in the world is that social techniques and technologies are just not keeping pace with other forms of technology.'

He took a sip of his water. 'How are you defining optimism? What's your framework? Is it philosophical, historical, sociological?'

Ian's sharp, analytical eyes seemed to pierce into the back of my head. My tongue felt thick in my mouth. 'It's a mixture of things. It's the belief that things are getting better, that humanity is evolving in an upwards direction.'

He frowned. 'I think your framework may need a little work.'

'Well, I have worked on it,' I said. 'I've definitely worked on it.'

'Because the question I'm wondering is: what are the *preconditions* for positive belief to actually sustain itself?

Optimism that doesn't succeed can create cynicism or a sense of despair.'

'Sure,' I said. 'Sure. Of course.'

Ian examined his biro as if it were a highly sensitive scientific instrument. 'Positive belief is a necessary, but not a sufficient, condition for success. It's not a guarantee.'

'Well . . .' I differed.

'And you haven't talked about the word risk,' he continued. 'Which is different from pessimism. You can be an optimist and still have a real sense of risk. You mustn't confuse the two.'

I blinked.

'I must say, I'm going off the word optimism a bit.'

'You are?'

I glanced through the window at the pavement below. There was a woman walking in the sunshine. I felt a sudden unexpected envy.

'Yes,' said Ian. 'I prefer the term positive belief. It's less open to misinterpretation. The question is . . .' He leant back in his chair and stared at the biro. '. . . if social techniques are not keeping pace with other forms of technology then are we always going to be on the cusp? If you look at history you've always had punctuated progress.' He looked up at me. 'It's not always a straight line. And now, because of our technological capability, punctuated progress could mean the end.'

'The end!'

'Well, it's binary isn't it . . . ? The trouble now is that technology allows negativity to express itself on a catastrophic scale. So you only need one rebel, one dissenter to break ranks and then . . . bang. My point is that now and for the next hundred years we're on the cusp. That's why it's so important that the benefits of positive belief become engrained within a large majority of the world's population.

Because if you have a world which is mostly optimistic but you have pockets which are deeply pessimist . . .' He stopped. 'That could be worse than everyone just feeling rather negative.'

'Yes,' I said, 'that's it.' I stood up and slowly shook him by the hand.

'I think you're onto something,' said the CEO. 'You need to clarify your approach, but I do think you're onto something.'

I walked down Kensington High Street, transported by the grace of pure mental intelligence. I felt as if I were floating slightly over the pavement.

The optimist project wasn't about lists of problems or famous people. It was about redefining the very concept of optimism. I needed to unlock this elusive quality and make it available to the world. I needed to develop my own intellectual framework. Maybe if I could find these 'preconditions for optimism' that Ian was talking about, then it would all work out from there. And if I could do that, Ian seemed to be hinting, then the doors of McKinsey and Davos and the Clinton Foundation and all those other wonderful places – a whole new, extraordinary life – would all open up for me.

In the meantime, one thing was clear. If pessimism was putting us at risk of nuclear annihilation, as Ian was suggesting, then the Harold Pinters and the John Elkingtons of this world, they weren't just an irritation. They were a danger to humanity.

4

There is nothing either good or bad, but thinking makes it so.

William Shakespeare, *Hamlet*

It was a sunny day, but I could sense the presence of rain. I poked my head around my father's door. The smell of silicon and Post-it notes, the desk, the manly chill: Dad's study, as it had always been. He had turned the radiators off again.

'How are you doing?' I said.

'I'm depressed!' he replied. *Of course*, I thought. 'I just shelled out a thousand quid for this laptop and now the broadband won't work.'

'I'm sure it will be fine.'

'I'm sure *it won't*. I've already spent two hours on the phone to the call centre.'

I sat down and looked at the computer. He was right. The spot where there should have been playful green bars was empty of all life.

'But why let it get to you?' I argued. 'It's just a computer.'

'It's not "just" anything.' He tramped upstairs. 'It's always the same. Everything goes wrong!'

I stared resentfully at the monitor. Why was my father so easily discouraged? And why was I so powerless to cheer him up? It seemed so obvious to me – that one shouldn't take faulty computer accessories personally. Especially Dell computer accessories. And yet there was nothing I could say or do to lift his mood. I sat for a moment on my father's chair, feeling the full weight of his disappointment and chagrin.

Upstairs there was sunlight on my desk. I went for it, with the conviction of an addict. I needed to work harder, make calls, see people. I needed to get things going. I ran my finger down my target list of problems and optimists. I wasn't even sure if I needed a list any more – not after my meeting with Ian Davis and his comment on the 'preconditions of optimism' – but it was all I had to go on. And I had already made certain plans. One of them was to speak to Jung Chang, the author of *Wild Swans*, a best-selling autobiography set in China during the Maoist Cultural Revolution.

China was item twenty-three on my list, and an important obstacle in my journey towards optimism. Even if I succeeded in totally redefining the intellectual framework for positive thinking, the problem of Communist China would always be there, looming in the background, preventing me from feeling really relaxed and happy about the future. It was something that troubled me more than it should, probably, given that the country was 5,000 miles away. But there was something about the mere presence of the nation that scared me. Because even if everything else went OK in the twenty-first century, there would always be the Chinese state to worry about – an alien culture with no concept of human rights, awful food and a 99 per cent chance of becoming the next world superpower. There was something terrifying about the place, something vast and unaccountable. It made me feel tiny, powerless.

I didn't like that feeling.

'I'm worried,' I said to Jung Chang. 'The Chinese seem so different from us.'

Jung tutted. You would never guess from her relaxed voice she'd once worked in a labour camp. The anger was barely visible, like nails under a carpet.

'People have this idea,' she said, 'that human lives are less valuable in China, that human rights is a Western concept. It's just not true! In fact, Confucian philosophy places human beings in the very centre of its philosophy. The Chinese have always been very individualistic. If anything they're *too* individualistic.'

'Really!' I'd never thought about it like that. Then I remembered the delivery boy at my local Chinese takeaway. He had sleepy, uncooperative eyes and looked as if he stayed up every night practising how to kill people with his numchakas. 'Even if they are individualistic,' I said, 'they seem a bit too . . . patriotic. I've heard that the Chinese view all foreigners as barbarians.' I shuddered as I imagined the treatment that would get doled out to writers and visionaries like me.

'China is not a militaristic state,' said Jung soothingly. 'It's unlikely it will ever become an aggressive, expansionist country. It's not going to launch some kind of crusader army which is going to invade the rest of the world.'

'Really?'

'That's just not going to happen!'

'What about Taiwan?' I asked. 'Isn't that a problem?'

'If Taiwan claims independence I fear the Chinese regime would use force,' she conceded, 'and that would be disastrous for everybody.' I stared dismally at my hands. 'But a gigantic war, it would be disastrous above all for the *government*, because the government itself might fall! If you bear in mind the "one child" policy – the state-imposed policy that each family may only have one child – it's extremely drastic and has caused tremendous human anguish; but it's also the policy of a non-militaristic regime. So you see, it's the last thing they would want.'

'Aha,' I said, my view of China slowly overturning.

We talked for another half an hour. I felt Jung Chang slowly warming to my theme. In my own small way, I believe, I was helping to create understanding between our two great and noble cultures.

The first thing was to tell Dad. More proof that the world was on track, and so much better than we realised. Now China! Soon there would be nothing to worry about at all, nothing to prevent us from being optimistic all the time.

I tapped on the study door. Dad was still leaning over the computer, his eyebrows bent into strange, agonised shapes. 'Hey, Dad,' I said, 'I just talked to Jung Chang!'

'Oh, great,' he said, tapping on his keyboard. I waited for him to say something else. He was totally engrossed. 'I don't suppose you know anything about wireless configuration protocols, do you?'

'No, Dad.'

That afternoon Xanthe called around. Xanthe and I had only known each other for a couple of years, but already we felt like old friends. I think we brought out the best in each other. Xanthe was very busy and very social. I was grounded and calm. I was an open person, generous, an optimist. Xanthe was a pessimist who had the extra misfortune of being a journalist. Amazingly, this didn't stop us from being able to discuss a whole range of subjects without ire. Mainly me.

'What if it's not problems that stop people from being optimistic,' mused Xanthe, 'but the way they think about things?'

'What does that mean?'

'Well, I often wonder why I'm not an optimist, and

sometimes I think it might be a psychological thing. You know – the way my brain works.' She swirled the tea around her cup. 'Maybe you should look into that side of things.'

'I don't know. I think what I'm looking for is more simple. It's something we all have, but everyone is telling us we shouldn't. That's what I'm trying to change.'

'So, is it working? Are you feeling better?'

My eyes found the wall. 'Well, yes. Most of the time.'

'I think it could really help you,' said Xanthe. 'Have you heard of Martin Seligman? He's an American psychologist. Very famous.'

'What for?'

'He's the world expert on optimism.'

'The world *expert?*' I looked into my tea. *I* was supposed to be the world expert on optimism.

'He's the founder of a movement called Positive Psychology and one of the pioneers of cognitive therapy.'

'Cognitive therapy?"

'Yes, they believe that anxiety and depression are created by our thoughts, and that's all – everything comes down to our thoughts. Which is what I was trying to get at before.'

'Right,' I said. 'Well, maybe I'll have a look.'

A week later this Martin Seligman was due to fly over from Philadelphia to give a talk in York. I found this out from his website. There was no need to say this to Xanthe, but she was right – I was morally obliged to check the guy out. *World expert.* I decided I would catch a train up there and sit at the back of the lecture. It wouldn't be so much a meeting as an observation. I figured that Seligman was a psychologist and I was a humanist, and we might have something to give each other.

On my way north, I browsed listlessly through Seligman's book, *Learned Optimism.*

Each of us has our own 'explanatory style' . . . a way of thinking about the causes of things that happen in our lives. The basis of optimism does not lie in positive phrases or images of victory, but in the way you think about causes.

The way you think about causes.

I liked it. Seligman made it clear that in his system there was no big deal with repressed emotions, penis envy or toilet training. Which meant, he hinted, that the Freudians were done for. This was good news. I had always disliked the Freudians. If the war on pessimism was to be won, they would have to be the first to go, along with their leather sofas, their Hampstead consulting rooms and their depressing view of human nature. I was convinced Freud had ruined the otherwise perfect brains of Harold Pinter and my father.

Maybe this Seligman was smarter than he sounded. Just like me, Seligman was calling for more optimism. Just like me, he saw negative beliefs as pointless and destructive. On the other hand, the doctor seemed to think you could reduce this shift to a few simple exercises. Optimism, he wrote, comes down to three things: when something bad happens do you: 1) take it personally, 2) expect it to last forever, and 3) let it affect other areas of your life? If so, then you're a pessimist.

I sat in the conference room and waited for the great man to appear. A murmur of excitement passed through the hall as a thickset American in his fifties walked up to the podium.

'Today,' said Seligman, in a deep voice, 'I want to talk to you about happiness.'

I listened impatiently as the doctor described his life-time quest to understand the scientific basis of happiness.

'We've actually found that happiness is measurable and that there is a formula for this . . .'

Seligman turned on the overhead projector and we all gazed up at his formula.

$$\text{Life Satisfaction} = \text{Positive Emotion} + \text{Engagement} + \text{Meaning}$$

Hold on, I thought. That is funny! A *formula* for happiness. That's what I needed to do for optimism.

'There are short cuts to Positive Emotion,' said Seligman. 'You can take drugs, you can have sex, you can go shopping – but there are no short cuts to Engagement. The Engaged Life is when you're totally absorbed in what you're doing, and it comes when your highest challenges meet your highest strengths. There's also Meaning. Human beings ineluctably want meaning and purpose in life, but this only happens when you use your strengths to serve something bigger than yourself.'

I watched, impressed. For every one of his statements, Seligman had done an average of thirty years' clinical research. After another hour of complex explanations, the doctor unveiled one of his favourite scientific techniques for raising human happiness.

'We call it the Three Blessings Exercise,' said Seligman. 'Every night for the next week, before you go to sleep, write down three things that went well today. It turns out that building gratitude is one of the main ways of developing happiness. This is hard data,' he added. 'The people I assign to this exercise, their happiness goes up and just *stays up* for six months.'

A smile crept up to my face. Had Seligman been reading Dr Seuss?

I introduced myself in the next interval. Doctor Seligman glanced around the conference room which still seemed to be orbiting slowly around his body. 'I wouldn't mind getting out of here,' he said. 'Shall we take a walk around York Minster? It's one of the most beautiful medieval cathedrals in Europe.'

The other delegates watched enviously as we made for the door.

'I enjoyed the gratitude exercise, Professor, but . . .'

'Please . . . call me Marty.'

'What's the connection with optimism?'

'The Three Blessings is an intervention for increasing Positive Emotion about the past. Optimism is related to emotion about the *future*. For that we use a different set of techniques.'

'Mmm.'

'The basic mechanism is simple,' said the doctor. 'When you're a pessimist you give up easily; when you're an optimist you try. Pessimists just have different thoughts about adversity.'

I stopped. 'That's it?'

'Precisely. Pessimists have habits of thought, which mean that they interpret failure very negatively. These negative thoughts then create feelings of helplessness, which in turn feed depression. Pessimists tend to take bad luck personally. They see bad events as a reflection on themselves. They also tend to assume they're going to last forever and they're going to affect all parts of their life. But if they can learn to question and dispute those thoughts, then they can shift their explanatory style from a pessimistic one to an optimistic one.' He paused. 'We are currently facing an epidemic of depression in the Western world.'

'An epidemic,' I said.

'Severe depression is ten times more prevalent than it was fifty years ago.' The doctor looked down at the pavement. 'That's why this work is so critical.'

I glanced at the doctor as we walked down the street. Maybe Seligman was a pessimist himself. If so, he was a pessimist like none I had previously encountered. He seemed to be aware of his condition. He was actually *trying to get better.*

'So, this . . . this pessimism can be cured?'

'Absolutely,' he said, looking at me kindly. 'It's a training. You teach yourself to recognise the negative thoughts you're saying to yourself *before you start believing them.* You become an expert disputer of your own beliefs.'

The doctor paused. We were standing outside the soaring granite of York Minster. Next to us an ancient Roman column stood uselessly in the middle of the road. 'Even if negative thoughts are true, those beliefs are rarely *useful.* Take someone who thinks they're fat. They might be fat by some people's definition, but to others they might look normal and attractive. Having the thought – *I'm fat* – makes you much less likely to go out and meet those people.'

'What about *real* things,' I asked, 'like Osama bin Laden?'

We walked through the doorway of the cathedral. 'If I asked you to describe the best thing that happened today and then asked you to describe the worst thing that happened, you'd give me about twice as many words to describe the worst thing, and that's because evolution has given you a *bad weather* brain.' Seligman stepped carefully across the tombstone of a medieval knight. 'Having a brain which always assumes the worst was crucial in the Pleistene period, when we had to fight to survive. But today it has become a liability. It also means that if you're in politics or journalism and you want to get people's attention it's much easier to do it by telling them what's wrong. Of course there's bad stuff going on, but when you actually tell people the good news, what's so interesting is that *people don't believe it*. What? We have three times more . . . what? There's less pollution? People in the Third World are getting richer?' He laughed. We both laughed. What a great guy, I thought. He really wasn't a pessimist at all.

'No, I'm deeply optimistic. I think when you compare today with the last century – two world wars, a great depression, Fascism and Stalinism . . .' The doctor's voice echoed off the flagstones.

At the end of the aisle Seligman turned and pointed in the direction of the altar. 'Do you see the gargoyles above the apse? Can you see the backs of their heads?'

I peered into the darkness, making out the faces of the gargoyles with their scary frowns and grins. 'I can only see the front of their heads. There's no back.'

'Exactly!' whispered Seligman. 'The medieval craftsmen who made those statues carved the backs of their heads in perfect and loving detail, only you can't see them because they're inside the wall. They did it because they thought God would appreciate it. Now that,' he said, 'takes optimism.'

I looked up towards the majestic vaulted ceiling. 'Great achievements of culture spring mainly from optimistic periods of history,' said the doctor. 'Pessimistic civilisations achieve little that is truly lasting.' He sat down on an ancient old pew. I imagined us meeting here again, secretly, in years to come – the godfather of optimism and his protégé. The doctor looked at me. 'Between you and me, I'm now being asked into meetings at the highest level of government to discuss this.'

'Oh!'

'There's a belief that this is the key to the future of British politics. And not just British politics. It turns out there are people pouring millions of pounds into scientific research to prove a pessimistic view of humanity. You know, there's quite a lot at stake on this issue. And I don't just mean science, there's a lot . . .' He lowered his voice. 'There are huge funders interested in this thing, private funders.'

I listened, rapt. I felt like Kevin Costner in *JFK*, when the dark secrets of power are finally revealed to him next to the Capitol building in Washington. Seligman regarded me with a distant blink. 'In the war of ideas this is the big one, Laurence. So, you see, what you're doing is important. But you do need a title. The whole movement needs a title: 'Positive psychology', 'happiness', 'wellbeing' . . . The person who can find a better label than that,' he looked at me, 'that person will be catapulted to political office.'

I gulped.

That night my father seemed in a cheerful mood. I could see no particular reason for this change of heart. It was dark outside and raining, and the pessimists still controlled the airwaves. But Dad had an amused look on his face. Did he think it was funny? Finally I had met someone who really grasped what I was trying to do, who saw it in its appropriate historical context. Like Ian Davis, Seligman had given me a new direction – one which was far more important and philosophically interesting than simply ticking problems off a list.

'Seligman says it's not our problems that makes us depressed. It's our thoughts.'

'M-hm.'

'That's why he shows people how to dispute them. Especially if you have a pessimistic explanatory style.'

'Aha. And if they're true, the thoughts?'

I hesitated. 'Well . . . those beliefs are rarely useful.'

'So, he's saying, I shouldn't have a certain thought, even if it's true? I should pretend it's not happening.'

'No. Listen . . .' I rubbed my forehead.

Dad switched off the light and walked towards the door. 'The computer's working again, by the way.'

'It is?'

'Yes. Luckily I believed my own thoughts enough to take it all the way back to the shop.' He smiled. 'They had sold me a faulty wireless card.'

I went to bed and lay on my back. *The person who can crack this will be catapulted to political office.* Seligman's words echoed in my head, comforting me with their oaky ring of great forces and destiny. These techniques of his, they were definitely interesting, but I didn't need to worry about that. My task was different – to bring wisdom to the people. All the people. To find that simple, clear, universally longed-for optimism that was true, underneath all the mess and discussion. To redefine the meaning of the word – make it something that everyone wanted and everyone could understand. Dr S had made a start. I would build on that.

The next morning I walked past a fruit stall in Euston. The salesman was muttering to himself. He looked annoyed: 'Bad, bad . . .' he said. 'Bad.'

'What's bad?' I asked.

'Things,' he said, looking up absently. 'Bad . . .'

'For who?'

'Who do you think?' he snapped.

I stared at him. Now was my chance. 'Cheer up,' I said.

'Why should I?'

I thought quickly. 'Evolution has given you a bad weather brain. Having a brain that assumes the worst was crucial in the old days, when we had to fight to survive, but today it's become a liability. Count your blessings. Even if you're clinically depressed you can always find something to feel grateful for.'

The man picked up an apple. 'Piss off!'

Notes to Pessimists

TITLE OF LECTURE: Preconditions of Optimism

INTRO: 'Now then . . .'
(Look at audience)

1) SENSE OF PURPOSE
Many people's sense of purpose revolves around trivial things like their house or their children. Most pessimists are extremely materialistic, to make up for their lack of other qualities. However, you can change this. Purpose is one of the biggest qualities that we optimists share. As Dr Seligman wrote:

> Human beings ineluctably want meaning and purpose
> in life, but this only happens when you use your
> strengths to serve something bigger than yourself.

(Give example)
(Discuss/anecdote)
Homework:
Set up a global movement of some kind. Ideally this movement will be an optimistic one, as people are attracted to cheerful and positive statements. If it's a really good idea,

like ending poverty or eradicating Third World debt, you will feel energy coursing through your body like a chainsaw. As a result of this glowing charisma you will be invited to speak at international conferences with the likes of Bill Clinton and Angelina Jolie. You will sit on panels with them at Aspen and Davos, drink Fairtrade coffee in high-altitude ski lodges and give your opinion on a range of world issues. Soon you will start your own lecture tour of the world and attract your own followers. You may be invited to star in a film of your own life. It will be great.

(Breakout groups/tea/discussion)

2) DISPUTE YOUR THOUGHTS

I will now introduce a powerful technique. (Joke here) What you have to do is talk to yourself – if necessary, out loud in the street – any time that you feel yourself worrying or submitting to pessimistic thoughts. That way your inner pessimist will become embarrassed and give up. Doctor Seligman – author of *Learned Optimism* – provides the following tip:

> Stand up and slam the palm of your hand against the wall and shout: 'STOP!' This is one of several simple but highly effective thought-stopping techniques used by people who are trying to interrupt habitual thought patterns.

If that doesn't work, then you need to give yourself a good talking to. Doctor S suggests pacing around the street like a highly paid barrister and treating your mind to a dose of nose-pinching cross-examination. Find the gaps in your argument, push yourself to come up with evidence. Even if your mind is right, it's bound to feel a little awkward.

On the other hand, I've often noticed, a lot of pessimists enjoy being negative. They just don't realise it. If you're one of these people, give up now. I don't know if any of these psychological techniques will work for you. And if we take the long view, you're probably right.

Everyone is against you and you'll probably die horribly.

(Breakout groups/tea/discussion)

5

Death, be not proud.

John Donne

'What about you, Loz?' Mark grinned and punched me on the arm. 'How's the optimism?'

Mark had just sold another company. Every time he sold a company, I noticed, his teeth got slightly bigger. They were imperial teeth. Alpha teeth. He showed just the right amount of gum. I sipped my lager and tried not to stare at them.

'It's going great,' I said.

Mark's eyebrows contracted. 'Have you found the answer yet?'

'There are lots of answers,' I said uneasily. 'I'm not sure I can fit them into one simple message.'

My friend looked worried. 'That's not very optimistic, Loz.'

I wasn't feeling optimistic. Almost a month had passed since my meeting with Dr Seligman and I still hadn't found the JBF, that mysterious energy I'd been searching for. Nor had I found this new definition of optimism yet. Without my list of world problems I felt at sea. What was this precondition I was supposed to look for? When would my life start to change?

That night I lay in bed, staring at the ceiling of my father's spare room. I thought about Mark and his large apartment in Mayfair. He was probably at his desk right now, staring at a printout of projected future cashflows. Mark certainly had the JBF. Where he got it from I had no idea. Perhaps it came with his teeth. I knew for a fact that he woke up at 6 a.m., canines at the ready, to do some kind of daily fitness. I had heard that he went running three mornings a week and took boxing lessons. And every day he went to his office and drank cup after cup of coffee as he plotted his takeover of the world. Maybe taking over the world was an absolute prerequisite for optimism? Maybe coffee was? I sank back in my chair. That couldn't be it. Both of those things give me stomach cramp.

Then there was Ian Wilson, the international rower who boasted that he got up at 5 a.m. every morning to sell rowing machines: 'Life is competitive,' he told me. 'You put people on a desert island they eat each other. That's why I get out of bed at five o'clock. Bang! Ready for business.'

Yet every time I set out of the house with the intention of being dynamic I ended up slowing down to a stop and looking at trees. I just couldn't get excited about my project any more – list or no list. I was more interested in feeling OK. I turned my head and tried to sleep. Something was still missing and I didn't know what it was.

A few days later I sat across from a gloomy-looking woman at a dinner party. She fiddled quietly with her chicken while everyone else chatted. A pessimist, I thought to myself. Maybe she would have some insight into this stifling cloud of apathy? I leant across the table and said: 'What are you most pessimistic about?' The woman looked thoughtfully at her plate. 'Oh!' she said, as if she had left it at home with her car keys. 'Death! Without a doubt. Death and the loss of loved ones.'

'Death?' I was taken aback. 'You mean normal, ordinary death?'

'Yes. There's no way to solve that one.'

I spent the rest of the dinner in silence. Death!

Wasn't it a bit small-minded to be worrying about death? Death wasn't so bad, was it? I had learned that, when people die – if you don't think about it too much – it isn't such a terrible thing, especially if you live in South London and have to walk fifteen minutes to catch a bus. I felt sorry for the woman.

The next day, however, her words were still rumbling in my head. I found a book by Carl Jung in my father's study. Fear of death, I read, lies at the root of all our sorrows. Everything we do to get attention, feel better about ourselves or win love and approval from our friends, is a subconscious strategy to avoid the clutches of death.

Good joke teller? Successful entrepreneur? Avoider of death!

Did I have a *subconscious* fear of death, a fear I wasn't aware of? Was that the explanation for the choking cloud of greyness hanging over me? Maybe it was really nothing to do with bad news after all. Maybe I was suffering from a sublimated terror of oblivion?

I tried my father on the subject.

'Yes!' he laughed. 'It's intolerable! We didn't ask to be born. We didn't ask to be put in this world and got all interested in it only to have it fizzle out on us. It's absurd!'

Maybe Xanthe would have a more optimistic angle on the matter. For a journalist she seemed to know a vast amount about psychology. And all sorts of other ologies too.

'I went to a conference last weekend,' she told me, 'and this man gave a lecture on the science of old age. Soon they expect to massively extend the human lifespan, perhaps even eradicate ageing altogether.'

'That's it!' I said, banging my fist on the grass. 'I knew they were doing something about it.'

'He's a gerontologist from Cambridge University, and apparently he's quite controversial.'

'I have to meet him.'

She leafed through the programme. 'His name is Aubrey de Grey.'

'Aubrey de Grey . . .' I rolled it around my mouth. 'He sounds like a medieval knight.'

'I think he spends most of his time on CNN.'

I looked up Aubrey on the internet. He was obviously a knight with html skills. His website explained the whole thing:

SENS (Strategies for Engineered Negligible Senescence)
A practical approach to developing real anti-ageing medicine

Think curing ageing would be bad? Think again

What's this nonsense about me maybe living 1,000 years? Answers

Bingo! I thought Immortality had an internet address. At the bottom of the website there was a link to the University of Cambridge genetics department. Despite his colourful writing style the doctor was for real. I called him on the phone.

'It's not a question of if, but when.'

'When?' I asked.

His voice was deep and doctorly. 'It'll take ten years for

us to double the lifespan of a mouse. If that happens, then there will be a huge public outcry to develop this for human beings. Things will happen very quickly.'

I felt the room grow cold. Now that we were getting down to it there was something grim and scary about all this. What if the process got out of control? What if terrorists used the technology to create ten-foot tall rats with infinite life spans? Technology was one of the things that many pessimists – *even I* – found ominous and depressing. What if it destroyed the human race?

It was a sunny, windy afternoon when I finally made it to Cambridge. I stood outside the train station and waited as autumn leaves made circles around my feet. Aubrey de Grey, like all my other optimists so far, had agreed to see me immediately. I watched as students came and went, wrapped up in their long scarves and petty concerns, unaware of my mission and the burden I was carrying for the world.

As I pondered my responsibility to mankind, a student careened through the traffic on an ancient racing bike. He had an immense ginger beard, capped with a purple and orange ski hat. Only in Cambridge, I mused, could students get away with looking like that. To my surprise, the cyclist spun in a semi-circle and dismounted, waving at me as he jumped off.

'Laurence Shorter?' he said.

'Professor!' I choked. I had been expecting someone sage and groomed, perhaps in a cashmere coat. Aubrey was wearing Converse trainers. A hand emerged from his donkey jacket.

'Welcome to Cambridge,' he said.

We sat in the back yard of a pub and I set up my recording equipment. 'Where shall I put my head?' asked the doctor. 'For your camera?' He tidied his hair with a fingerless glove.

'How old are you?' I asked.

'I'm forty-three,' he said, glancing at my hands. 'But I happen to know that I'm unusually healthy.'

'Right,' I said. 'And you're finding a cure for death.'

'It's not a cure for death,' he corrected. 'It's a cure for ageing. In fact it's a mix of things.' He sucked the foam off a pint of Guinness. 'We're combining seven different fields to come up with a solution which might actually have a chance of working. Let me explain. These therapies are rejuvenation therapies that fix the damage that has been accumulating in our metabolism throughout our lives. That damage has to accumulate to a certain level before it's bad for us. This means that in order to maintain youthfulness indefinitely we don't need to cure ageing once and for all – we only need to keep the overall level of damage *below the threshold* where it starts to become functionally problematic. In other words, we never have to fix ageing perfectly, and yet in terms of our health it will be the same as if we had. Do you follow me?'

'You're saying that this would be an ongoing therapy, a finger in the dam approach?'

'Exactly. Which will give us time for the technology to advance. Every time you hit fifty or sixty we'll put you back another thirty years.'

I rubbed my temples and tried to keep up. 'This is actual rejuvenation,' Aubrey reminded me, smoothing his hair. 'You would be youthful, both physically and mentally, right up to the day you mis-time the speed of that oncoming lorry.'

'That's clever!' I said. I felt myself being swept along by the doctor's fast-talking enthusiasm. But what about the other side of this? A future ruled by scientists in lab coats with bad breath and no knowledge of popular music.

'And the nightmare scenario,' I said. 'Genetic engineering out of control, nano-agents, clones, terminator genes, overpopulation . . . ?'

Aubrey stroked his beard, amused. 'One hundred thousand people die from ageing *every day*,' he said. 'If we can bring the defeat of ageing even one day closer by our actions, we'll save one hundred thousand lives. In one year, that means 35 million lives. I don't know about you, but those are pretty staggering numbers.'

'Right,' I said. 'Well, that's certainly a strong point.'

'If Fleming had halted his work on penicillin,' continued the doctor, 'because he was worried about the effects on population, we wouldn't have antibiotics!'

I watched him take a glug of his Guinness. Was Aubrey really the next Alexander Fleming? He had his critics. Before coming up I had managed to get hold of an open letter written by the professor's colleagues in the academic world. It wasn't positive. The eminent US gerontologist Rich Miller had persuaded twenty-eight other scientists to sign it.

> Each of the specific proposals that comprises the SENS agenda is, at our present state of ignorance, extremely optimistic . . . it commands no respect at all from within the scientific community.

I drew this to Aubrey's attention.

'Ah, the letter,' he said. 'If you talk to a mainstream gerontologist they may scoff. But ultimately because my ideas are so radical and my predictions so extreme, I can't just be a nice, kind diplomatic scientist.' He smiled to himself. 'You know what Gandhi said: "First they ignore you, then they laugh at you, then they fight you, then you win." Yes, that letter was a definite step forward for me.'

He raised an eyebrow, suavely. 'I don't kid myself but I am definitely the spearhead of the worldwide war on ageing right now.'

I leant back, impressed. 'What does it involve, this . . . therapy?'

'When it first arrives,' replied Aubrey modestly, 'the therapy will be extremely elaborate and expensive and *dangerous*, quite honestly. It will involve going to hospital for a month, maybe more, and getting all manner of stem cell therapies and gene therapies and a bunch of other things . . . basically I have no idea really yet, but it will be very elaborate.'

I flicked a peanut off the table. 'So . . . what chance do you think I have?'

'Of making it?' blinked Aubrey. 'If you look after yourself, and the rest of your body doesn't do what your hair is doing,' he glanced at my forehead, 'you have a fair chance.'

'You think my hair is a problem?' I touched it cautiously.

'There are lots of things you can't predict . . . but if you're able to access these therapies immediately, and if they don't kill you before they cure you, then you've got . . . I'd say . . .' He paused. 'A 30 or 40 per cent chance?'

'Of living to a thousand?'

The doctor licked the foam from around his lips. 'Yes. Well, of being healthy enough to survive until the therapies come along. And then I'd say it's fifty-fifty whether you make it to a thousand or not.'

'That's quite a strong chance of living to a thousand,' I said.

He smiled. 'Exciting, isn't it?'

A breeze blew over the tops of our glasses. I had a 40 per cent chance of having a 50 per cent chance of living to a thousand. Was that good or bad? I pictured myself at the moment of truth – a red pill sitting on the table in front of me. Ahead lay the scary future, behind the pessimistic past.

'Do you think this will actually make us happier?' I asked.

'I haven't the faintest idea whether it will make us happier,' said the professor forcefully. *'But I don't care . . .* All I know is I'm not in favour of ageing. And I don't think I need to have a better reason.'

'Won't we be terribly timid? I mean, if life is so long we'll be scared to take any risks.'

'Yes,' he conceded. 'People may become more risk-averse. That is one of the potential problems. But I'm not too worried about that. Things will become safer. They'll have to. They'll develop risk-free automobiles with highly advanced guidance systems. They'll never crash.'

'Technology can solve everything!'

'It has so far,' said the doctor.

I hesitated. 'What about pandemics, and housing, and over-exploitation of the environment?'

Aubrey checked his nails impatiently, as if this and any other wasted moment might lead to his untimely death. 'We will have plenty of time to figure that out later. For the time being our priority has to be: end the slaughter. Everything else is detail.' He sipped his pint. 'You know – premature, involuntary death is generally frowned upon in most other contexts – so one only needs the most utterly primitive sense of proportion to say that whatever the problems might be that will result from defeating ageing . . . they're worth it.'

I fell silent, pondering this undeniable argument.

'People won't be frail any more,' said Aubrey, leaning back into the sunshine. 'Everyone is going to be youthful. There won't be any old people. That's quite a difference. It'll be just like when we were students: you've got your entire life ahead of you, you have a million choices to make and a million years to make them in; it feels pretty good to me!' Then he added: 'My mother's in hospital at the moment. It would be great not to have to worry about her.'

I watched an empty crisp packet as it got yanked around by the autumn wind. 'You're an optimist, right?'

'Yes, well, I don't give up easily. When I was a kid people always said, Don't get your hopes up too high, you'll only be disappointed. Well, I always ignored that advice and I've never had a problem!'

I looked into the black mirror of my Guinness. Aubrey had the ability, enviable in a bearded man, to create a universe that revolved endlessly around himself. Maybe that's what I needed. Maybe it was nothing to do with death.

I went home in a philosophical mood. Perhaps it was the uncertainty. I was still waiting for the information about my massively extended lifespan to sink in. Rain started down from heavy grey clouds, spattering the windows of the train. We rolled through the flatlands of East Anglia and I pictured the countryside crowded full of people: their vehicles, their space-age buildings and their thousand year-old children.

Somehow it made no difference to anything.

6

It is hard to conquer burning passions towards relatives and close friends. The best way to quench them is to break all associations.

The Hundred Thousand Songs of Milarepa

It was only at the end of our long encounter in the cathedral that Doctor Seligman told me about Matthieu Ricard. We were about to leave York Minster when the famous psychologist turned to me.

'If you're looking for optimists, there's someone you have to meet.' The professor raised an eyebrow. 'Matthieu Ricard is a Buddhist monk. He also happens to be the Dalai Lama's interpreter and a high-powered research scientist. In France he's a major celebrity.' He weighed his words carefully. 'The amazing thing about Matthieu is, he's taken all my tests, and every time it's the same. He is the happiest person I have ever met.'

Coming from Doctor Seligman this was no small statement. After all, Seligman was the godfather of Positive Psychology. He had met a lot of happy people and he had tested all of them. By the laws of probability that made Matthieu Ricard the happiest person in the world.

'There's an important neuro-scientist called Richie Davidson,' he continued, 'who has isolated the parts of the left frontal lobes that light up when you're happy. And in Richie's curve there's this one person who is four standard deviations happier than anyone else in the world, whose brain lights up more . . . it's Matthieu.' The doctor shook his head in admiration. 'Statistically, it means he's on another planet. And he has this aura,' he said, trailing off wistfully. 'Auras aren't really my thing . . .'

'Is he an optimist?'

'That's the paradox,' he exclaimed. 'Buddhists aren't *supposed* to be optimists. For Buddhists everything is an illusion, including "good" and "bad". Yet Matthieu is the biggest optimist of them all. If you can get him to explain that to your satisfaction I'll be extremely interested.'

I nodded dutifully. Whatever Seligman said, I would do. Besides, I was badly in need of a fresh angle on the subject. After all, I had now tackled the single most important problem of the universe – death itself – and yet I could see no significant improvement in my feelings. Was there something deeper going on?

As soon as I got back to London I sent an email to the monk, crossing my fingers and praying that I hadn't missed his annual visit to the internet café. He replied almost immediately:

Dear Laurence,

Thank you for your warm and kind message!
I think that optimism is much deeper than people often think and that it reflect a deep confidence in the potential for change and flourishing that we all have deep within.

Three occurrences of the word 'deep' in the same sentence – the guy was obviously a believer.

I live in Nepal but I will be passing through Paris on
21 January. Would you like to meet then?

Yes, I would.

The Happiest Man in the World!

My father knocked on the door.

'Guess what?' he said. 'I've found a buyer for the
house!'

'Wow.' I felt a lump in my throat. 'Dad, that's . . . great.'

I knew we were trying to sell the family home. I just
hadn't foreseen it going through the very moment I decided
to quit all paid work and dedicate myself to the search for
optimism.

'Don't worry,' he said. 'I'm sure we'll find a place for
you.'

I shook my head. 'No, Dad . . . I have chosen my path.
I must face it alone.'

Life had obviously got wind of my promise to defeat
pessimism and had decided to take me seriously. It was all
part of the strange and disturbing power of the book. It
was making stuff happen in my life, it was *forcing* me to be
optimistic.

There was more, too.

Zara was a tall, spirited Dutch girl I had met two months
earlier at a yoga centre – a place I had started attending after
noticing the high density of attractive women in the vicinity.
I hadn't paid much attention to Zara at first, but on my
third or fourth visit, I stopped and studied her across the
room. She seemed more at ease than the others – and yet
she didn't wear sandals or have unseemly henna tattoos. She
even had a sense of style. But what caught my interest was
something else: she was full of brightness and enthusiasm.
There was something exciting about her presence. When
she laughed, I noticed, the cupboards in the kitchen actu-

ally vibrated. It was an optimistic laugh. A laugh I could imagine travelling around the world with.

I felt a rush in my tummy. *My God*, I thought, *what if Zara is the one?*

I had been waiting for 'the one' for ages – as long as I could remember in fact. But recently this search had intensified. I had suddenly noticed – as if waking from a long and troubled sleep – that most of my friends were already married and already on their first or second baby. How did that happen? Had I been dreaming all this time? There was not a moment to waste.

'Do you know Professor Martin Seligman?' I quizzed her, as we sipped a cup of tea one winter afternoon. 'Are you aware of his groundbreaking work on cognitive therapy?'

Zara smiled faintly. 'I'm familiar with Seligman. I studied with the existential psychotherapists. Like cognitive therapy the existentialists are concerned with the self-conceptualisations that lie at the heart of the human struggle with sex and death.'

I was stunned. Zara was smart enough and beautiful enough to be a serious contender. There was only one problem. She didn't believe in the concept of marriage. She didn't believe in the concept of relationships, either – or, for that matter, any concept. Like me, Zara was on a personal voyage of discovery. Unlike me, her passions were freedom, non-attachment and the illusory nature of all existence.

'What do you mean you don't believe in marriage?' I asked her, on our first date.

'It's just a concept,' she explained. 'And concepts cause problems.'

I frowned. We were clearly meant to be together. Everything pointed towards that, from our love of roses to our shared taste in Chopin. And yet, she had these ideas,

ideas which were bizarrely radical and inconvenient. I felt my shoulders tensing for the task ahead. I would have to change her mind. It would be a struggle, but I would succeed. I was absolutely certain.

Four weeks later Zara told me she was selling her flat and leaving London to travel the world. A chill coursed through my being.

'But why?' I said. 'Where?'

'India!' she said. 'I've been planning it for years!'

My nerves lunged, sickeningly. *Wait*, I told myself. It's a test. It would take Zara a while to realise that her life had changed, changed for good. In the meantime I would humour her, and encourage her plans for a short break from London. As our intimacy grew, it would soon become obvious that going away for a year off just wasn't going to happen.

Luckily, she hadn't booked her flight yet. She was waiting for the results of a long-standing legal case and she had nothing to do except hang out with me and meet optimists. This didn't surprise me. It was merely destiny playing its hand and keeping the two of us together.

That's when I remembered Matthieu Ricard: 'happiness' . . . Buddhism . . . It was exactly the kind of thing that Zara loved.

I told her about the meeting.

'Wow,' she said. 'You're finally approaching optimism from an interesting angle!'

I shrugged shyly.

'Do you think this guy is *enlightened*?'

'I don't know,' I said. 'What does that mean anyway?'

'Achieving Enlightenment is every Buddhist's goal. It means an end to suffering, a state of bliss.'

'Oh.'

There was a boy at my school who used to call himself

a Buddhist. Benjamin used to walk around in his judo outfit telling people they were deluded. He was fat and he had freckles. If you said good morning he liked to say: 'Ah, but *is it?*' And if you got angry he would flip you with a judo throw.

'Your own anger has defeated you,' he would say.

Was that Enlightenment?

Unfortunately I only had a few more weeks to persuade Zara how spiritually advanced I was. It was Matthieu Ricard or nothing. I asked her if she would like to come see him with me in Paris. She said yes.

At least there was some certainty in my life.

The next day I agreed to help my father clear out the basement – a cavernous cellar which contained my entire childhood. It was a big job. When I came down Dad was cramming something into a bin bag. I caught him in the glare of my torch. 'What are you doing?' I said. 'You can't throw away *Brown Ted!*'

He sighed and tossed my teddy onto a pile of old toys. 'You're going to have to let go of this stuff one day, Laurence.'

'Why?'

'There's not enough room,' he said. 'How's the book? Or is it a radio series now?'

'It's bigger than that.'

I told him about Matthieu Ricard.

'Ah, Buddhists: the ultimate optimists. They believe it's possible to escape from suffering. Hah!'

'"Buddhists don't believe in God",' I said, quoting from a website I had just printed off. '"They only believe in a supreme consciousness. All entities including the self are an illusion. The only way to avoid suffering is to escape from all human attachments."'

'Ah, yes,' he said, 'I find that rather reassuring. Maybe you'll learn something from this guy.'

I grabbed my bear from the throw-away pile. 'Why would I need to learn anything?'

My father shrugged and broke a picture frame over his knee.

Friday.

The doors closed and the Eurostar glided soundlessly out of the station. We were on our way to France. I sipped a coffee and glanced up at Zara. She was looking sexy and windswept in a casual, understated way. Like Ashley Judd, Zara had a subtle beauty that most people couldn't see, a beauty which resonated perfectly with my own, superior tastes. I watched her, indulgently. What a catch! Even if Zara had weird ideas about spirituality – things like 'freedom' and 'universal love', which had caused me so much anguish in the last few weeks – I knew they wouldn't last. Any day now she would wake up and become a normal, grown-up person. She was simply going through a phase. And while she did I was happy to take a friendly interest. It was bringing us closer together. Maybe I could afford to be a bit more relaxed about Buddhism? I opened my book, *Introduction to Buddhism*, at the first page. There was a list of precepts entitled 'Buddha's Four Noble Truths'.

THESE ARE THE KEYS TO HUMAN PERFECTION

I bridled slightly as I scanned the list. They weren't exactly light-hearted. Truth number three was particularly stern:

Freedom from suffering comes when a person rids himself of all desires.

I hunched over the book. What about healthy desires, like love? I had been looking forward to this weekend for days. If Zara was merely an illusion – or part of some formless supreme consciousness – then how could I explain the long brown hairs that had started appearing on my jacket? And why could I not stop thinking about her?

I turned the page.

Inside every pleasure is the seed of future sorrow.

'Oh, my God.'

'How's it going?' asked Zara, looking over curiously.

'Fine,' I said quickly. If I didn't take precautions the girl would join a Buddhist monastery and I'd never see her again. Maybe I had made a serious mistake inviting her to meet Matthieu.

'You don't have to come to this meeting, you know,' I said. 'You can walk around Paris or go shopping.'

Zara laughed. 'Are you joking? I didn't come here to buy clothes. I want to meet the Buddhist.'

A few hours later, Matthieu greeted us in the corridor of his apartment. As he waved us in I stood hesitantly in the hallway, sniffing the air. There was something strange about the atmosphere in there.

A saffron nun appeared and offered to take my coat.

'No, thank you,' I said, smiling thinly. I scanned the room for signs of incense – a favourite trick of hippies and meditators. A strange light glowed off the mantelpiece. I was determined not to get sucked into their 'aura'. No doubt they would like me to stay here and become a devotee. I could arrange the flowers and welcome visitors. And that would be the end of my quest for optimism!

'Is it normal,' I asked, 'for a monk to have such a beautiful flat?'

'It belongs to a friend of mine,' said Matthieu warmly, adjusting his toga as we sat down. 'You accept whatever comes your way. One day I was in Tahiti at the house of Gauguin, the famous artist, sitting by the swimming pool. Imagine: the sunset, the palm trees. I thought to myself, Suppose I owned this place? Suppose this *belonged* to me. So what!?' He chuckled. 'Which way is that supposed to make me happy?'

Aha, I thought. Non-attachment to material things. Noble Truth five no doubt.

Matthieu glanced at his watch and I recalled a comment from my Buddhist manual:

Time is a human invention, an illusion which doesn't exist.

This didn't seem to bother Matthieu.

'We have one hour,' he smiled.

Before we could go any further the nun appeared with a tray of tea and cakes. I was relieved to note that the Noble Truths didn't forbid the eating of cookies.

'Is it true that you're the happiest person in the world?' I asked.

'*Bof*,' said Matthieu, looking embarrassed.

'Dr Seligman told me you were the happiest person he had ever met.'

'Possibly . . . whatever . . .' Matthieu shifted uncomfortably. 'He did some scientific tests. Sure, I came out 200 per cent above the average . . . but so what? It's silly!'

There was an anxious pause. Matthieu laughed and

changed the subject to gamma waves in brain activity, but it was too late – I had found his weak spot. He couldn't take a compliment.

'That's the great thing about science,' continued Matthieu. 'If something is true, it's true. It's just science. And that's what Buddhism is. Science. The Buddhists have been practising it for over 2,000 years, and now it's coming to the West.'

'So pessimism and self-denial are available to everyone,' I said sarcastically.

Matthieu smiled. 'Buddhism is the most optimistic system you can imagine. We are the only people who believe that you can actually escape from suffering. True optimism is a deep confidence that you have the inner resources to deal with whatever may come your way.' He touched his heart. 'It's an inner happiness which is not dependent on outer circumstances.'

I gave him a shrewd look. Matthieu seemed to have inner happiness *and* outer luxury. 'If you're optimistic, does it mean you'll have a better life?'

The Frenchman laughed. 'Are you joking? I usually live in a monastery. I have to wake up at 5 a.m. and eat rice cakes for breakfast.'

'But isn't there some kind of mass consciousness at work,' asked Zara suddenly, 'that creates its own reality, like with earthquakes and natural disasters? Don't we make these things happen somehow?' I looked over, annoyed. 'The more optimistic you are,' I interpreted, 'the more things work out for you. Right?'

'No!' said Matthieu. 'This is stupid optimism. Stupid optimists think that everything is going to go their way. Imagine 6 billion people in the world, all getting their wishes. That's never going to happen . . .' He giggled playfully. 'Not ever! Remember,' he said, 'external situations can *never* make you happy, because they are *never permanent* – so, if you attach too much of your happiness to external things, like a relationship, for example . . .' He glanced at us both. 'Then of course you will be unhappy, because eventually it will die.'

I laid down my biscuit.

'But relationships are important,' I said, fixing him with a look. 'You can't just cut yourself off and withdraw from the world.'

Matthieu reached for his tea. 'True love can't be restricted to one or two specific beings. Love between men and women is limited, very limited. It can be mixed with very selfish feelings.'

He smiled innocently. I had fallen into his trap. Like all spiritual types, Matthieu was determined to convert us to the path of Nothingness. But I hadn't even achieved Somethingness yet!

I reached for Zara's hand. 'Is that how you see the future?' I asked him. 'A world with no possessions, no relationships, no desires?'

He shrugged. 'It doesn't matter about the future. What matters is your perception. What matters is training your mind to learn happiness.'

'But I'm happy already,' I said.

He shook his head. 'Genuine happiness is a skill. It takes time to develop. You don't expect to learn chess in one day, or to ride a horse – no! All the more so with your mind – it's your main interface to reality. That's why training it is so important. People who are negative and unhappy get stuck because they have a distorted vision of reality. They get attached to *things* because they believe that they are either good or bad, but this is wrong. For example . . .' He made a shape with his hand '. . . what is a woman? To you it is beautiful. To a *whale* it means nothing!'

His voice rose poetically. 'You must lose the illusion that some things are good and some things are bad. You have to end your dependency on external situations . . .'

Zara pulled her hand away.

'But . . .'

' . . . Then you can maintain your happiness, whether you're thrown in jail or . . . your girlfriend leaves you, or whatever!'

'I'm *already* happy,' I said, feeling the blood rise to my face. 'I'm an optimist.'

'What's more optimistic?' he said. 'To accept you are ill and look for a cure, or pretend you are not? We only emphasise suffering in order to fix it.'

'But I *am* happy,' I insisted. I glanced at Zara.

'What are you holding onto?' she asked suddenly. 'Ask yourself that question.' She watched me carefully.

'Look, can you not . . .'

Matthieu joined in. 'It seems you are hanging onto an idea of your *self* which no longer works . . .'

' . . . which doesn't make you happy,' concluded Zara.

'Because it is an illusion,' said the monk. 'Do you believe in yourself?'

'Of course!'

'Exactly,' he said softly. 'And as long as you hold onto this idea . . . this illusion of your *self* – then you will always suffer. The self is not possible. It's like a rainbow – you see it, but it is created by the sun, the cloud, the angle you are standing at. You think it is there, but if you take away one element it is gone. *Paf!* It never existed! You understand? Let go of it! That is the way to be happy.'

'I don't want to be happy,' I moaned. 'I want to be me!'

The video recorder clicked and whirred to a stop.

'You need to change the tape,' I said weakly, and Zara

started switching the cassettes. Outside a siren sped along the street, bending sound as it passed the building.

I felt a strong desire to lie down.

Maybe Matthieu was right. Perhaps I didn't exist, after all. Maybe I could just relax and let it all float past me. Zara would join a monastery and I could become a yoga teacher. It wasn't worth the struggle.

Then, I remembered something. 'A man like you,' I said, watching Matthieu. 'So peaceful and, yet, so . . . busy . . .' His eyes glazed over. 'May I ask . . . have you attained *enlightenment?*'

The monk blinked. I could almost hear Zara flinching from the other side of the room. It was the ultimate no-no.

'No, no,' he said, quickly.

There was a pause.

'Listen,' he said, 'you don't have to be enlightened to be happy.' He stood up and wrapped his gown around his waist. 'There's no right way of doing it. You don't need to become a monk and give up all your possessions and relationships.'

'You don't?'

'Of course not! This is what I spend my life telling people. You live in the world, you do the best you can, you take some time to meditate every day, and you recognise that things outside yourself cannot bring you lasting happiness. I have to go now, unfortunately, I have an interview with a television station.'

'Maybe we can go together?' I suggested.

The Buddhist agreed to drop us at our hotel. Sitting in the back of a taxi, crammed between my love interest and the red-robed priest, I swayed back and forth as the cab took the high-speed roundabout of the Arc de Triomphe. Miraculously, everything seemed to be in one piece. Matthieu had imparted his opinions without brainwashing my girlfriend, and I had survived the conversation without having to abandon my beliefs. Zara didn't even seem interested in the guy.

It had been a lucky escape.

'That was interesting,' I said, gratefully sipping a café au lait. 'So, what he's saying is, you can be spiritual *and* normal. You don't have to give up all your relationships and go and live in an ashram.'

Zara looked at me over her book. 'I don't necessarily agree with everything that Matthieu said.'

'Still,' I said, 'it was a good point, I think.'

'Maybe, but he was definitely right about one thing. Attachment can only lead to suffering. Love can only exist in freedom. And freedom in love.'

I sighed. Zara had some mild psychological problems. It was normal for a therapist.

Back in England I emailed Matthieu to congratulate him on our interview. He replied with an extract from his soon-to-be-published book about happiness. To my surprise he had written an entire chapter on optimism. Apart from my annoyance that the monk had stolen my idea, I had to concede that it was a well-written piece of prose. It was also a noble admission of defeat. Matthieu had cleverly summarised my most important points:

> For an optimist, it makes no sense to lose hope. We can always do better (instead of being devastated, resigned or disgusted), limit the damage (instead of letting it all go to pot), find an alternative solution (instead of wallowing pitifully in failure), rebuild what has been destroyed (instead of saying 'It's all over!'),

take the current situation as a starting point (instead of wasting our time crying over the past and lamenting the present), start from scratch (instead of ending there), understand that sustained effort will have to be made in the best apparent direction (instead of being paralysed by indecision and fatalism), and use every present moment to advance, appreciate, act and enjoy inner peace (instead of wasting our time brooding over the past and fearing the future).

I smiled. Optimism 1, Buddhism 0.

7

When I greeted Archbishop Tutu, I enveloped him in
a great hug; here was a man who had inspired an entire nation
with his words and courage, who had revived the people's hope
during the darkest of times.

Nelson Mandela

The next day someone smashed in the window of my car.
I spotted it from fifty yards away. 'I'm detached,' I said
to myself, as I approached the vehicle. 'This is nothing,
merely a transient material object.' I looked moodily at
the street. 'Fuck.' There were hundreds of cars to choose
from. Why did they have to choose mine? I kicked some
glass against the wall. Was it a sign from the universe?
Had I messed up again? I was failing as a positive thinker,
that was it. If I had been a proper optimist, this wouldn't
have happened.

Zara called. She sounded happy and excited. 'I've
bought my ticket to India!' she announced. 'I'm going,
I'm finally going!'

'That's wonderful,' I said.

'I bought a one-way ticket,' she added.

I walked back home and tried to work. It was no good.
I paced in circles around my room. I had to think, hard.
I had to figure out this situation.

The radio was on in the kitchen. I guiltily overheard

the day's news: an earthquake in Pakistan; a suicide bomb in Delhi; fifty deaths in Iraq. I put the kettle on. I had no time for this now. Zara's flight was leaving in three weeks. After all my work, she somehow still believed that relationships were illusory social constructs designed to prevent her from achieving self-actualisation.

The world would have to wait.

'You know,' said my dad, switching off the *Today* programme, 'Voltaire wrote *Candide* – his great masterpiece about optimism – after the city of Lisbon was destroyed by an earthquake.'

'You see!' I replied.

'Not really. Voltaire's book was a *satire*. He thought that optimists were idiots.'

Maybe Voltaire was right. Maybe I was an idiot.

It was time to change my approach.

As a young management consultant in the 1990s, my employers once posted me an American self-help book called *The Seven Habits of Highly Successful People*. It was sent along with my starting bonus as required reading and a taste of things to come. I was only twenty, but this innocent paperback seemed such an insult to my identity as a young, sceptical Englishman that I invited some friends around to witness its immolation in my dustbin.

'It seems like an OK book to me,' said Steve.

'Yeah,' said Daniel. 'Why the hatred?'

'Give me the book,' I said. I tossed it into the bin. 'It is evil, because it makes losers think they can be winners. And when winners are losers in disguise – and they're running the world – then we're in trouble.'

Daniel looked confused.

'Most Americans fall into that category,' I added.

Things had changed since those headstrong days. Now I was older, more desperate, and in love with someone who held cruel and unusual views about interpersonal relations. What is more, I was supposed to be investigating positive thinking.

I slipped into the Self Help section of Waterstone's, reminding myself I was a trained business consultant and had no cause to be afraid of a few paperbacks. Besides, I didn't know who else to turn to.

I looked around, hoping that no one would take me for a hippy.

This one looks quite innocent, I thought to myself, sliding out a weightless paperback with a cheerful, floral cover. The book was called *Creative Visualisation: Fulfilment of your Desires through the Art of Affirmation*. I opened it at the beginning.

> In creative visualisation you use your imagination to create a clear image, idea, or feeling of something you wish to manifest. Then you continue to focus on the idea, feeling, or picture regularly, giving it positive energy until it becomes objective reality.

Strange as it sounded, this instantly rang a bell – as if it were something that I had always known, deep down. I read on. Maybe I could use this method to visualise a technical problem for Zara's aeroplane? Maybe I could visualise someone just like her, but more convenient – perhaps with a dog and a house in Fulham.

I moved along the counter and opened another book. Strangely, this one also had flowers on the cover. It was called *The Cosmic Ordering Service*, and it stated that all you had to do was ask the universe for whatever you wanted, and it would happen.

Be aware of what you wish for and order; it could come true at once!

Interesting, I thought, *they all seem to be saying the same thing.* I slid the book back onto the shelf and sneaked out the back entrance.

I felt an invigorating burst of confidence, a freshness something akin to the feeling you get when you first shave with a Gillette. A sudden clarity of purpose filled my bones. Zara's determination to go travelling was nothing more than a challenge, a test of my will. As long as I didn't deviate and fall into panic, then everything would be OK – I just had to stick to my belief. What I had to do now was get my project back on track. Optimism was my trump card. It was something that Zara understood, something she admired, something we could collaborate on.

In the meantime, action was required: clear, decisive action on some pressing world issue, something that worried everyone and would be impossible to ignore. I needed something simple and straightforward, something depressing and universal, like starvation or poverty or . . .

'Africa,' said Zara, when I saw her that evening. 'Are you not going to tackle Africa?'

'That's it!' I said.

How could I forget Africa? It had been on my list from the start – item 35, between Food Prices and the Absence of a Tangible, Interventionist Deity – but I had put it off, intimidated by the scale of the problem. It was right in the pessimist sweet spot, a constant source of worry and guilt, the perfect excuse for cynics to feel bad about humanity and give up on the world. Forget Buddhism or psychology. Africa needed serious attention. But who could help me figure it out?

'Desmond Tutu?' suggested Zara.

'Tutu!' I said. 'Why not?'

Archbishop Tutu, surely, was the ultimate optimist: legend of the anti-apartheid struggle, founder of the Truth and Reconciliation Commission, and veteran campaigner for peace. He was so busy bringing forgiveness and reconciliation to the planet, and so ubiquitously present in every global initiative, I sometimes wondered if he had cloned himself and offered himself for commercial release.

Would he have time for us?

That evening I sat at my desk, trying to visualise a meeting with Desmond Tutu. I pictured myself in a grand office with alabaster statuettes and oil portraits of churchmen. Tutu was wearing a purple gown and I was in a suit.

I waited. Was something supposed to happen? The self-help books had said quite clearly that I was supposed to make my request and then leave it in the hands of the universe. But then what? The image faded.

Unwilling to put my trust in wishful thinking, I fired off an email to Tutu's office, asking when we could see each other. I told him I would be bringing my assistant, Zara, who was a trained psychologist, and that we had matters of importance to discuss with him. My tone was confident, masterly. Within an hour his secretary had replied.

I'm sorry, the Archbishop is travelling constantly and I can't crowd him with meetings.

I picked up the phone. As if that was going to stop me! I knew if I could get this meeting, then Zara and I could have one last, epic holiday together – and our union would surely be sealed. I would not give up. I called Tutu's office and pleaded, with ruthless and irresistible persistence, until his secretary finally gave in.

Two weeks later we were in Cape Town.

6.45 a.m. The chapel of St George's Cathedral, waiting for the morning service to begin. We didn't exactly have a meeting, but Tutu's secretary knew that I was here. She said that she would do her best. It was good enough for me.

I smiled at Zara. Amazingly, we hadn't had an argument about emotional commitment for days. She had even stopped arguing when I introduced her as my girlfriend. It seemed she had finally accepted her destiny as my future wife. The tide was beginning to turn.

I scanned the chapel for Desmond's secretary.

Strangely, my hands were beginning to sweat.

'Relax,' said Zara. 'Trust that things will work out. That's what optimism is all about.'

'What do you mean, trust?'

'Make a clear and positive intention that the meeting will happen, and then it will.' She smiled, brightly.

'I'll try,' I said.

A rustle of anticipation passed through the congregation as a small man in a purple dress walked up the aisle. He gave the crowd a long-suffering grin. I tried to catch his eye but he didn't seem to notice me.

Tutu delivered the service and then closed his Bible with a look of relief. 'Welcome!' he shouted. 'Welcome, welcome!'

The congregation clapped as if they had just witnessed God himself giving communion.

'It wasn't *that* great,' I whispered.

Tutu's secretary appeared and led us outside to a bustling café. Inside there was a committee of at least fifteen Tutu fans waiting for their hero.

'We're hungry!' cried Desmond, appearing in the doorway.

I crammed myself next to two other worshippers – a lady priest from Canada and a silent German. The archbishop was squashed in the middle like a birthday boy, with an oversized cup of chocolate in his hand. He was doing his best to talk to everyone at once. The Canadian priest – with her upturned collar and Margaret Thatcher handbag – was dominating the early running with stories about her diocese. Her object of worship looked bored. I seized my chance.

'Archbishop,' I said, 'I'm Laurence Shorter, the optimist . . .'

The room went swimmy as my eyes tunnelled in on the international celebrity.

'Mmm . . .' said Tutu. 'The optimist. Well, let me tell you, *I am not an optimist.*' He looked around the table as if to muster support. 'I'm *definitely* . . . not . . . an . . . optimist. I am . . . a Prisoner of Hope!'

I felt as if I had just been shot in the chest. A chorus of admiring sighs ascended from the Tutu fan club.

'*Optimism*,' he said, pointing his finger to the ceiling, 'can turn far too quickly into *pessimism* if conditions don't go well. *Hope* is different!'

He cackled meanly. I was now the object of attention – possibly hatred – of the entire cafeteria. 'But isn't hope the same as optimism?' I persisted.

'Not optimism . . . no!' He grimaced at my dictaphone.

'Hope is an article of faith! That despite all appearances to the contrary it's going to be OK!'

'That *is* optimism,' I insisted, but the archbishop ignored me.

By this time my fellow breakfasters were beginning to look at me as if I were an ambassador from another species, probably in the insect kingdom. The Nobel Prize winner himself was giving my project the thumbs down, in public. Carol from Canada shifted her seat slightly to the left. Didn't she know who I was?

Tutu grinned. 'For example, we always said that apartheid would end . . . but all the signs indicated that we ought to give up *hope*! That we ought to be totally *pessimistic*! I mean, the international community *supported* the apartheid government. *Your Prime Minister* actually called Nelson Mandela a *terrorist*. If you were only *an optimist* you would have given up!'

He looked around, appealing to the crowd.

'This is a moral universe,' he declared. 'There's no way that injustice . . . *ha ha ha*! . . . will ultimately prevail. But that's an article of faith! It's not something that depends on how things look. Things look awful.'

I took a gulp of tea. I had to let him know we were talking about the same thing – that he really was an optimist, that I wasn't a naïve fool but a very nice young man. Maybe then he would stop talking to me like some kind of colonial idiot from the 1980s.

'But aren't optimists better at being hopeful?' I reasoned.

Desmond frowned. 'Now you are *cheating* because you are making me talk about what we are supposed to talk about later. So you needn't come! *We've finished our interview.* Goodbye!'

I was shell-shocked. I didn't even know we had an

interview. And I had already blown it. I ran to the toilet
and did a yoga move to calm myself down. If I gave up
now, the whole reputation of optimism would be in jeop-
ardy.

When I got back, breakfast was over. The archbishop
had gone. I ran out of the building and followed his secretary down the street.

'Do you have a car?' she asked.

'No!' I cried.

'We can give you a lift to the office.' She caught up
with Tutu. 'They're going with you,' she ordered.

'Oh, *man!*' he sighed. 'Only if you promise not to
talk!'

Next thing I knew I was sitting in a BMW. Zara was
in the back and Tutu was in the driving seat. Desmond
looked out the window. 'No talking!' he said.

It took twenty minutes to get to his office. Tutu gazed
contemplatively at the road, still hoping that I would
somehow disappear if he didn't look at me. I wasn't sure
what I had done to offend him but I didn't care any
more. I was sitting in a car with Desmond Tutu – and
he was driving! I felt as if the doors of the universe had
opened and finally let me in. From now on, everything
would be OK.

At the next junction, Tutu twisted around in his seat.
'Let me give you some advice. 'Don't be optimistic. Be
hopeful. Hope is not dependent on reality.' He looked at
Zara in the mirror. 'Hope says that *good will ultimately
triumph over evil*. But in the meantime you have to put up
with poverty and torture.'

He waved at the traffic. An ocean of cars waited
politely at a crossing, giving way without a honk.
'Incredible! People can actually be quite considerate on
occasion.'

'Maybe I can persuade you,' I said.

Tutu ignored me and steered his vehicle into a business park. A gateman waved us past.

'I have a firm faith in people,' said the cleric quietly, as he parked the car. 'I believe that people are fundamentally good.' He looked me up and down. 'Now most of the evidence contradicts that, you know, and yet . . .'

He put his head in his hands. 'Oh, *man!* Why am I talking to you?'

Tutu led us up a stairway past some numbered, prefabricated business units. I looked around, confused. Where was the palace? Where were the liveried guards and the ornamental fountains? Had I made some kind of mistake?

To my relief, the archbishop's study was covered with awards and plaques from the nations of the world. I could feel the warmth returning to my cheeks. It felt good to be surrounded by the hushed approval of great men. I could do this, I thought to myself. I could be a world leader. Why not? I gazed longingly at a framed medallion cast in gold.

'Have you met my girlfriend?' he asked, pointing to a portrait of Aung San Suu Kyi, the Burmese dissident. 'I've never met her, but I like to call her my girlfriend.' He winked at Zara and stared back up at the picture. 'They wouldn't even let her see her husband when he was dying. They are such vicious creatures. Vicious, vicious, vicious. But they are also God's children. *Oohh!* I'm glad I'm not God! *Ha ha ha!*'

I laughed politely. No wonder Tutu was getting hope and optimism mixed up. He was a Christian!

The old man sat down. 'Yes?'

'Optimism,' I reminded him.

He put his hands together and frowned. I frowned back in return.

'You might not agree with optimism,' I said, 'but at least it's better than pessimism.'

'Nah,' he said, stubbornly. 'I think optimism leads far too easily into pessimism . . . really. Because as soon as the material circumstances change then you are for the high jump.'

'But . . .'

'Listen, pessimists are usually people who are not actually doing too badly. But they're cynical because they're holding onto the wrong kind of things. They're holding onto *externals* . . .'

Oh, no, I thought, *not again.*

'You're cynical because you think that external things can make you happy . . . you know, a smart car, a nice house, a beautiful wife, but it was discovered long ago . . . you don't have to be a Christian to realise that. Ha! All of these material things, wealth, success, sex . . . they don't actually have the *capacity* to satisfy.'

I cast a doleful look at Zara. Did every optimist I meet have to get involved in our personal relationship? Everyone *knows* that material things are superficial and unsatisfying. But some are less superficial than others. Like joint bank accounts and two-bedroom apartments in West London.

'So what is hope?' I asked, my voice steady.

'I think there is a deeper thing that people have. Human beings have a remarkable resilience. I was in Haiti just now and the poverty is . . . it just knocks the breath out of you. And yet people could laugh, people are smiling, people are neat, and they call that . . . home! You know, that dingy, squalid shack . . . home! There is something in us that tells us we're made for something better.'

'And Africa?' I asked cautiously. 'Do you feel "hopeful" that it can sort itself out?'

He looked up sharply. 'If you were just a little more modest and remembered just a little bit of your own history you'd not be so hoity-toity.'

'I'm sorry?'

'I often say to Europeans, *I just wish you didn't have such short memories.* You know, you produced two world wars, you produced the Holocaust and you've most recently produced ethnic cleansing! I mean you are experts!' He laughed, full of mirth, 'Yes, Africa,' he said, as if he were thinking out loud to himself. 'It will take some doing, but it will be done. Yes, it will be done.'

There was a knock and his secretary poked her head around the door. 'Time is up!'

Tutu smiled faintly and carried on in a whisper. 'We used to do a lot of funerals. When we were talking to our people we would say to them, "Do you know what? Some of you are going to be killed. Some of you, they are going to torture you. You're not going to see this wonderful *denouement*. But it doesn't matter, it's going to happen!" And there was an incredible time in the struggle when people were remarkably altruistic, when they said, "It doesn't matter if I'm tortured or killed, as long as it contributes to the attainment of our freedom." Now there must be something that makes these young people say, "Even death doesn't matter. My total . . . my apparent . . . total ANNIHILATION doesn't matter."' He slapped his hand on the chair leg. 'And it's not *optimism!*'

By now, I had figured out Tutu's system. Hope was a code word for optimism. And optimism was a code word for stupidity. We were talking about exactly the same things. We just had different vocabulary.

But the old warhorse wasn't going to budge. 'You know, the police . . . they used to have photographs of Mandela and lesser mortals like . . . like me. And they liked to use us for target practice! They have your face and that was . . . *he hehe hehe heh ha ah aha!*' He rolled his eyes and hooted. 'Hope,' he said. 'Yeah . . . Hope is a God who accepts everyone. Even killers. And that is when you say, *I think I've got to be a better person*. Not because that is the grounds on which God accepts me. No, God has accepted me already!'

He put his hand on my knee. 'You know, the Bible says some extraordinary things. It says, God chose you before the foundation of the world. God said, *Laurence, this is going to be my special child*.' I looked down, mesmerised, at his giant fingers. 'And then because you are God's special child you then evolve into . . . a *saint*.'

'That's very interesting,' I said.

'Every one of us has the capacity to become a saint,' said Tutu slowly. 'The best thing that God ever created is *you*.' He smacked my knee. 'You! Especially! There's nothing better, God couldn't have done better. You're the best thing that God ever produced . . . ! You see?'

I nodded.

'Good!' He cranked himself off his chair. 'Now get out!'

8

*The question is, when did you stop growing? When did
you stop having those Aha! moments? And that's the moment you
died. Most pessimists are the walking dead. It doesn't matter that
they breath and they get up and eat . . . they are dead.*

Taddy Blecher

The Cape of Good Hope.

We turned the corner of the headland and the sun
angled kindly through the pine trees, shading our eyes
as we gazed on the great city below us. I had been looking
forward to this moment – leaving Cape Town for a few
days of holiday before travelling back home. The scene
below us – gleaming white ships, industrious docks, the
cranes and pulleys of a busy, maritime city – filled me
with a sense of relief. This was Africa at its best: clean
and prosperous and safe. This was the continent's future:
boutique hotels and vineyards, orange groves and restaur-
ants. 'You see,' I said, as we took another bend, 'what
positive thinking and free enterprise can do for a country!'
Zara smiled. I put my foot down on the pedal. 'Tutu
knew exactly what I was talking about. He was just too
stubborn to admit I was right.' *Oh, yes,* I thought, *things
were unfolding exactly as I had planned.*

Soon we reached flat ground. The sun was going down

and it wouldn't be long before dark. I decided to take a short cut.

'Wow,' said Zara. 'This must be a township.'

'That's funny,' I said, peering at my map. Small fires appeared at the side of the road. The surface became tarry and broken. I fixed my gaze on the way ahead.

'We should have hit the coastal road,' I said, trying to stay calm. 'This isn't marked. I think this is . . . this is Khayelitsha. The one they told us about.'

Zara rolled down her window to lean out. The shanty town stretched for miles around.

'Can you roll that up?' I said. 'Please.'

'Look at the view!' said Zara. 'Can we stop?'

'I'm not sure that's a good idea,' I mumbled. 'We're running a bit late.'

'Late for what?'

'Just . . . late,' I said, feeling annoyed. I scanned the side of the road.

'But we're on holiday!' she protested.

I pulled over and Zara opened the door. 'Wait, I'm going to take a picture. I'll only be a second.' She hopped out of the car. The sun was dipping slowly towards the horizon.

When I looked up Zara was gone. I cursed and got out of the vehicle, just in time to catch her red dress disappearing between rows of huts. Was she totally oblivious? 'Zara!' I yelled. I looked back at our hire car, gleaming with new paint and piled with electronic equipment. I stood for a moment, agonised. By the time I found Zara she was halfway into the shanty town, crouching to talk to a little girl. A small crowd had gathered around. I looked at them. 'Hey,' I said. 'What's up?'

Zara grinned. 'Can you take a picture of us? I've promised to send them a copy.'

'Sure,' I said, sweating. 'That's a lovely shot . . .' She

beckoned to the rest of the family to join her. A young guy with bleary eyes ambled over and called his friend. Was that a machete I saw in his belt?

I looked back towards the car. If someone stole it now we would be done for. Would we be shot or beaten to death? Would they force us to drink castor oil? 'It's getting dark,' I said, calculating the fastest escape route. *Maybe I should go now*, I thought to myself. I started walking backwards.

'Wait,' said Zara. 'I'm coming.'

Back in the car I gripped the steering wheel.

'That was nice!' said Zara. 'We're probably the first outsiders they've spoken to for days.'

I clenched my teeth and nodded.

'Why are you so nervous?'

'I'm not nervous,' I snapped.

She looked out the window.

I spent the rest of the journey in silence. Once I had completed my mission and saved the world from pessimism I would come back here and walk through that shanty town without any fear. I would walk right in there with my pockets full and my hands open. But right now I had unfinished business to attend to. I had a book to write, I had a relationship to work on. I wasn't ready to die. I brooded as the horizon disappeared into darkness. Africa was a mess. A man shouldn't have to worry about this kind of thing when he is on holiday.

We had one more optimist to meet before catching the plane back to England – an entrepreneur in Johannesburg who had started his own business school.

I had heard about Taddy Blecher from Desmond Tutu

– or rather, Desmond Tutu's secretary, who had passed his name to us as we left. The interesting thing about Taddy, it seemed, was that he had come up with a solution to poverty: a university designed to educate poor South Africans and make them into entrepreneurs. The whole thing sounded genius. All we had to do now was roll this out across the world and the problems of crime, poverty and gang violence would be solved in one fell swoop. I would never have to fear for my life again.

We drove in through downtown Johannesburg. It was forty degrees and the streets were mobbed, but I wasn't afraid. Soon we would be at CIDA, Taddy's business school. I sat back and waited for his campus to roll into view. It would be a welcome relief from the squalor of the Jo'burg streets.

The taxi pulled over and I looked up from my newspaper. There were still pedestrians everywhere. We were on a busy main street, under a row of skyscrapers. 'Why are we stopping?'

'Look,' said Zara, pointing to a building. 'CIDA City Campus.'

I frowned. Where were the playing fields and the neatly mown lawns? And the quiet students sitting under trees? A secretary met us and took us inside. It was an old tower block, a 1980s skyscraper from Johannesburg's merchant banking days. I felt the sweat creeping up my back. This is not what I had envisaged. We followed the girl across a gutted, open-plan floor. 'What's that noise?' I asked, glancing nervously towards the ceiling. The sound of stamping and shuffling reverberated from upstairs.

'Salsa class,' she smiled sleepily. She led us past a makeshift lecture theatre curtain. *Chaos!* I thought, gripping Zara's hand.

'Mr Blecher will be with you in a moment.'

'Is he running late?' I asked. 'Because we don't have much time.'

We sat down on a sofa and I thought longingly about our pretty guesthouse and the gin-and-tonic I would be holding in my hand that very moment if I wasn't currently in the most dangerous downtown on the planet. Why had I dragged Zara here? I *hated* charities. Charities were *depressing*. The very existence of NGOs implied a world of unfixable problems, and usually some hate figure to campaign against, like the American government or big multinationals. I was only interested in solutions, ideally involving the graceful expansion of coffee chains, organic supermarkets and internet companies with free drinks cabinets – across the entire world. I sniffed the air for the smell of freshly ground coffee.

At least CIDA was a business school, I told myself. I looked at the framed certificates on the wall. One of them commemorated the opening of a new faculty, endowed by the Virgin Group. 'Look, he knows Richard Branson!'

Zara shrugged.

'Hi guys!' said Taddy, appearing in the corridor. 'I'll be with you in a second.' I watched him hand some documents to his secretary. He had the soothing manner and careful modulation of a mental nurse.

I knew his type. I looked down at the CIDA brochure:

> Taddy is a former senior project leader with international strategic management consulting firm Monitor Company, where he was voted consultant of the year three years in a row.

Taddy was the kind of bright-eyed achiever who charms everyone. No doubt he was loved by everyone – the secretaries, the senior partners *and* the boys in the print room. When he was a teenager he probably ran the debating society, the school magazine and the lacrosse team: all at the same time.

Taddy reappeared. You could almost see the halo of 'yes' around his head.

'Can we get you some tea, coffee, hard spirits?' he chuckled smoothly and we followed his slipstream into the boardroom. I could feel Taddy's energy scooping me up like some kind of human-flavoured ice cream. He was a boyish fellow – a spitting image of Harry Potter in his late thirties, complete with glasses and oversized tie. Behind us on the wall was a poster entitled QUALITIES OF THE UNIFIED FIELD LOCATED IN THE LAGRANGIAN OF THE UNIFIED FIELD – a pattern of crisscrossing lines with mysterious labels, like a map of the universe from Elizabethan times. What the hell was that?

'Are you guys together?' asked Taddy.

My heart leapt. Even Taddy Blecher could see it. Our togetherness was now a fact of life.

'I'm helping out with optimism,' said Zara.

'We're together,' I told him.

'That's great!' Taddy spread his hands like a talk show host. 'Why didn't you say?' We sat down at his boardroom table, and drinks were served. 'Let me tell you guys, I love what you're doing.' He put a hand on his heart, and then another. 'I think it's awesome. Optimism is very important to me. Through optimism we've created a whole university. We aim to create the first university that runs on no money at all . . . because why should anyone be poor in Africa? It's insane!'

The door opened and a student appeared in the room. He needed to talk to Taddy.

'So I've got Laurence here . . .' said Taddy. 'And

Laurence is going to interview me now, and he's come all the way from England. Isn't that wonderful?' He sounded genuinely torn. 'So the answer is *yes*, but *later*, OK?' The boy retreated. '*Great.*'

Taddy paused for a moment to let the silence settle around us again. 'You have no idea how insane and how crazy it is, what we've done,' he said quietly. 'I've lived through eleven years of people thinking I'm insane, people just thinking that we've completely lost the plot. Words can't describe . . . You have absolutely no money, no buildings, no chance of a government grant, your students are not going to pay *anything*, no teachers, no curriculum, no accreditation. You owe 40,000 Rand to a bank and you decide you're going to start a *free university*, and you have absolutely nothing, and you want to create something incredibly beautiful and EVERYBODY tells you you're crazy.'

'The pessimists!' I said.

'Yes! And you go through incredibly challenging times because you're surrounded by an entire *system* of people who have forgotten that it's possible to *create beautiful things*. Take this campus . . . We came into the city of Jo'burg, the crime capital of the world, and everybody said, "You're crazy, you're going to get killed, your students will get mugged." But we saw what Johannesburg could be. And now, seven years later, nobody's moving out of the city any more, they're all moving back, crime has fallen about 80 per cent. And it's the same with everything we do.'

Of course! I thought. If I had been Taddy Blecher I would have done exactly the same thing.

He swept his hands across the tabletop, as if he were conjuring a spell from inside the varnish. 'People always think changing the world is about tangible things, it's about getting 50 trillion dollars from somewhere and giving it to Africa or building road systems, but here's the point – and this is why I'm optimistic – *it's nothing to do with money.* No one gave anything to America, no one has given anything to India or China. They're building it themselves.'

He looked at Zara. 'Do you know what education means? The word education came from the Latin 'educare' – *to lead out.* It meant leading out the genius out of every human being, the beauty in everybody. So that's what we're doing – we're reinventing education, we're taking it back to what it really should be. We're creating the most beautiful university in Africa. Every day we see the genius and brilliance of these students: they win international awards, they get jobs in corporate finance. They come from squatter camps, street kids!'

I sipped my water stealthily. I felt like the geologist who, on his first month of a three-year expedition in the rainforest, chances accidentally on the seam of gold he has been writing about for years, which no one believed existed. A proper optimist! This required careful handling. Taddy was dangerously charismatic, possibly even irresistible – especially to women of a spiritual inclination. But what he was saying was pure gold. I looked down at my dictaphone, which was faithfully recording every utterance. *Keep it coming, kiddo.* All I had to do was sit back, nudge him every now and then, and let the goods roll in.

'We live in a field of infinite possibility,' said Taddy. 'We just have infinite possibilities for creating solutions to the problems we have.'

'This work makes you very happy,' I said.

'The last time I was sad was eleven years ago,' he said. 'Truthfully. But I work very hard at that: I do work which

I find intensely meaningful, I take care to rest, I spend time with people I love . . . I meditate three, four hours a day.'

'You meditate?' I gripped my water glass. 'Is that something to do with the . . . uh, Lagrangian field?' We looked up at the strange wall poster.

'Guys, everyone has their own way. All I can say is, I was schooled in a traditional school system.' He scanned the surface of the table as if the criss-crossing lines of the Langrangian field were also embedded in there. 'And at a certain point, I stopped exploring and questioning – and I forgot how I felt when I was a child, how beautiful life was. And all that mattered to me was when I would make a million Rand and when I would make 10 million Rand, and then I learned to *meditate* . . . And one day I was meditating with this big group of people and somehow I just had this flash of Enlightenment experience . . . And I went running out into the street and I started jumping up and down and I started to hug the trees, and I was laughing and I was crying and I was incredibly happy and I had this absolute realisation that I had been in prison and I had this huge awakening of who was the jailer, and who was it? It was *me*.'

I watched Zara from the corner of my eye. Her face was glowing with appreciation.

'And I realised,' said Taddy. 'I don't have to be in prison any more! I can do anything! I could be sailing down the Amazon, I could be picking rice in China, why am I just thinking minute by minute, day by day, I'm going to get to this level, then my boss is going to do this, then I'm going to do this, a tiny little narrow awareness of a life, a pitiful, miserable little life that I'd created for myself when actually I was a giant who could be completely free! And believe me, I was on the verge of leaving South Africa, about to emigrate, I'd packed up forty-three boxes of clothes and belongings – and I turned my back on six jobs and multi-million Rand salaries and all my clothes and all my everything, and decided I was going to start a new life and go into the black townships in South Africa and try and help people find themselves.'

I scanned the newsletter he had handed me earlier.

CIDA Consciousness Newsletter
Transcendental Meditation is an easily learned, natural mental technique which opens the awareness to the infinite reservoir of energy, creativity and intelligence that lies deep within everyone.

'This Transcendental Meditation . . .' I said.

Taddy opened his hands. 'Whatever you believe in, whatever system you follow,' he said, 'what matters is that you do it. Our university has educated thousands of kids – street kids, glue sniffers, gang members – now they are working in merchant banks, accountancy firms, starting their own charities. We've just had the honour of Mrs Mbeke – South Africa's First Lady – becoming our chancellor. *Anyone* I might ever have wanted to meet, I've met – Nelson Mandela, Bill Gates, Bill Clinton . . .'

'You've met . . .'

'*Listen.* Everything that anyone believes heaven could look like, is how our world could be. There is no reason we could not have heaven on earth!'

I felt the hairs on my arm stand up. I could feel the purpose of my life peeling away underneath me, as if to reveal the smallness of everything I had ever worked for. Bill Clinton!

'We're not saying to anybody you've got to go out there and start a free university for the poor. What we're saying is, in your heart somewhere very quiet is a powerful and very important voice – whatever you call it, your soul, intu-

ition, God, whatever you want, it doesn't need a name –
which is telling you what you should be doing. You have
a higher purpose, you're on this earth for something and
you've ignored that voice for ten years, fifty years, seventy
years, but at some point if you can break through the boundaries of fear and just listen to what you really believe you
should be doing, *a life of unparalleled beauty waits for you*.'

He paused. Zara was transfixed. I looked uncertainly
at my coffee. Maybe if I talked in enormous sweeping
metaphors like Taddy I too could transcend the boundaries
of fear and become the giant that I truly was. Maybe that
was the secret.

'What do you eat for breakfast?' I asked.

'Oats,' said Taddy. 'With raisins.'

'Thank you,' I said. 'That's perfect.'

It was still hot when we stepped back onto the street.

'What an amazing man!' said Zara.

I nodded calmly. Soon I would be as big as Taddy. Or
bigger. 'I feel so aware,' I said to her. 'Aren't we lucky to
live in such a beautiful and infinitely wonderful world?'

'Maybe you should try meditation, Laurence. It might
help you overcome your fears and find your higher purpose.'

'Fears?' I said. 'What fears?' I grabbed her hand as we
crossed the street.

'It's about letting go,' she said. 'Taddy let go of everything that mattered to him before he could find his real
purpose.'

'What can I let go of?' I laughed. 'I don't have a career!
Or a house. No one would want my car.'

Zara stopped on the pavement and gave me a searching
look. 'What do you care about most in the world?'

I looked at her and blushed. 'I'm not attached to
anything, if that's what you're talking about.'

Notes to Pessimists

Please return to your seats.

1) TRANSCEND THE BOUNDARIES OF FEAR
Somewhere in your heart is a powerful voice which is telling you what you should be doing. If you can break through the boundaries of fear and just listen to that voice, then everything will be beautiful. Or listen to the voice, then break the boundaries. It doesn't matter which way around you do it. If you have problems hearing the voice then you can meditate, although this is only necessary if you have a tiny narrow awareness of life and you absolutely need it.

(Exercise here)
(Invite audience participation)

2) MEDITATE
As above, this is not necessary unless you're at a very basic level of pessimism. Remember, you don't really exist, so whether you meditate or not makes little difference. Give up and go for a swim. Note: any time you stare out of the window of your office, that's also meditation. iPods may disqualify you. (Joke here)

Some useful notes on Buddhism:
- The world is illusory. Don't confuse yourself with a whale or any other inanimate object
- Don't rely on one person for your happiness. Better to have several partners so they never know where you stand

Remember, nothing is permanent, not even your girlfriend's faulty and ungrateful view of human relationships.

9

One truth is clear, Whatever is, is right.

Alexander Pope

What happened next I found difficult to explain. After our magical holiday in South Africa and a whirlwind introduction to our future life, Zara went to the airport and left for India. She had been talking about this for so long I'd decided it was never going to happen. Then it did.

I stood at the departure gate and put down her bags. She tilted her head. 'You're not going to be sad, are you, Laurence?'

'Sad?' I shrugged. 'Why should I be sad?'

A tear trickled down her face. 'Oh, Laurence.'

Three days later I woke up in the middle of the night. Up on the doorknob Zara's fur jacket hung eerily in the moonlight. I groped across the bed for her arm. She was gone. My body started quaking, seized by a wave of fear. I hadn't felt this scared since my babysitter accidentally left me in a filling station on the New Jersey interstate.

Over the next week I sank into a pit of anxiety and despair. I felt as if reality were being torn in half, and I was in the middle. How was I meant to write a book about optimism now? An optimist was supposed to feel confident about the future – not gripped by terror and uncertainty. If I could get derailed so easily by a few days of this, then how was I going to cope with the next six months? And how would I handle a real problem like, say, thermonuclear attack?

I sat down and looked through my interview notes. I must have missed something. I had had absolute faith in our relationship yet my future wife was at this moment hanging out in a free love ashram in a diaphanous maroon gown. It was grotesque and inexplicable. It was entirely wrong.

I closed my eyes and tried to meditate, but my mind was running in circles like a brain-damaged mouse. What if I could change her plans? Make her see sense? I unfolded a scrap of paper and started making notes. It was quite obvious that Zara had psychological issues with commitment and was afraid of giving herself to one person. Only in the context of a loving relationship could she finally get over her unhappy view of the universe and become whole. I worded this as carefully as I could and sent it off, along with a hint that I would come out to visit her next time I had a chance.

She didn't take it well.

I'm worried about your last email. I simply can't be in a 'relationship' right now.

I told myself to stay calm. It was a case of stay calm or die.

Luckily I had a plan. And a new role model: Taddy Blecher didn't spend hours alone with his computer, sending emails to celebrities and making notes in his diary. He worked with *other* people, *lots* of other people. That's where he got his energy from. It was the same with Tim Smit. It was the key to their optimism. I needed to transcend the boundaries of fear and ego, and get everyone else involved too. I needed to get the optimist movement going again – start a think tank, a charity, a revolution. Then I would have a purpose.

Then I could stop this constant thinking about Zara. I might even forget about her completely.

I ordered business cards and commissioned a designer to build me a website. He unveiled the finished product in a café on Victoria Street. It looked clean and empty, like a brand new supermarket. I approved. Soon its message boards would be crowded with the discontented pessimists of the world.

Then I wrote a letter to President Clinton. It was discreet but inspiring. It was respectful but dignified. We were talking man-to-man.

> Dear Bill
>
> The Optimist Project is a pioneering initiative drawing together the learnings of the world's outstanding optimists, with the purpose of applying them on a global – or organisational – level.

I smiled to myself. It sounded so professional. I was particularly pleased with the phrase 'or organisational'.

> As one of today's most experienced leaders you are in a position to help us communicate the importance of optimism as a force for collective change. We invite you to share with us your vision for the future.

Bill would notice the spark of genius, the tone of a future leader. He would never guess that there was only one of me, and that my office was the spare bedroom of my father's house in North West London. He was bound to say yes.

It was my destiny.

My next stop was New York.

★

Central Park.

I lay on my back in the sun and watched the towers of Manhattan looming over the treetops, like ancient magnets built to suck the optimists of the world into America.

They had got me, anyway.

'Do you ever see Clinton jogging around here?' I asked an art student casually. She was sitting on a rock overlooking the path.

'I'm busy,' she said.

I reeled backwards. The girl had obviously been traumatised by years of aggressive chat-up lines. It was nothing to do with me. 'We live in a field of infinite possibility,' I told her, opening my palms. 'I'm writing a book.' She picked up her pad and moved to the other side of the rock.

Maybe it was the city, I thought. Even the narrowminded behaviour of the locals couldn't get me down. And I hadn't thought about Zara for over an hour. My escapade was working. I had come to NYC to attend a conference of New Age speakers and enthusiasts in the 7th Avenue branch of the Sheraton Hotel. The gathering was called BEING FEARLESS and it was my best chance yet to show Zara I was a superior spiritual person and not the materialistic Neanderthal she thought I was.

The lobby was thronged with delegates in a state of happy panic, rushing from workshop to workshop. A man in a white dress was spinning a stick gracefully around his head, grinning at the crowd as they milled around him. I winced as the soft cotton of his scarf brushed my face. Middle-aged women in tye-die skirts strode past, laughing happily.

I walked to registration and glanced at the conference schedule: past-life regression, astral hypnosis, kundalini meditation . . . lectures on being 'free' and finding your 'internal warrior'. *Jesus!* It was the sinister world of Buddhists and spiritual seekers, the world which had dragged my sweetheart off to India. I moved cautiously through the lobby, feeling a frisson of unexpected fear – I was in enemy territory. A woman in a flowing gown approached me with a welcoming smile. Her costume looked as if it had been designed in the lost kingdom of Atlantis. 'Are you a delegate?' she asked.

'No,' I said firmly, 'I'm a journalist.'

Delegates spilled out of the main ballroom as the welcome ceremony ended. I pulled out my microphone and held it in front of my face like a crucifix.

'Why are you here?' I asked a lady.

'To feel the love,' she sighed, holding her hand on her heart. 'To recharge and connect and just feel wonderful!'

'So you're an optimist?'

'Oh, yes . . .' she nodded, '*such* an optimist.' She leant towards the mic. 'If you ask me whether the glass is half full or half empty, I would definitely say "half full".' She beamed, delighted with her contribution.

'What if you had two glasses?'

We were standing in a queue for autographs, and at the top of it was a bald, smiling man in a Hawaiian shirt. 'That's Wayne Dyer,' said the woman, glowing. 'You know Wayne Dyer?'

Wayne Dyer was standing at the top of the stairs, signing copies of his book, *Inspiration, Your Ultimate Calling*. On the book's cover, which everyone in the queue was holding, was a photo of himself in a white shirt with a butterfly perched on his hand. Wayne innocently joked and flirted with the middle-aged women who were waiting to meet him. He was obviously a popular man. Why not interview him?

'Hi, Wayne!' I said. 'I'm from England.'

The smile faded. I was the only man in the entire line and I wasn't holding a copy of his book. 'It's pretty tight,' he said, when I asked him for an interview, 'but talk to my PR. He's over there.' Just as I thought: when you got past the handshakes, the guy was a showman, an impresario, like all the other 'spiritual gurus'. I met him later in a studio downstairs. They were polishing his head while he sound-checked and smiled into the camera.

Wayne agreed to let me ask him three questions, but only the last one seemed relevant: 'The butterfly, is it real?'

Wayne Dyer looked tired. 'The butterfly on the cover of my book? No, I think it's digital.'

'Thanks,' I said.

'That's all you want to know?'

'Yep.'

The afternoon dragged on. The initial excitement of breaching enemy lines had passed and I was starting to feel downcast. What if this made no difference to anything? What if Zara took no notice of my break for freedom? What I needed now was some novel spiritual technique for changing her mind. That's why everyone was here, wasn't it?

I decided to try my luck with Caroline Myss, one of the conference speakers. Caroline was famous, apparently, for clearing 'psychic blocks' from people's bodies – blocks that prevent your life from running smoothly. I was pretty entranced by this idea. Presumably I had one of these blocks and now it could be got rid of, thus making every-thing work again. I spotted her in the lobby, deep in conversation.

'Excuse me. Could I talk to you for a moment?'

She looked up, startled. 'No, you can't,' she said. 'I'm having lunch with my friends.'

'Sorry,' I said.

I watched her finish a mouthful of salad. Was she scanning my energy field for psychic blocks? She sighed and looked back up. 'Thirty seconds,' she said, 'but that's all. Walk with me back to the hall.'

She paced through the foyer, nodding briskly at well-wishers, while I told her about my mission. I wondered when she was going to do her psychic clearing.

'On the spiritual quest,' she said, striding up the stairs. 'You must go beyond optimism.'

'Where to?'

She looked at me. 'Do you know what acceptance means?'

I stood helplessly at the entrance to the hall. A media assistant was waiting to pin a mic to her shirt. She handed me her empty cup of coffee.

'You accept the negative,' she said. 'And you don't turn away from reality. OK?' A swell of applause met her as she climbed up on stage.

I walked away, depressed. What good was that going to do me? The whole point of life was to *change* reality.

I only had time for one more interview: Byron Katie, a woman who had taught herself how to be happy all the time – by not believing her thoughts. Not believing my thoughts seemed like a fairly desperate measure, but maybe, I mused, it would give me the ammunition I needed to change Zara's attitude. I approached Byron Katie's stand. Her latest book was piled up on the side. I flicked through it carelessly.

Since the beginning of time, people have been trying to change the world so that they can be happy. This hasn't ever worked, because it approaches the problem backward.

Hmm, it didn't sound like optimism to me.

'I am an optimist,' said Byron Katie, as I set up my mic. 'Now that we're talking about it, I'd say I'm constantly optimistic. Whatever happens I immediately see why, and it's *always* good.'

'What, anything?'

I glanced at her assistant, Melony. She smiled tranquilly.

'There were several years when I was unable to see,' said Katie. 'And it absolutely did not slow me down. I would fall and I would stumble and I would bump into things and it was magical and wonderful.'

'Right.'

'I'm a realist. Most people aren't. Most people are at war with reality. They are never at peace because they believe their thoughts and their thoughts do not accept what *is*. And so they suffer.'

'Are you saying I just have to accept reality, and everything will be OK?'

'Everything is already OK.'

'What if I want it to be *more* OK?'

'Then you're not getting it. That's not acceptance. That's pretending to accept, while still wanting to change things. Remember, when I believe my thoughts I suffer, but when I question my thoughts, I don't suffer.'

I looked down. Katie was an attractive-looking woman and she had hypnotic brown eyes. There was always the danger that I would start agreeing with her for the wrong reasons. Yet it was vital that I maintain some form of mental control while this lady attempted to dismiss the last two thousand years of Western civilisation – a civilisation built on rational thought. What about the benefits of thinking? Compared to my father's laptop my brain was really a faultless work of creation. It had been switched on continuously for more than three decades without a single software failure.

I had only had to reboot it once, and that was after an eighteen-hour drinking session.

I reached for the hospitality nuts. 'What if it's a true thought,' I argued, 'like, say, the war in Iraq? What are we supposed to do then? Pretend it's not happening?'

'How do you feel when you have that thought?' she asked, holding my gaze.

'Iraq? It makes me feel . . . anxious.'

'What thought is there? What is the stressful thought? "I feel terrible because of all the people dying"? "People *shouldn't* be dying"? Is that it?'

'That's a good start.'

'Well, let's question that thought . . . People *shouldn't* be dying. But they are. Now can you think of one good reason to keep that stressful thought that doesn't agree with reality?'

'Well, for a start, it might motivate me to change the situation.'

'So does feeling stressed help you to change it? Or could you try your best to change things without feeling like that?'

I was no longer sure of myself. She seemed to have talked me in a circle. 'All I know is that some things aren't as they should be.'

'I used to think that too. I was very depressed. I was agoraphobic, paranoid. My self-esteem was so low I used to sleep on the floor.'

'And then?'

'I woke up one morning and there was a cockroach crawling over my foot . . . and at that moment I opened my eyes and I was born into a world that no one had told me existed. There was no fear, there was no pain, and there was no suffering, and basically what I saw in that moment was that when I believed my thoughts I suffered, and when I question my thoughts I don't suffer. It's as simple as that.'

'So, you're saying . . .' I massaged my temples. 'You're saying that the problem with the war in Iraq is not the killing and the bombs . . . it's just the thoughts we're having about it?'

She nodded.

'And if I have a problem in my life . . . Like now, I have these negative feelings, anxiety for example, I can feel it in my stomach . . . but it's there. I can't pretend it's not.'

'What do you name it?' she asked. 'Anxiety? So question that. Do you *know* it's anxiety? Everything is OK until we name it, until we attach some kind of problem to it. But you have named it "not OK". When you're with a true optimist you might say "This feels terrible" and they'll just smile and say "You know, well, what's so terrible about it? Nothing!"'

I looked within, trying to imagine the feelings in my gut as temporary flutters, non-existent creations of my imagination.

'They're still there,' I concluded.

'OK,' said Katie. She smiled and looked in my eyes, glowing in her armchair like some previously undiscovered radioactive element. Minutes passed. I waited for her to signal the end of the interview, but all she did was sit there. She seemed entranced by my presence. I didn't know where to look. We listened to the honking of the mid-morning traffic thirty floors below. 'Isn't this great?' she said eventually. 'What an amazing place for us to end up.'

'Well,' I said, stiffly, 'thank you.' I stood up and shook her hand – I couldn't think what else to do. Downstairs I bought myself a latte and swallowed it almost in one. A bell chimed and the lobby flooded with people. I watched them gratefully as they milled around my chair, smiling and laughing, unaware of the bizarre experience I had just survived. Suddenly the caffeine hit my blood.

I had to get out of there.

On the subway I looked at the glum faces of the commuters. *Acceptance!* I laughed. *Why should I want to accept this?* I felt lonely and tired.

That evening I called up a friend of a friend, someone I had been connected with as a possible contact in New York. I spoke to him on the phone and explained my project. Then I asked him if he could think of anyone I should meet.

'Anyone?' he asked.

'Anyone at all,' I said. 'The first person who comes to mind. As long as they're optimistic.'

By now I was desperate. I stood and watched the wind blowing sandwich wrappers down Avenue of the Americas. The initial rush of confidence I had felt on arriving in New York had passed and now, after six days in the city, I still hadn't made any progress towards my main objective – achieving some kind of breakthrough in my communications with Zara. When I hinted to her in my last email that, now I was in the land of the free, I felt careless and liberated and on top of things, she didn't rise to it. She even sounded pleased for me, which made it ten times worse. My only hope now was that something magical would happen in my last few days in America to boost my confidence and thus shift the balance of power which was so stubbornly stuck in her direction.

Hence the call. It was time, I figured, to activate the element of random chance, to cast my line out into the black waters of synchronicity and haul in some unscheduled and life-changing experience. Isn't that what a quest was supposed to be? Random?

The next afternoon I made my way to a café on Fifth Avenue. All I had was a name and a job description: Srikumar Rao, a business school lecturer from Long Island University.

My contact had explained that Srikumar was the most optimistic person he could think of. At such short notice anyway.

When I arrived, Srikumar was sitting at the bar in a puffa jacket, cheerfully humming a tune. I was thirty minutes late.

'Sorry,' I said.

'No problem!'

Srikumar held out his hand. I looked down at his neatly clipped fingernails. Why was he being so friendly? Was he trying to sell me something? I could feel my body retracting like a snail's head.

'Before we start,' said Srikumar, courteously, 'may I ask, what is your definition of optimism?'

'It's hard to describe,' I said. My definition of optimism was beginning to dissolve. 'I'm looking for . . . how to feel OK about everything. How to jump out of bed in the morning. I thought you might have some ideas.'

'I certainly do!' He grinned and led me to a table. Before I had even had time to take out my microphone Srikumar had given me a potted history of his career and his ultra-successful lecture course: *Creativity and Personal Mastery.* Apparently it was one of the most popular courses at Long Island Business School. Not only that, but Srikumar had just written a book about it, which he pulled out of his briefcase now and laid on the table before me.

'Are You Ready To Succeed?'

'I don't know,' I said.

Srikumar leant towards my mic. 'I believe that if when you get up in the morning you don't come *alive* at the thought of what you're doing for a living . . . if *many* times during the day you don't *go down on your knees* in involuntary gratitude at the good fortune that's been bestowed on you . . . if you're not *vibrantly alive* every day . . . then you're wasting your time.'

Wasting my time!

'It *is* possible to craft an ideal life. Let me repeat that – it is possible to craft an ideal life. I believe that anyone can do it. Every day I get up in the morning I am literally *overcome* with gratitude that I do what I do . . . and get paid for doing it.'

'What, *every* morning?'

'Yes!'

I gazed peevishly at Srikumar's puffa jacket. The JBF, I thought. It was kind of sickening when you saw it this close up.

'So, tell me,' I said coldly. 'What's the secret?'

'You're not living in reality!'

'Ha, ha,' I said.

'No, really. We all have mental models for how to see the world, but most of us make the mistake of mixing them up with reality. They're *not* reality. For example, you probably have a mental model that your ideal job or your ideal partner is *out there.*'

'You're describing your business students,' I reminded him.

'Everyone,' he corrected. 'Everyone uses mental models. For example, you may well have some fantasy relationship or fantasy career, which you define in terms of what it looks like – the external environment. What's my boss like, how much money I'm earning, who am I working with, and somehow if all of these elements come together then you're going to be happy. Not true! It doesn't work that way. Even if by some miracle everything that you've postulated is there in one place I guarantee you'll be equally unhappy in six months or less. Because the ideal situation *isn't* out there, it's in between your ears.'

I didn't like the way he was lecturing me. 'You know,' I said, 'I'm quite familiar with all this stuff.'

'Good, then you'll know that the first thing you have to do is clean up your internal furniture. Stop living in the *me-centred* universe. You know, everything that happens – what's its impact on *me*? There's a traffic accident and your immediate reaction is, oh no, how late am I going to be? Your wife gets offered a promotion abroad and the first thing you think is, how is this going to affect me?'

I gazed tiredly at the table.

'The trouble is,' continued Srikumar, 'if you're always concerned with "me" you'll *always* be unhappy, it's inevitable. The universe is never going to conform to your idea of how it should be and you *are* going to have angst in your life. If your optimism is always focused on yourself, you're doomed.'

'I'm stuck in this body,' I said, suddenly annoyed. 'I can't *be* anyone else. Why shouldn't I want my life to go well? It seems to go all right for lots of other people.'

'That's what they all say,' laughed Srikumar. 'And it's not true. So what I recommend to my students is this. Try consciously asking, what can I contribute? What service can I render? Rather than always thinking the other way around, what can society or life give to me? What can I get from this relationship? I tell this to my business students, people who are training to run multinational companies.'

A waiter came by. They were closing for the afternoon and they needed to cash up. I sprang to my feet.

'Wait!' said Rao. 'We haven't finished cleaning your mind.' He gestured to the waiter and I sank back into my seat. 'The next thing you need to be aware of is what I call your "mental chatter" – your inner monologue, your mind's commentary on life – which never stops. Sometimes it even keeps us awake at night. Most of the time we don't pay attention to it, we assume it's part of life.'

I glanced down at my chocolate. It was almost finished.

Amazingly, Srikumar hadn't even taken a sip of his coffee. Why couldn't I be that focused? Was I in the wrong job? It's easy for Srikumar to preach, I thought. He's found the perfect career. If I were a management guru with thousands of students and my own lecture course I would be happy too.

'Actually it's critical to be aware of it,' said Srikumar, 'because mental chatter – and mental models – are what we use to *define and create our reality*. We think of it as reality but actually it's a construct that we've created with our mental chatter. You can't turn it off, and over time the negative judgements start to accumulate. Eventually they form a huge barrier on the path to your ideal life. The bad news is, you can't kill it and it won't shut up. The good news is, you don't need to! All you need is to be aware. When you're conscious of what you're permitting to germinate inside you, the weeds in your life will wither away of their own accord.' Rao gathered his papers. 'It's that simple. What I suggest to you, Laurence, is this: carry around a notebook or a sheet of paper for the next few days, and keep note of what's going on inside your head. Especially the negative thoughts.'

I raised an eyebrow. 'I know what you're going to say next. I should question my thoughts and never believe anything my mind says. And I should accept reality.'

He looked taken aback.

'Exactly!'

I sighed.

'The trouble is,' he said, 'you get stressed when things don't go the way you expect them to. When reality doesn't meet your dreams.'

I stood up. There were dreams and there were dreams. My dreams were real. Some people's weren't. 'There's a difference between dreams and destiny, isn't there?'

'Maybe.' He zipped up his puffa. 'But the stress in your life is caused only by one thing, your reaction to not getting what you want.'

He opened his arms, the host of a shopping channel for spiritually-starved Americans. 'Detach yourself from the outcome. Accept whatever outcome the universe provides. You may get what you wanted, or you may not. And let me give you one final tip . . .'

'Thanks,' I said, 'but I think they need us to leave the café now.'

Years of teaching students had given Srikumar a thick skin: '*Whatever you are truly grateful for and appreciate will increase in your life.*'

'Oh, gratitude,' I said. 'Sure. You probably know Martin Seligman?'

Srikumar ignored my reply. I followed him out into Times Square. The afternoon sun was coming down in streaks across the plate glass of the Ernst & Young building.

'Interesting that you're investigating optimism,' he said. 'My philosophy of life is that everything that happens to you happens for the best. In other words . . .' He looked at me pleasantly. '. . . it's impossible for you to make a mistake.'

I shrugged. 'I'm afraid I've made plenty of mistakes.'

'Listen,' he said, standing at the top of the subway stairs. 'Regardless of whether it's true or not, if you believe it's true, your life will be a heck of a lot better. And if you go one step forward and say, maybe it *really is* true – there's no such thing as a mistake – then heaven on earth is no longer a fiction, it's what you're living in.' He held out a comradely hand. 'Thank you, Laurence. Stay in touch. And good luck!'

Lover

10

The Terrible has already happened.

Heidegger

London, 2007.

A season had gone by since my journey to New York. Winter had passed into spring, and I had moved from my father's house into Xanthe's flat in St John's Wood, a beautiful and affluent district of North London. Zara was still in India but we were now in regular touch. Life looked pretty good, especially from St John's Wood, with its delis and flower stands and white houses thick with cherry coming into bloom. I had landed on my feet.

My new housemate turned out to be even more pessimistic than my father.

'I told you,' said Xanthe. 'I don't want to be an optimist. Everywhere you look things are going wrong. It's the law of averages. The war in Iraq is a mess. Innocent people get killed and maimed all the time. What, are you just going to pretend that everything is OK?'

I looked serenely out of my bedroom window at the swaying trees of St John's Wood. 'Everything is perfect, Xanthe. You only have to question your thoughts and then, when you are free from attachments, you will understand.'

'I don't know about this detachment. Aren't emotions the whole point of being alive?'

My laughter came like a trickling stream on a calm summer's day. 'The world is an illusion, Xanthe, and everything in it has a purpose. Accept reality. That's *true* optimism.'

I glanced down at my computer. An email had just arrived from India. 'Excuse me,' I said, 'I need to be on my own now.'

'Yes, oh Master.'

My hands trembled slightly as I opened it.

Hey!
I've just found a new house. It's wonderful! I can see myself staying here for years.

'I am accepting reality,' I intoned. 'All reality is good.'

The next morning I met a woman called Immaculée Ilibagiza. Immaculée was a survivor of the Rwandan genocide and had just published a book about her experiences. I was enthusiastic to see her. Now that I had understood the true nature of optimism I was no longer moved by famous names and big words. I found myself drawn to ordinary people, everyday people who had lived through extraordinary events. Optimism is good wherever it comes from, I concluded, but when you hear it from someone who has lost everything, then you really pay attention.

I stood in line at the book signing and peered at her from the back. To my surprise Immaculée was rather beautiful. I had thought that anyone who had been in the genocide would be stained by age and grief. But this lady seemed young and full of life, not at all the image of a person who had lived through one of the worst massacres in recorded history.

'Immaculée,' I said, 'I am writing a book about optimism. I want to change the way that people think and return hope to the world. Can I interview you?'

'Oh, thank you,' she replied, smiling gratefully. She handed one of her books to me, *Left to Tell: Discovering God amidst the Rwandan Holocaust*. A Christian, I noted. What was it about these spiritual people? I glanced at myself in the mirror of the reception room. It must be my aura. They can sense it.

'I am definitely an optimist,' said Immaculée, as she signed her final book. 'Even if a person has done you wrong, they are always able to change.'

We settled down on thick leather sofas in the lobby of the hotel and she told me her story. 'I was hiding in a bathroom for weeks,' she said. 'I couldn't move, I couldn't do anything. They were searching for us twenty-four hours a day. Three months of becoming a skeleton!' She giggled, as if we were gossiping about some embarrassing social event, some nightmare date or dinner party. Yet the Hutus had hunted for Immaculée every single day. They were only inches from her head, behind a door that could have been opened at any moment.

I sat back, delighted. Not only was Immaculée beautiful and optimistic, she had been through a near-death experience. Why had I wasted my time talking to businessmen and psychologists? This was exactly what I needed.

She flicked a strand of hair from her forehead. 'You know when you're waiting for someone to kill you?'

'No!'

'There's an instinctive thing in your mind telling you, they're going to kill you – there's no way to escape! – Maybe they're going to cut you in your stomach, maybe they will hit your head! You just keep wondering, how is my spirit going to fly away from my body?'

I pictured the machetes scraping along the corridor walls. 'They were still outside looking for you?'

'Oh, yeah.'

'They still wanted to kill you?'

'Oh, they wanted to kill me . . .'

I leant forward.

'Those things were scaring me so bad that I made a decision to pray, to shut off those imaginations, so my brain don't have any time to think about anything else. I'm like praying all the time! I'm having the Bible in my mouth! I was praying to keep myself from going crazy. I tried to tell myself, *to die is not punishment. How many billions of people have died since the world began?*'

'And the killers?' I said. 'Tell me more about the killers.'

Immaculée crossed her arms. 'I was so disappointed with them, I was so disappointed with my fellow human beings. So I was just praying, and meditating on the life of Jesus, and then a vision came: *forgive them!*'

I frowned. 'Forgive them?'

'Yes! There was Jesus was on the cross and he said FORGIVE THEM, THEY DON'T KNOW WHAT THEY DO.' She laughed. '*Yes!* I thought, *there's no way they can know what they do.* This cannot discourage me.'

'Aha,' I said calmly. 'You're talking about the power of acceptance.'

'Right!' said Immaculée. 'I was able to forgive them. You know, a child can do something to hurt you or even kill you, by mistake – a child can hold a gun and *boom!* all of a sudden it kills you – but do you get angry with them? No!'

She sank happily into her armchair.

'Interesting,' I said. 'So you questioned your negative thoughts . . .' I sat back and rubbed my chin. Immaculée was a Roman Catholic, but that was just a cultural thing. In fact, she was actually practising advanced-level optimism: acceptance, detachment and self-disputation. Christian or not, she had questioned her thoughts and thus gained power over her fear.

It fitted perfectly into my new intellectual framework for optimism.

ADVANCED OPTIMISM (Figure 1)

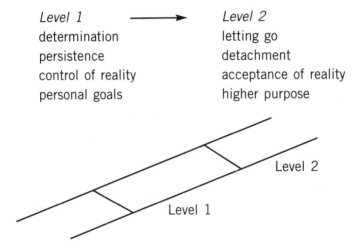

Level 1   ⟶   *Level 2*
determination   letting go
persistence   detachment
control of reality   acceptance of reality
personal goals   higher purpose

Level 2

Level 1

Of course, I thought – it's a ladder! A ladder you have to climb up. This revelation had come to me days before during a moment of deep thought: there isn't just one kind of optimism, I realised, *there are different levels of the stuff.*

It was nothing to do, I realised now, with news bulletins or economic progress in the developing world. The JBF I was looking for was totally internal. It was a state of mind.

Old-fashioned optimism – persistence, purpose, never giving up – that was down there at Level 1, along with forcing yourself to smile and making affirmations. It was an important survival mechanism, but it wasn't the true optimism that I was looking for, the 'preconditions' that Ian had urged me to track down. To get that, you needed to move up the ladder. Then you got to all the clever stuff, the stuff that Srikumar and Matthieu Ricard went on about. Of course they didn't realise that what they were talking about was optimism. They thought it was something special, like Buddhism or spirituality. But now I was redefining the word – and making it available for everyone.

I wasn't sure where all the bits went yet. I would figure that out as I went along. For example, some things like self-disputation – Martin Seligman's technique for questioning your thoughts – might not be Level 1 *or* Level 2. They might be rungs you had to climb on between levels. If I wanted to restore the reputation of optimism and find the JBF, I had to locate the rungs and I had to locate the spaces between the rungs, and I had to identify the highest rung of the ladder. At the moment there were only two. An intellectual framework based on a ladder can't have just two levels. Then it wouldn't be a ladder. I would have to find another rung.

I came back to the room. Immaculée was still talking. The greatest thing about Level 2 optimists, I thought to myself, is that everything *works out* for them. Immaculée, for example, had saved her own life by being detached.

'There was a moment where I lived pure happiness in that bathroom,' she sighed.

'Yes.' I gave her an approving smile. 'You questioned your thoughts and thus remained in control. It's all about acceptance of reality by a process of re-interpretation. No doubt your change of heart saved your life.'

'Oh, so much,' she said. 'There were moments when I felt like just going out there and ending it, the torture! Many people did it . . . my neighbours, my grandmother. She just said, I can't wait any more, and she went on the road and they killed her!'

As Immaculée continued her story, I asked myself, what

if I weren't the advanced twenty-first century optimist that I am? What if I were a visitor from a super-intelligent species of the future, where my book about optimism had become the standard training manual for all sentient beings, especially the psychologist-explorers who would be sent back in time to analyse the goings on of the human race?

If so, then maybe I would write Immaculée's story like this:

REPORT TO FUTURE UNIVERSE: A CASE STUDY OF LEVEL 2 OPTIMISM

Item: Immaculée Ilibagiza's unusual attitude to death

The subject, afraid of death, is only seconds from being discovered by her killers. Her mind is full of horrible thoughts, so awful they threaten to overpower her. In an effort to control herself, the subject employs the following strategies to gain power over her own mind:

1) She 'prays', in order to give no room to the terrifying thoughts. Quote: 'So my brain doesn't have any time to think about anything else'.

2) When the thoughts come anyway, she questions them. Quote: 'To die is not punishment. How many billions of people have died since the world began?'

3) From her new understanding, the killers are still a threat, but they have no power because she has let go of all negative and disempowering thoughts concerning them. Quote: 'A child can hold a gun ... but do you get angry – no!'

Conclusion: the subject used powerful cognitive techniques to successfully overpower her negative and non-useful thoughts, therefore increasing her chances of survival.

P.S. Please bring me back. I hate the food.

'Are you still optimistic now?' I asked.

'So much! Especially about my country. I saw it come from nothing, destroyed completely. I remember the time I stood in Kigali right after the genocide and I saw dead bodies all over the road . . . all you can see is dogs running, eating people . . . those are things you never even saw in a movie . . . things that never existed in your imagination . . . it's like, is this the end of the world? Am I dreaming? Is this a nightmare? To see it from there, and where it is now . . . Oh, I have a lot of hope.'

Immaculée stood up. 'I know many people are still broken-hearted but it doesn't discourage me. In Africa things go wrong and wrong and wrong again, but it's just a click away. I know if the people of the world get it – about caring for another human being – it can be done so quick. They can care, and Africa can be healed right now.'

'Good,' I said. We walked together through the lobby as a tall black man ambled through the door. Immaculée smiled. 'My husband.' The man stopped to buy something at a counter.

'How did you meet?' I enquired politely.

'In New York,' she said. 'I visualised him.'

I stopped. 'You did what?'

'I wrote a list of his qualities, the husband that I wanted. I imagined every detail. I even drew a picture of his face!'

I turned around. 'You cosmically ordered your husband?'

'Yes,' she said. 'And he was exactly like in my picture!'
I felt a girlish flutter in my heart.

'Do you think I could do this for someone I know already?'

'Why not! But you need to be open to whichever way God chooses to show it to you. You need to trust.'

'Oh,' I said. *Trust.*

'Trust who?'

'Listen,' said Immaculée. 'When I was looking for my job at the United Nations my husband said, "You're crazy! You are new in this country; your English is not good. Do you know how many people want to get a job at the UN?" But I visualised it. I just knew I had to leave my CV somewhere and come and pray to God. And I kept reminding God: *You can do all things, you know what that means – it means all things. You know how much I need this job.* And believe me, miraculously, I went, without knowing anyone, met someone who was standing beside me, I asked her if she can show me the personnel office, I gave them my CV and I left. Three weeks later, they called me. It's just trust,' she added. 'In trusting there is a power to see clear, a power to be able to see in the future.'

'To see the future,' I repeated. It was an aspect of positive thinking I hadn't considered for my new intellectual framework. If anything I had relegated it to some dubious aspect of Level 1. After all, Visualisation and Cosmic Ordering had nothing to do with acceptance and they sounded suspiciously like wishful thinking. But maybe I had missed the point. After all, Immaculée wasn't a middle aged Californian with ambitions for a bigger swimming pool. She was a Rwandan who had lived through one of the worst events of the last 2,000 years.

'Our duty is to clean our hearts,' she said seriously. 'What is in your soul, that is important. What is outside is just like an illusion.' She flicked her long fingers. 'It can go, any time.'

Whatever! I gave her a hug.

Outside it was sunny, for the first time in days. I could feel my endorphins returning to pole position in the fast lane of my major arteries. My feet sprang neatly on the tarmac. If Immaculée could live through the Rwandan genocide and still believe in the power of positive thinking, then maybe it wasn't necessary to accept 'reality' after all. Maybe those people were wrong. Optimism, faith, dreams – they were absolutely respectable. It was OK to want things; it was OK to dream . . .

And dreaming is what I would do.

11

The purpose which guided him was not impossible,
though it was supernatural. He wanted to dream a man: he
wanted to dream him with minute integrity and insert him
into reality.

Jorge Luis Borges

Xanthe was standing in the corridor, looking glum about something. 'What about you?' she asked. 'Don't you ever get down?'

'What would get me down?' I said. 'There's nothing I desire.'

'Really?' said Xanthe. 'Even Zara?'

'It's not like that,' I said. 'We're in touch. That's enough for me.'

'Is she coming back?'

'I don't know. Love can only exist in freedom. You have to trust,' I said. 'You have to trust that everything will be OK. That's how it works.'

Xanthe looked doubtful. 'Don't you miss her?'

'I live in the present, Xanthe. I try not to think about the past or the future.' I glanced down at my notebook, where I had drawn a sketch of Zara's face. Next to it I had written a list of her qualities:

CLEVER
SPIRITUAL
GOOD TASTE
.   JUST LIKE MY MOTHER

'Anyway, we don't *need* to be together. We're connected.'

'Right,' she said, leaning against the wall. 'So you're accepting reality, like a true optimist.'

'That's right.'

'I assume you've seen this film everyone is talking about?'

'What film?' I sat up.

'It's called *What the Bleeping Hell*. It's all about this . . . positive thinking and visualisation stuff. Everyone in my psychotherapy class was talking about it.' She skipped away, looking pleased with herself. 'I can't believe you haven't seen it!'

I crept upstairs and switched on my computer. Visualisation was supposed to be my domain. I had tracked down Immaculée, and now I was busy working it into my general theory of optimism. It would be terrible if everyone else knew about it.

To my dismay, however, it turned out there were two major films all about positive thinking. The first one was called *What the Bleep*. The second one was called *The Secret*. I browsed, anxiously, as page after page of commentary spooled in front of me. It was all the stuff I'd encountered in Waterstone's – Creative Visualisation and Cosmic Ordering, and all the tricks that Immaculée had told me – but with an extra layer of science. I found a metaphysical blogger who had dedicated his website to explanations of this phenomenon. There was all this stuff about 'quantum physics'.

Quick Fact: The essence of this 'secret', according to researchers, relies on both the spiritual & meta-physical truths that if you were to break down every-thing you see, the net result would be a pure, 'non-physical' energy, which can be *physically* directed to create what we desire' . . . (see: *thought energy* or *psychic energy*)

Obviously, I wasn't going to watch these tawdry films myself. The idea actually horrified me. But it was vital I find out what they were on about before these ideas seeped into the general public.

I found an article on the web by a guy called Khaled. He claimed that he regularly 'created his day' by 'infecting the quantum field', an idea he had picked up from watching *What the Bleep*. Khaled had posted a phone number on his site. I rang him.

'I'd like to talk to you about visualisation,' I said. 'I'm writing a book and a major TV series.' This was perhaps an exaggeration, but it was important to make an impression. I was in a hurry. 'I need some help with . . . certain diffi-culties.'

'Why not?' he said. 'You can come to my office.'

'Somewhere private,' I added, 'if you don't mind.' I gave him the name of a bar near Victoria.

I met Khaled the following evening. He was a Lebanese guy with a trans-Atlantic accent and friendly blue eyes.

'You've tried this visualisation stuff,' I said.

'Yes,' said Khaled.

'Tell me about it.'

We ordered a beer and the young man gave me a quick rundown of his life story. Brought up as an expatriate in the African nation of Liberia, Khaled's life had been struck by tragedy three years earlier when Liberia had fallen into civil war. The family business destroyed, Khaled went bankrupt and his whole life was turned upside down.

'That's how you found creative visualisation?'

'Yes. It was like, nothing else seems to be working, maybe this will work.'

'You were desperate.'

'Definitely desperate. My finances were shot and my personal life fell to pieces. But I started to pick up these old books, and my mind slowly started to re-expand. I don't know if you know the quantum physics theory about infinite universes? There's this whole thing about parallel realities . . . how each atom has got an infinite amount of replicas across infinite universes?'

'Yes,' I said, 'of course.'

'Well, it's a theory. I'm not going to go into specifics of how it works but based on that I started to feel, well, what if it is my *belief* that is going to take me there?'

'To the parallel reality?'

'I thought, what if I just make the leap of faith that I actually have to feel things are better, before they do get better? That somehow I could just *will* it to get better?'

'So what was your first act . . . of visualisation?' I thought about Immaculée.

'I got a new job,' said Khaled. 'And it was just what I had visualised. Since then my life has been expanding in every direction.'

'You got a new job?' I felt disappointed. 'But you're in London, probably the most dynamic job market in the world. What makes you think it's anything to do with positive belief?'

'Indeed,' said Khaled, hesitating, 'but I saw colleagues in a similar position who didn't have that belief and who didn't go as fast. It infused my actions with a certain amount of energy. You have to be open-minded; you have to believe that you can go from A to B, that you can make a shift. You have to think, things could be a million times better. Then, if they're only half a million times better, that's great.'

'What about the "science" stuff?' I glanced up from my olives. 'The stuff they mention in the *film*.'

'Fair enough, the science. Well, for a start, the more they examine the world the more they find it is holographic.'

'*Holographic?*'

'It's like a constant motion of atoms whirling around each other. This material,' he pressed the surface of our table, 'if you looked at it under the electron microscope it is not solid at all.'

'Is that what you meant by the "quantum field"?'

'Yes, this is a big amalgam of atoms that is all inter-connected and . . . and thoughts are also connected, and by using the power of thought in a clear and directed way you can "infect" the quantum field.'

'And how does that happen?' I squashed an olive with my finger.

'I don't know. It's like sending out a good thought . . .' He paused, unhappily. 'These are only fragments, only pieces of the puzzle. I'm not a scientist, but deep inside of me there was always this belief . . .'

I interrupted him. 'It just happens.'

'You could say that.'

'And you're saying that even desperately poor people . . . people in Liberia, in the direst poverty, if they thought differently their lives would be different?'

He took a big breath. 'I would have to say yes. I would have to say . . . this is quite a sensitive area . . . who's to say that visualisation can't help them? I can't say that it won't. It is a universal thing, not just for us people in the West. And I do think if the human spiritual evolution was far enough down the line we could fix a lot of things

quite instantly, including poverty, including absolute
desperation in the worst possible places in the world.'

'By using thoughts.'

'Absolutely, definitely. And the whole thing of natural
disaster . . .'

'Natural disaster?'

'Yeah, I really do believe a lot of it can be prevented if
the mass consciousness of that country or that area is willing
to believe that it will or won't happen . . . It's not necessarily that people *create* earthquakes, but people *incarnate*,
they choose their experience before they were born . . . God,
this makes me sound like a complete nutter.'

'I can change your name,' I said.

'But I really do believe there is no such thing as an
accident. There is a universal force and it is a single
universal energy; we are expressions of the same thing . . .
The thing is, I've had my own experiences. It was a spontaneous thing. I was walking in the hills and I experienced
a complete loss of who I am as a person.' He opened his
eyes wide. 'It just sounds so clichéd, but there was just
this moment of dissolving into everything and it was
extremely blissful.'

I fell silent and contemplated my olives. 'Do you
meditate?' I asked.

'I don't.'

I went home and ruminated on Khaled's words. Maybe
if I could take quantum physics and stick it together with
cognitive psychology and Buddhism, and come up with
a grand scheme for saving humanity from destruction,
get Bill Clinton involved, and possibly the President of
Iran *then* I would really have an intellectual framework
worth talking about. Then I would have a sense of purpose
like Desmond Tutu, and a boardroom like Taddy Blecher,
and a swivelling chair like Tim Smit.

A few days later I went to a dinner party in East London. There was an Italian girl there called Rafaella. For some reason the conversation got onto cakes.

'I love cakes more than anything,' she said, in an expressive, Bolognese kind of way. 'Sometimes I think more even than my boyfriend. But then . . .'

'Rafaella's amazing!' said her friend suddenly. 'She has this system. Tell them about your system!'

My ears perked up. Any talk of a system and I sniff the proximity of an answer to the fundamental question of the universe: how can I get what I want, all the time, and be permanently happy?

'When I need something important,' said Rafaella slowly, 'I promise God I will give up cakes for two weeks. If it is a big thing, three weeks. But he has to give it to me first,' she cautioned. 'Then I give up the cakes.'

'It's a win-win situation!' I cried.

Rafaella's credit must have been good with the deity, because apparently the system had never failed. Once, on the morning of her cousin's wedding, it had started to rain, so Rafaella walked outside and made a special deal. 'OK,' she said, 'if you make the rain stop I will give up cakes for three weeks. And chocolate!'

I sipped wine and scribbled Rafaella's name down in my notebook. 'This may be more important than you realise,' I told her.

Next morning, I made my own deal with the universe. Although I wasn't a Christian, I was pretty sure that God and I had a special relationship. On the other hand, it wasn't a very talkative one. Any time I tried to pray the words would get stuck in my throat. It seemed silly to use English vocabulary with an omniscient creator. Ideally he should already *know*.

But visualisation was different. I felt that visualisation

was probably a metaphor for some power of belief inside our heads and only indirectly connected with the Almighty, who was busy doing other things on an unimaginably cosmic scale. Either way, it seemed to be a metaphor that worked, at least when it came to cakes.

I knelt down by my bed. 'I will,' I whispered, 'give up tea and coffee . . . *and* alcohol for a month, if Zara comes back to England this summer.' I bowed and stood up. There was something a bit voodoo about it, but I liked that. As Doctor Seligman put it:

> Optimism is all about control . . . At the root of depression is the feeling of being powerless. (*Learned Optimism*)

Well, I had had it with being powerless. It was time to get back in control. As well as being the obvious next step in my relationship with Zara, which was critical to my mission to save the world – for all sorts of reasons – it was time to prove that positive thinking actually *worked*. Once I did that, then optimism would be unstoppable. I would patent Rafaella's cake system and take my place among the great and the good. For the moment, at least, I had found the missing rung on my ladder.

ADVANCED OPTIMISM (Figure 2)

Level 3 Optimism

Mastery over the psychic mirroring between mind and reality, known by Californians as:

Visualisation
Cosmic Ordering
or
Creating your own reality

A few weeks passed. I kept it going with my promise to the universe. I became crotchety and difficult with caffeine deprivation. I was beginning to wonder: Was I keeping my side of a cosmic negotiation or was I a self-punishing control freak with borderline OCD? Then, just when I had forgotten about Khaled and his sparkly blue eyes full of conviction, I got a call from Zara on the crackly long-distance line from Bombay.

'I'm coming back for the summer. You want to go travelling?'

Notes to Pessimists

TITLE OF LECTURE: (unscheduled)

Everyone is pessimistic about something. And even pessimists are optimistic about most things.

I was at a party recently and I was talking about optimism. A man approached me and told me he was a pessimist. He looked pleased with himself.

'Isn't pessimism just another form of optimism?' he asked.

'Not as far as I know,' I said.

'Well, I'm definitely a pessimist,' he said, 'and the way I deal with life is – I underestimate everything. Then when the future arrives I'm never disappointed.' He looked at his wine glass. 'I know the future is always going to be better than I expect. That's got to be optimism.'

I frowned. He obviously wasn't an optimist at all.

Still, it made me think. Pessimists can be optimists, and optimists can be pessimists. It depends what subject you're talking about. For example, optimistic as I am, it turns out there are certain things . . . let's say there are certain subjects where I am less steady. Of course, I am still optimistic about them, it's just not such a relaxed, optimistic feeling. Maybe that's the point. I'd rather be a relaxed optimist than a stressed optimist. Stressed optimism is right down the ladder at Level 1. Confident optimism is right at the top. So that's where I want to go. The question is – how?

12

The most intelligent thing you can do is to appreciate everything, no matter how bad it is. It won't take long before life will give up. It will adapt to your mind and deliver only good things.

Barbel Mohr

I AM THE MASTER OF MY EXPERIENCE.

I CREATE MY OWN REALITY.

I put down my pen and stared out the window. Maybe that's why I felt so tired.

The phone rang. It was Vicky. We were putting together a proposal for my radio show.

'I've got news,' she said. 'I've heard back from the BBC. They've decided to shortlist it.'

'Shortlist!' I said. 'That's great.'

'It means they've decided not to go ahead. They've put it in a list of possible future projects. I hope you're not disappointed.'

'No, no . . . I'm not. "Shortlisted", huh?'

'Well, I've never heard of them shortlisting anything before. So they must be fairly interested.'

'Don't worry,' I said. 'I need to work on my intention. My intention isn't clear, and that's creating this ambiguous situation. Through the quantum field, probably.'

'Great. Well, you work on your intention, and I'll talk to the commissioning editor. Are you going to the library today?'

'Actually, no. I'm about to "create my own day".'

Vicky laughed out loud. 'What does that mean?'

'I'm not sure – I'm just going to walk out there and see what happens.'

'That's hilarious,' said Vicky.

I glanced over at the pile of books in the corner. 'Not as hilarious as you think.'

After my meeting with Rafaella I had gone back to Waterstone's and bought the entire set of personal development classics. It was as if a valve had burst in my sense of discretion and I was now willing to read anything. What an open-minded person I had become! The books on Visualisation and Cosmic Ordering sat a few inches from my bed. I hadn't actually opened them yet, but it was enough to look at their shiny, encouraging covers to remind myself of that burst of inspiration I had felt when Immaculée told me about her magic-husband trick.

'Cosmic Ordering is the key to advanced-level optimism,' I told Xanthe later that morning when she came upstairs for some tea. I tried to make my voice sound objective and scientific.

'I thought you said that optimism was all about Acceptance? That sounded like an interesting direction.'

'Well, I did. But this is more . . . revolutionary. You know, Xanthe, if you put forth a clear enough request . . . Wait.' I scooped up *Creative Visualisation* from its place in my shrine.

'"Just put forth a clear enough request, and everything

your heart truly desires must come to you." . . . I'm quoting to you from Shakti Gawain,' I said.

'Right. Shakti . . .' Xanthe sounded temporarily derailed.

'"Because of our own deep-seated negative concepts about life, we have automatically and unconsciously expected lack, limitation, difficulties and problems to be our lot in life . . . the use of Creative Visualisation gives us a key to tap into the natural goodness and bounty of life." You see?'

'Not really.'

'This is going to change the world! We could get entire countries to do it. Think how things would change if Israel and Palestine sat down together and did affirmations. Or the Democratic Republic of Congo. We could get them to visualise peace and abundance. It's all about expectation. They just have the wrong ones.'

I pictured the first meeting of my new International Manifestation Task Force. Bill Clinton would make the opening speech and I'd have President Ahmadinejad finish with a global affirmation of peace and human rights.

The world is now becoming an abundant place of well-being for all nations.

'I don't know,' said my housemate, unwilling to offend me but equally unwilling to betray the entire history of Western rational thought. 'It all sounds a bit wishy-washy.'

'OK,' I conceded. 'That's your upbringing. In Europe these ideas are only just beginning to enter the mainstream and they still don't have much credibility. In parts of America Creative Visualisation is actually the state religion. Listen to this . . .' I opened up *Cosmic Ordering* by Barbel Mohr. '"If you feel funny about putting in an order with the universe and think nobody will be able to hear you, imagine that you are talking into an imaginary cell phone that has a direct connection to the universe. That's it. Done!" . . . One day I'm going to California,' I said. 'That's where the real action is.'

'How'd it go?' asked Vicky, the next morning.
'What?'
'Creating your own day. How was it?'
'Oh, that!' I had already forgotten about it. 'I'm not really sure. I walked to Covent Garden, got tired, came back. I don't know if anything happened. Then I got stuck on the train and got frustrated because it was a beautiful day and I was missing it and I wondered, if I was a more laidback and trusting person could I actually influence reality and *make the train move*? Or would I just not mind so much when the train got stuck?'
'I think you should think less,' said Vicky.

Later that week I met David Cameron, the leader of the Conservatives.
'Do you visualise the future?' I asked him. Cameron's eyes narrowed. I looked across his office at the stately view of the Thames. 'When you were younger, for example, did you visualise being PM?'
'No, God!' he exploded. 'I didn't at all.'
'It's a common trait in optimists,' I mentioned.
'No, no. I never saw it like that at all.' He threw his arm bluffly across the sofa. 'I think that *issues* matter and *people* matter and the *decisions* we make as a country *matter*. No . . .' he shook his head, energetically, 'I've never had some sort of great personal plan.'

I looked at him, puzzled. Maybe he had transcended Level 3 completely.

'Do you see yourself as quite a spiritual person?'

David coloured slightly. 'I . . . I'm sort of very typical sort of Church of England, sort of vaguely religious and go to church,' he stammered. 'I see that in a very personal way.' He burst into laughter.

'What are you least optimistic about?' I asked.

'What, politically?'

'Personally or politically, what brings you down?'

'Uhhhm . . .' Cameron thought carefully. It was early on a Monday morning. 'I worry about failing,' he said, eventually. 'I worry about not doing my best, about letting people down.'

'Really?'

'I think fear of failing is quite an important motivator in life. That doesn't sound terribly optimistic, I know.'

He rubbed his hands together and stood up.

'Wait,' I said. David was clearly on the verge of an emotional breakthrough. A few more minutes and we would be talking about his childhood, his aspirations, his deep inner pain. It was just as Seligman had predicted: the person who could crack the code of optimism would gain access to the highest levels of power. It was the biggest life coaching opportunity of the decade. Sadly David's secretary entered at that moment and handed him his media schedule. It might be another decade before I got such a perfect entrée into British politics.

'I'll stay in touch,' I said.

Our paths would cross again, no doubt.

Soon afterwards I met Mick Jagger. He was kicking a deflated football around Kensington Park.

Whoa, I thought to myself, this visualisation thing is getting out of hand!

'Mick,' I said.

'Yeah?' He looked up.

'Are you optimistic?'

'Course I am!' he grinned.

I took a step closer. 'Why are you optimistic?'

'It's a long story.'

'Tell me more.'

He glanced anxiously at his friends. 'It would take too long.'

'There's no hurry,' I reassured him. 'I've got all the time in the world.' Mick broke into a trot. 'Come back!' I cried. Mick was afraid, afraid of the therapeutic journey. I watched his thin figure pirouette around the ball.

All in good time, I said to myself. All in good time.

That night, I picked up Zara from Heathrow. This was the moment I had been waiting for all spring. It had been five months since we had last seen each other. My journey into positive thinking had finally reached its end. I hugged her calmly. The woman had returned.

India had tanned my future wife and added bangles, but other than that she was the same as when I had left her – even down to the long hair and the sudden, wall-quaking laughs. Here she was, in my car again, exactly where she belonged. I was full of excitement and a mellow kind of contentment. Life had resumed its rightful course.

We made a plan to drive down to the West Country for a festival. Zara was intrigued by the new theory of Creative Visualisation and wanted to give it a try.

'Why don't we manifest a camper van?' she asked, as we sat in St John's Wood.

'Sure,' I said, 'but there's something we need to clarify before we can give a clear intention to the universe . . . camper vans are very small. They usually only have one bed.'

Zara looked at her hands. 'A lot of things have changed since I stayed in the ashram,' she said, speaking quietly. 'I've become more aware of my true feelings and I am committed to following only my feelings from the heart.'

'Which means?'

'These things will take time.'

I examined the carpet. 'Well, I just wanted to bring it up.'

'That's good,' she said. 'I respect that.' Zara was a therapist. Therapists make excellent wives.

'Let's visualise the van,' she said.

We sat down and closed our eyes. I imagined a VW camper, the sort that surfers cruise around in while having picturesque breakdowns on country roads. I had fantasised about such a van for years, and wondered if it would ever happen to me.

'Do you see it?' said Zara.

'I see it!'

We looked on the internet for our imaginary vehicle but all we could find were transit vans with their roofs cut off. I asked a couple of friends, randomly, if they knew anyone with a VW. Other than that, we left it to chance. This time I was determined to do it properly: 'Trust . . .'

I just knew I had to leave my CV somewhere and come and pray to God.

A day passed, then another. I felt myself getting tense. We only had twenty-four hours before the festival was supposed to begin. If I didn't get a van now then my romantic break with Zara might evaporate. But somehow, I managed to put it out of my mind.

The next morning I logged into my email.

'Zara,' I cried. 'Look at this!'

From: Gordon
Subject: Re: blank
Date: 28 June 2007 16:14:39 GMT+05:30
To: laurence

mate, I've got a van – VW, full works. K and I are house-bound this summer so it's yours if you want it.

She read it in a second. 'Yes!' she squealed. 'We cosmic-ordered a van!'

We held hands and jumped up and down. 'We cosmic-ordered a van! We cosmic ordered a van!'

I coughed and sat down. 'No need to get excited,' I muttered. 'It was only to be expected.'

Together, we had great and unstoppable powers of manifestation.

We picked up Gordon's van and drove towards Cornwall. On our way we camped in farmers' fields. They seemed empty and deserted. It was the same everywhere we went.

'It's Tesco's,' complained a cattle farmer. 'The cows have to be thirty months old when we kill 'em otherwise they don't want 'em.'

'It's Tesco's,' said a dairy farmer. 'I got a letter from the buyers last week reducing the price to sixteen pence per litre. It's ridiculous.'

'It's Tesco's,' said a potato farmer, who had just finished harvesting. 'They get potatoes cheaper from France. In ten years this will be a wasteland.'

I looked out over the wind-blasted headland. The tiny heads of cabbages were spinning in the rain. 'Can't you ... can't you retrain and start a small business or something? Things may seem bad,' I said, 'but if you trust that everything will be OK, then it will be.'

The farmer seemed unimpressed.

'Have you tried visualising yourself as infinitely creative and prosperous?'

One evening we parked the van in a farmer's field on the edge of some rugged cliffs. I gathered herbs for tea while the setting sun warmed my skin. It was pretty idyllic. This was Level 3 in action, I told myself. We were living it. My struggles with optimism – the painful separation from Zara, the lonely nights, the scraps of paper full of notes – they all seemed worthwhile. Things really do work out if you believe in them enough. For a moment I imagined us as the only people alive on the planet, the last survivors of a world gone mad.

'What about the farmers?' I said to Zara. I felt troubled by the farmers.

I opened Srikumar Rao's book where I had left it that morning.

The universe always acts in your best interests and always brings into your life exactly what you need at any instant ...

I gazed through the windshield. 'So if those farmers understood that the world was perfect and that everything happens for a reason, presumably in some coincidental, synchronistic way that defies human logic ... unless within the context of multiple lives or a karmic system of cause and effect ...' I trailed off, 'then they wouldn't be going out of business?'

Zara smiled to herself. 'The way I see it,' she said, 'the

world *is* perfect. But it can be very challenging. I learned this in my therapy practice. Everything in life happens to confront you with some deep inner fear. So that you can let go of it. But you can't let go of things before you know them. The process is about facing your deepest beliefs and emotions.'

'Oh,' I said.

'You go into your emotions and you see what's there. It's important to be with whatever you feel inside, because all pain, all challenge and all imperfection come about when we're trying to escape these feelings. That's all we're ever doing. Trying to escape.'

'Trying to escape,' I repeated. 'OK.'

Since meeting Zara I had been getting psychology lessons on a fairly regular basis. But even by my standards, her theories were extreme.

'You're saying those farmers are creating this reality in order to confront their inner fears?'

'Exactly!'

I looked doubtfully into the teapot. 'What about self-fulfilling optimism? And visualisation? That's the whole point of it. You can make things better.'

I unfolded a page from my notebook on the dashboard.

FIRST LAW OF OPTIMISM

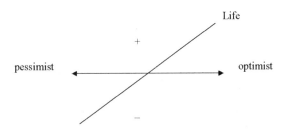

The more optimistic you are, the better life gets.

'In your case, I think, it's more like this,' said Zara. I watched her as she reached for my pen. She added a squiggly line to my chart.

SECOND LAW OF OPTIMISM

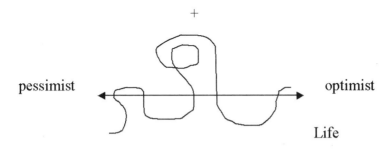

'Life gives you what you need, whether you want it or not. Although on some deep level you probably do want it.'

I crossed my arms. 'You think those farmers want to go out of business?'

'Everything happens for a reason – to teach you something. Take us,' she said, pouring out the tea. 'We're together at the moment because we have something to learn from each other.'

'Right,' I said, picking at the shell of a nut. I wasn't sure I liked the analogy. 'You make it sound quite . . . temporary?'

'Listen, all relationships have a purpose. When that purpose is served, the relationship ends. Or rather, you move onto another form of relating.' She gazed at the meadow. 'Unfortunately that's usually where the problems begin . . . because most people can't accept when something is over.'

I stared at my tea. The smell of wild fennel floated upwards from my cup.

'Right,' I said. 'But they don't *have* to end. Right? They don't always *have* to end.'

Later that week I got a call from Richard Branson. This was interesting, because I hadn't cosmically ordered an interview with him. I had just sent an email.

Branson was travelling in Canada but he had promised to ring me from his car on the way to the airport. I set up my dictaphone and flicked through his Quick Read autobiography, *Screw It, Let's Do It: Lessons in Life*. Now that I was getting to grips with optimism, I was pretty sure that the Virgin founder was a standard-issue Level 1 optimist. 'Screw it, let's do it' – one of his favourite mottos – seemed to sum this naïve, beginner-level optimism up. Branson was a clever entrepreneur who had fooled the world into believing he was cool and 'plugged in' when in fact he was just another ruthless businessman who happened to have an out-of-date beard.

The afternoon drifted on. Reading his life story I started to realise I had been hasty in my judgement. Branson wasn't as superficial or insincere as I had thought. He really did have some interesting and profound insights into life, although nothing like as interesting as the advanced psychological theories I had been developing with Zara. He even seemed like a rather nice person.

> I have found that, if I have fun, the money will come. I often ask myself, is my work fun and does it make me happy? If something stops being fun, I ask why? If I can't fix it, I stop doing it.

When you have goals and a positive outlook on life,
you have something to aim for.

It was quite possible that the billionaire had achieved Level
2 or even Level 3 optimism. He certainly seemed to have
the art of visualising mastered.

But there was no way he had reached Level 4. Yes – I
had now identified a new rung on the ladder. Level 4 optimism, I realised, was a whole step above visualisation.
When you got Level 4, you no longer *needed* to visualise,
let alone have goals. Great stuff would just happen. All by
itself.

ADVANCED OPTIMISM (Figure 3)
Level 4 Optimism
– Life is perfect.
– Everything you need will be supplied.
– Simply face your deepest fears and remove all
  psychic blocks from your energy field.
– (Otherwise things will not be perfect. They will be
  shit.)

The phone rang. It was Richard's PA. His plane was running
late, so he would now call me when he got back home to
his private island in the Caribbean.

The hours swelled and collapsed, like waves breaking
on my bedroom wall. I slipped into a state of trance-like
calm. 'So this is detachment,' I said to myself. Then the
phone rang.

His voice was faint but unmistakable. I could hear the
sound of waves lapping in the background.

'You're on your island,' I said, wonderingly.

'Yes,' said Richard.

'Thanks so much for . . .'

'Not at all,' he interrupted, politely. 'It sounds like a great idea. So you're talking to people about the future?'

I laughed nervously. 'Not exactly the future,' I said. 'The future is a secondary preoccupation. I'm more concerned with the *now*. I want to understand the true nature of optimism. You're obviously the absolute consummate optimist . . . Your sheer . . . everything you could describe about optimism . . .'

Words failed me.

'I think that's true,' said Branson cautiously. 'In my own dealings with people, being optimistic, being positive, being caring . . . it ricochets forwards.'

His voice was hesitant, formal. What was wrong? Where was the chummy Richard I had been expecting?

'Partly it's an attitude of mind,' he continued. 'At the turn of the century I heard a Radio 4 programme. It was a vicar, and he said if everyone in the world could befriend one enemy on the first of January of the millennium what a difference that would make, so the next morning I called up the head of BA – Sir Colin Marshall – and asked him out for lunch.'

'Wow.'

'Life is too short not to overcome your differences, and on a global basis that is equally important. It's one of the reasons why Peter Gabriel and myself set up The Elders.'

The Elders – this had been my pretext for talking to Branson – were a group of twelve older statesmen whose job was to fly around to the world's trouble spots making peace.

'That's a very lofty goal,' I said.

'Yes. Well, if you send people like Nelson Mandela or Archbishop Tutu, and they say we'd really like to get you together over a round table, it's really impossible for these people to say no to something like that. A group of individuals with high moral authority and the respect of the world . . .'

'Do you think it's possible?' I asked. 'Do you think there actually might ever be a time when we have world peace?'

'I must admit, I used to think that was very naïve.' His voice became grave. 'But as I've got older I really sincerely believe there is no need for war. All the peoples of the world must rise up – peacefully – to make sure we don't allow it to happen again.'

'Sure,' I said, 'But there's something we're missing here. Before we can change the world,' I ventured, 'there's work we need to do on ourselves. On our *inner development.*'

'I'm sorry,' said Branson. 'I can't hear you, you're breaking up.'

I winced. 'Our inner development,' I repeated, clenching my jaw. If I got the timing wrong I could blow the whole thing.

There was a crackle on the line. 'You're breaking up,' he said.

'You're extremely driven,' I continued, losing my nerve. *The telephone line was synchronistically intervening to guide the process of our therapeutic voyage.*

'What drives me,' answered the entrepreneur, 'is being in a position to change things, to keep learning and to be in a position to make a difference. Throughout my life I've been trying to get into that position, and now I'm in that position I don't want to waste a minute of it. But I also have an attitude in life that however hard I'm working and however tired I am, you know, to make sure I just enjoy every single second of my life, and, you know, if you just make sure you enjoy *every person* you're with and *every second* of your life, the pleasure you're going to get out of life – and the pleasure you're going to give other people – is enormous.'

I listened gleefully: the desperate need to enjoy the present moment, the exhausting urge to squeeze every particle out of life . . . Branson definitely wasn't ready for Level 4.

'I don't want to be an armchair psychologist,' I said, 'but in your book you mention the "serenity" of those Japanese fishermen you saw in the Pacific. Don't you ever wonder what it would be like if you just *sat still*?' I laughed awkwardly. 'Obviously you do sit still sometimes.'

There was a pause while Branson took in the significance of my question.

'Look . . .' He sounded ruffled. 'I've sat alongside my son on a surfboard off the coast of Australia for three days without a phone. I'm not the kind of . . . If I didn't have the opportunity to make a difference I could be very happy bumming out in Bali, but the problem is I have an opportunity and I can make a difference. If you're a successful entrepreneur, then the wealth and power that come with that are unreasonable, and a massive responsibility comes with that, to utilise that wealth and power in a constructive way. If you take global warming, it's a very, very serious issue. One could arguably be quite depressed about it, but equally it's wonderfully challenging to see if we can collectively do something about it and actually avert a disaster and in the process address another problem – running out of oil. How wonderful it would be if the world were covered by windmills and solar panels and wave machines, and the crops we grew were powering our cars and trains and buses and our planes! It's something I truly believe is possible and therefore we do have an optimistic future but we all have to work hard to make it happen.'

'Work hard?' In my most optimistic moments I imagined a world with no work at all.

'If you're an optimist you have to work hard to make sure that your optimism is justified. If we all sat on our backsides we'd have no cause to be optimistic. And it's very gratifying, and at the same time it's hard work.' He sighed. 'You know, the last three nights I've shaken hands with about three thousand people, done pictures and signed things and . . .'

'But did you have to start a record company and an airline and a soft drinks company and . . . and a train line, just in order to help people?' If Branson had been a real optimist he wouldn't have needed to *do* anything. He would have sat in his room and just concentrated on *being with his emotions*. True optimism is about following your heart. It's about visualising things and letting them flow effortlessly into your life. Besides, it wasn't right that someone less advanced than me should be flying around signing autographs. That was my job.

'It's all very well trying to change the world,' said Branson sharply, 'but unless you've got some financial resources you're not going to be able to do it. In the process, I like to think that airline and train travel is a lot more pleasant.' He paused. 'I am sorry, I've got to stop now.'

'Oh!' Branson was the first optimist I had spoken to who ended when he said he would. I could feel the longed-for invitation to Necker Island slipping from my grasp.

'I hope I haven't . . .'

'No. Look, if you wanted to continue some other time, I'd be very happy. It's just . . . I'm very, very tired.'

'Could I ask one final question?'

'Sure,' he sighed.

I lowered my voice and moved the receiver closer to my ear. 'Do you ever have to force yourself to get out of bed?'

'Never,' he said. 'No.'

'Never? You literally *spring* out of bed in the morning?'

'Yes.'

I stared through the window at the branches of a leafless tree.

'Right,' I said.

13

When people are suffering they go to the heart of reality. People who really have been up against it emerge with a quality of life and aliveness which those of us who haven't had those kinds of experiences, we don't know about. It's very, very striking.

Diana Witts

Outside the trees were waving deliriously in the breeze. I sat in the doorway and read a newspaper, looking up from time to time to admire the houses across the road. People walked by in jogging kit with smoothies and bagels in their hands. It was high summer. I was glad to be in London.

Then I turned the page.

A boy had been knifed to death for intervening in a fight. He was a young footballer who had stood up for a friend. My stomach turned over.

'You don't just *die* for no reason,' I said to myself. 'What you *expect*, you *get*.' If only people realised the truth – that their thoughts create reality – then life would no longer seem so meaningless or painful. As Viktor Frankl, the Austrian psychologist who survived the Holocaust, wrote:

I was struggling to find the reason for my sufferings
. . . an ultimate purpose . . . Has all this suffering,
this dying, around us, a meaning?

Yes, I thought. Of course it does. Nothing is random.

I wrote it down in my notebook and underlined it three times. Since my conversation with Zara in the summer, it was as if a veil had been lifted. Life was fair after all! Knowing this made it so much easier to deal with things. Especially now that Zara was back in India. At the end of our summer around England, she had bought another one-way ticket. But this time it was different. 'It's exactly as it should be,' Zara had said. 'The universe is supplying us with everything we need.'

'Right,' I nodded. 'And right now we need to be apart?'

'Exactly.'

'But soon we'll see each other again.'

'Of course,' she said. 'Life will bring us back together at exactly the right moment.'

We made a provisional plan to meet again in the winter. Until then, it was a matter of killing time and filling the pages of my book with interesting characters. I also wanted to start benefiting others with my radical new understanding of the world. After all, I had a totally comprehensive and universal explanation for everything. All I needed to do now, before I wrote about it in my book, was to test it out.

I met Trude Levi in her small suburban house in North London. A contact of mine had passed me her details, confidentially, and in great excitement. 'She's a wonderful woman!' she told me. 'She's such an optimist!'

Trude took me through to her kitchen. I watched as she poured me a glass of water. Bent by age, she had the nimble movements of a puppet from a fairy tale. She had survived sixty years of life in Barnet, North London. And before that, Nazi Germany.

'I think it's about the ultimate experience one can have,' she said.

'In seven and a half weeks, four hundred and eighty thousand Jews were shipped out of Hungary. We were taken into a ghetto for seven weeks, then to our first concentration camp. Ninety per cent of those who arrived were taken straight to the crematoria. Only the women who looked strong enough were allowed to remain alive.'

She said it in a matter-of-fact way. I looked around Trude's living room, crammed with Eastern European books and photos and paintings. It felt like an entire culture preserved in amber. The afternoon sunlight spilled through the grates on the window.

'What did it take to survive?' I asked.

Trude's eyebrows arched sceptically. 'Luck!'

'Luck? What about your attitude?'

'Your attitude doesn't matter. It doesn't matter at all because, if you don't get food or water, you die.'

'What if you're an optimist?' I argued. 'Were there optimists who died?'

'I'm sure there were lots of optimists,' she said. 'I didn't tell you yet about the train journey to Auschwitz. People went mad, people became hysterical, people had heart attacks. We travelled with the dead and the mad and the screaming for five days and nights. We had no water and it was a very hot summer. My mother collapsed on the way. The rails were extended straight to the crematoria, and she had to be dragged out.'

Right, I thought. Maybe they weren't *real* optimists.

I felt my heart contract. 'They say . . . they say, what you expect you get.'

'I don't think we expected *this*!'

'But was there . . .' I fumbled with my water glass. 'An expectation on a *deep* level?'

'On a deep level.' Trude thought for a moment. 'I don't know.' Her eyes became distant, like oracles. 'You always hoped that in the new place you were going to be allowed to settle, to build something. And then every time it was broken down. People moved from one place to another but somehow they carried on. We carried on, we carried on for quite a long time. I mean, the Greeks disappeared, the Romans disappeared. The Jews are still here!'

Her fingers danced on the table. 'Last year I went to Nuremberg parade ground and stood on the rostrum where Hitler used to address 70,000 people. I shouted into the empty, enormous, parade ground: "Hitler and your minions! Where are you? You tried everything to annihilate me. But I am still here! And I'm still enjoying very much life!"'

At the end of our meeting I walked around Trude's living room, admiring the work of art that she had made it. She had protective blinds all over, and a triple lock on the door. After several burglaries, she told me, she wasn't going to let it happen again.

I drove back home, uncertain of myself. My model of the universe was still valid, I felt sure. It was just a matter of perspective. I could hardly mention creative visualisation to a survivor of the Holocaust. It wouldn't be appropriate. I pictured myself walking around the concentration camps, reading from one of Shakti's books:

> This, or something better,
> now manifests for me
> in totally satisfying and harmonious ways,
> for the highest good of all concerned.

It might not have gone down too well.

I spent the rest of the day writing an email to everyone in my address book. Did they know anyone who

... had stayed optimistic in the face of overwhelming odds?

I waited a day or two for the email to snowball. This was the element of random chance I had been longing for, which I had been too busy to activate until now. I wanted miracles of serendipity to emerge through my inbox – characters of such brilliance and weirdness that they would change my life forever. Sure enough, I soon started receiving calls from people who had never heard of me – friends of friends of friends – introducing themselves as optimists. Over the next few weeks I spoke to child abuse campaigners, car crash victims and a man who still lived with his wife after she tried to kill him with a kitchen knife.

There were also some optimists.

Emma ran a recruitment firm in the City of London. We met outside her office on a bright summer's day. She gave me a dashing smile and flicked her hair over her shoulder. She was on her third round of chemotherapy.

'I know what you're going through,' I said.

Emma leant towards me, confidentially. 'You know, it *really* doesn't bother me.'

'What doesn't bother you?'

'Having cancer!' she said. I glanced cautiously at her hair.

We walked to a park where office workers ate their lunch, showing their white legs in the sun. I thought about the footballer. Two days ago he would have been having lunch himself, maybe in this very park.

'I don't have any sense of "why me?"' said Emma, sitting

down on a bench. 'Because, you know, why not me? Why anybody?' She pushed a strand of hair from her face. 'It just happens. Everybody gets their thing. There's something. It comes later in life, or . . . something happens in your life and you deal with it. It's really very simple.'

Well, I thought, not that simple!

'Yesterday,' she whispered, 'I heard that an Al Qaeda leader had been killed and it coloured my entire day. I realise I'm so unimportant compared to all this stuff, I feel as though literally I'm a . . . particle! And these other things are so much more important than the fact that I've got cancer. My individual problems are just not that important, they're just not that interesting . . . to *me*.'

I squinted in the sun. 'Has it always been like this?'

'Oh, completely.'

I gave her an understanding smile.

'Let's go back,' I said, 'to when you were first diagnosed.'

She leant closer. 'This is going to sound a bit odd,' she confided, 'but I was kind of *expecting* something . . .'

'Aha,' I said.

'Yes . . . I had got myself into a corner. I didn't know what to do with the rest of my life. I was working very hard, my life was becoming narrow and quite small – and I didn't know how to break out of it. Odd,' she smiled.

Not odd at all!

'So I wasn't surprised when it happened,' she continued. 'And *I didn't mind*. My life was becoming very ordinary . . . and this isn't ordinary, it's interesting! You go through things you've never been through before. I've never *done* hardship or discomfort or fear, or any of that stuff before in my life. So it's a kind of opportunity.'

I looked at her with disbelief.

Emma smiled. 'When you get diagnosed, everyone tells

you the bad stuff that's going to happen: you're going to go through surgery, you're going to have this kind of pain, that kind of pain, then chemotherapy . . . But they can't tell you all the good stuff you're going to have as a result of it. They can't tell you what opportunities may arise. They can't tell you how it may change your life, because that's up to you.'

'Well,' I said, 'that's wonderful.'

She shrugged. 'It's not as if I've gone through the pits of hell. Actually, it's quite easy having cancer because everyone thinks you're amazing all the time, being so brave and extraordinary. You know: I make a joke and everyone thinks it's hilarious – they fall off their chairs – but I'm not really brave at all, because to be brave you have to be fearful . . . and I'd much rather it was cancer than something happening to my family, or that I went blind, or that . . . I can think of a million worse things. So, for an experience . . . it's not a bad one.'

I steepled my fingers. I was beginning to get a lock on the situation. Emma had 'created' this illness in order to expand her consciousness and now she was pretending that it didn't bother her: a classic escape strategy!

'But when you're feeling really sick and ill,' I said, screwing up my face, 'you know, *really* bad, how is it then?'

'The first time you have chemo it's all a big shock, but then you get your head around it and you know what to expect, and it's about putting things into boxes that you can manage, bite-size pieces. If you look at everything as one it's overwhelming but if you divide things into little pieces you can deal with each specific problem.' She pushed a hand through her hair. 'For example, a set of symptoms or side-effects you get from medication – you learn to deal with each one, and as soon as you've got them done they're done! You just need the time to figure out how to manage each thing. And fear of pain is so much worse than the pain itself. I've found that to be the case every time.'

I smiled tensely. Emma's delusion was complicated. Like Trude, her determination to be strong had made her life an endless series of obstacles. But how could I explain that to her? 'You've really learned to cope,' I said.

'I've learned all sorts of things. For example, you can't tell – because I'm good at covering it up – but I've lost a lot of my hair. I've always had long, blonde hair and my hair has always been one of my bigger features, and so what I've learned is – there are a lot of times when I feel extremely unattractive – and it doesn't make me unhappy! And I didn't know that. I can feel unattractive and not mind! That's an opportunity I wouldn't have had.'

'It's an opportunity,' I said.

'Well, it is. It really is.'

I looked down at my sandwich. 'But it might, you know . . .'

Emma shook her head. 'That thought doesn't really upset me.'

'You're not afraid of . . . ?'

'Death? No. See, I'm not afraid of death. I *would* mind dying from this cancer now, because my family would never get over it, but I don't personally feel any strong attachment to life . . . I've had a really, really happy life, a lovely life, and my brain is constantly full of wonderful things, and I find life fascinating and interesting, but if it was over tomorrow I wouldn't feel a sense of loss myself.'

'Your mind is full of wonderful things!'

'I just think life is wonderful and I don't have, like, stuff I need to get over, or things I'm still desperate to do. My brain is full of wonderful memories of my whole life and I enjoy every day. And even last year there was lots of stuff which I was bashing my head against the wall about, but even then I was happy to get up every single day and I think that life is fabulous, so I don't really mind that it ends . . . So, maybe not really minding what the outcome is . . . maybe that's why I'm happy.'

'Right,' I said, staring at her. 'Right. Well, that's nice. You're a positive thinker. That's great.'

'I don't really feel like I am. Depending on your disposition I think your boiler breaking down can be harder than having cancer. I don't think life is meant to be tickety-boo, and then if it goes wrong you should be angry – that's not the package, that's not how it happens. You just have to open a newspaper to see that.'

I shifted uneasily in my seat. 'There's no guarantees,' she said. 'Who's the lucky person who gets nothing wrong with them?'

'You act like it's random,' I said, steadying my voice, 'but from what you're saying it doesn't sound random at all.'

She answered lightly. 'I think you can sense when something needs to change, so when it does arrive you invite it in . . . I don't think you're ever going to know why, or if there's a reason. I don't think there's some "fate" thing.'

A gust of wind blew early fallen leaves across the lawn. I gazed at Emma over my fingers. 'You'll definitely recover,' I said. 'You've got the right attitude. I mean, if anyone is going to . . . you will. You will. You're very advanced.'

'I don't really mind,' she said, 'whatever happens. Really.' She looked silently at the grass. 'I've never been happier. I can't really explain it, but it's true.'

Notes to Pessimists

NOTHING IS RANDOM: THE PROOF

Gottfried, Wilhelm Leibniz (1646–1716): Everything is perfect because – mathematically – nothing in this world could be any other way than it is. For similar reasons, anything that can happen will happen. Leibniz proved this, then invented differential calculus. So I believe him.

Buddha, Zara, et cetera: Suffering is caused only by believing painful thoughts. Life will keep presenting you with situations until you finally stop believing them. Everything that happens to you, happens because you 'need' it.

Viktor Frankl (1904–97): If you're afraid of something, it's much more likely to happen to you: 'Fear brings to pass what one is afraid of.' Suffering is an achievement in its own right.

Quantum physics, Einstein, Shakti Gawain (1921–): The 'Law of Attraction' states that like energies attract.

Therefore whatever we think about the most we will experience.

I think that sums it up.

14

*We have found that merely repeating positive
statements to yourself does not raise mood or achievement very
much, if at all. It is how you cope with negative statements that
has an effect.*

Martin Seligman

2 a.m. I reached for my water glass and tried to clear my
throat. Something evil had taken up residence in my tonsils.
It felt threatening, unnatural. It had bad intentions. *Negative
feelings*, I said to myself, *trapped energy*. The more I became
aware of these things, the more they came. It was endless.
I coughed. My inner pain had got stuck in my lower thorax.
Now it was being cleaned out. What would Zara say? I was
being confronted with deep unconscious patterns that
needed to be released. Still, I was afraid. What if my inner
pain killed me? Did it know that I had long-standing plans
for the weekend?

I lay in bed, listening to the road outside, the constant
drone of ignorant people driving nowhere late at night. I
imagined the bad *feng shui* ripping through my brain cells.
If only I could sleep. What was wrong with me that I
couldn't sleep? 'If you can break things into bite-sized
pieces,' said Emma, 'you can handle anything.' I counted
off the symptoms: a painful swallowing, a dangerous cramp

in my tonsils, a dribbly inconvenience above my lungs. Yes, on their own the individual feelings were manageable. It was just when they got together and decided to take me out for lunch that things went wrong. 'Everything is OK until you give it a name,' said Byron Katie, 'but you have named it "not OK".'

All the same, I thought, even if I don't give it a name it's still bloody painful.

What's more, I had been analysing my cold for three hours and it still hadn't gone away. What was the point of that? Maybe if I wrote down my negative thoughts and read them out, then maybe I could detach myself from them and the symptoms would finally disappear. Isn't that what Srikumar Rao had told me to do? 'Carry around a notebook or a sheet of paper for the next few days, and keep note of what's going on inside your head. Especially the negative thoughts.'

I switched on the bedside lamp and groped for my pen. Beside me piles of papers and books covered the dusty floor. *Home.* I scanned the room. Everything I owned was here, packed into a few cardboard boxes. Outside the cars drilled up and down the road, from Croydon to Peckham Rye.

I had moved into this small bedroom two days ago: carried my belongings to the Fiesta and driven away from St John's Wood while Xanthe was out shopping. I had had no choice. Money was getting tight and a friend had offered me her spare room in South London. Besides, I would soon be leaving on my travels around the world – or so I hoped. I couldn't tie myself down with monthly rental payments and other petty, practical concerns.

All the optimists I really envied had gone through some major crisis like this, forced to let go of everything they held dear. Now it was my turn. There was something heroic about drifting from house to house, dependent on the generosity of friends. Soon I would free, like Immaculée after the holocaust, free to wander the earth without any ties or constraints. I saw myself weather-beaten and heroic, like David Banner, with only the shirt on his back, drifting from town to town. Behind me I would leave my belongings, parcel by parcel, in the attics and storage units of London. Eventually I would have nothing at all and, finally, I would be reunited with Zara and we would buy a large villa in the Mediterranean.

Still, it was awkward not to be able to find my pen.

The next morning I wandered into the living room. Gabrielle – my host – was sitting in her nightgown, chanting softly to a tape recording of whale music. I stared, blinking, at the sunlight on her back. Next to her was a small altar covered with Tarot cards and incense sticks and images of female deities. A year ago this would have scared the shit out of me. Now I looked at it with a feeling of distant amusement. I knew Gabrielle had a weakness for this stuff. Chanting, yoga, meditation . . . it was merely a lower form of spirituality, useful for people at a less advanced stage of psychological development. I could hardly hold it against her.

'Hey,' she said, opening her eyes. 'How are you?'

'Fine!' I said. 'I'm off to see my therapist.'

'Oh yes? What kind of therapy is that?'

'It's called rebirthing. You hyperventilate until your body goes into spasms and you release all your trapped energy. You know, painful experiences stored up from childhood, that kind of thing.'

'Sounds wonderful,' said Gabrielle.

'It's great,' I said. 'I'm finally facing my deepest fears. It's so much easier than I expected!'

My friend smiled, kindly.

'You see, Gaby,' I explained, 'by facing your deepest fears you become free from emotional blocks and negative self-beliefs. Then,' I held up my finger, 'you can be detached, because you're not trying to escape from anything. Then, when you are trusting and relaxed, you can have whatever you want. It's simple.'

'Are you OK?' asked Gabrielle. 'You sound a bit . . . funny.'

'I'm fine,' I said. 'Why would I not be fine?'

Gabrielle looked at me in a certain way.

'How's Zara?' she asked gently. 'Is everything all right?'

'Oh yes,' I said. 'She's always all right.'

My father put down the menu and ordered a glass of beer.

'Drink, Laurence?'

'Water. Thank you.' I watched him with concern.

We all knew the reason for Dad's recent upturn in mood. Dad's new girlfriend – an American woman he had met on a blind date – had had the mesmerising effect of making him cheerful for the first time in years. This was very welcome, of course, but if there was one lesson I had learned in the last year it was that optimism shouldn't depend on interpersonal relations. It should be a constant. Otherwise it would be like a yo-yo – vulnerable to all of the vagaries of life: weather, hormones, the punctual arrival of London Transport vehicles. Not to mention relationships. Dad seemed to be missing this important spiritual perspective.

'You look well,' I said.

'I feel great,' he said, smiling roguishly.

I fingered my chopsticks. I knew that all I had to do was steer the conversation onto George Bush, or Iraq, or pretty much anything else in the news and my father's customary cynicism would pop back into place.

It was tempting.

'Hey, Dad,' I said, 'you've finally become an optimist.'

'Oh, no,' he grinned, 'I'm still as pessimistic as ever. I still believe human beings are fundamentally screwed up and that our time on this planet is limited.' He opened the menu. 'But it doesn't bother me so much any more.'

I watched my father ruefully.

'How's Zara?' he asked.

I sighed. Why was everyone so concerned about my long-distance relationship?

'I must admit,' he said, 'to being a bit confused about you two. I thought you were an item. And now she's in India again.'

'Yes,' I said. 'But that's perfectly OK. Because we're both totally committed to being with our own negative feelings and taking responsibility for them without projecting them onto each other.'

'As long as you're happy,' he said, 'that's all I care about.'

'The point is, Dad, it's great to be in a relationship. But it's vital to work on your own stuff first. That's why therapy is so important.'

'Believe me,' said my father. He took a swig of beer. 'I've tried them all in my time . . . I've had a Jungian analyst, I've tried bio-energetics. I've done CBT and Group Energetics. I'm not sure *any* of them work, not for me at least. I'm still a raving rat bag.' He wiped his mouth. 'Well, anyway. I'm glad. I always thought you would end up in therapy sooner or later.'

'What do you mean?' I put down my chopsticks.

'Come on,' said Dad. 'You know that things weren't always easy when you were little.'

'But that's normal,' I protested.

He gave me a frank look. 'Things weren't easy for you growing up, Laurence. Relations between you and your mother were often fraught. You were the first and you had the toughest time. As you know.'

I hesitated. 'Do you think that might have affected my relationships with, you know, with . . . with . . .'

'Women?' said my dad. 'Oh, I'm sure it did.'

The following week I met an American economist called 'Woody' Brock. I didn't really want to meet him because, theoretically, I already knew everything I needed to. I was on a therapeutic journey. I was exploring my inner pain and I knew what optimism was. The last thing I needed was for some economist to tell me I had got it all wrong. But Doctor Brock was a friend of a friend, and when I ran into him one morning in Piccadilly he claimed he had essential information for me, if I could be bothered to track him down next time he was in London. Just from the way he looked at me, I could tell Brock thought I was a woolly-minded liberal who hadn't given optimism proper thought. *Ridiculous!* This – plus the evident assumption that I would be desperate for his advice – annoyed me enough to call him up.

First, I did a bit of research. I found out that Woody was one of the world's top five experts in Decision Theory, that he was a 'leading economist whose speciality is to understand the future' and that he had once exchanged letters with Bill Clinton. This put a different complexion on things. Whatever Decision Theory was, it sounded impressive and theoretical. If I wanted to generate an income from the optimist movement I was going to have to start sounding impressive and theoretical.

But Woody was in a hurry. 'I can't have this conversation,' he snapped, when I called him on his mobile. 'I can't do this on the phone. Call me back at noon. I'll be in an antique store on the Fulham Road. I don't know where it is. Look it up. Get your ass out to Fulham Road. Call me ten times! That's how it works.'

I looked at the telephone, shocked.

We finally met in a restaurant in Fulham. Everyone else was wearing suits. I felt like a smudge of paint on a spotless Chinese vase. Luckily, our encounter was a short one. Woody only had half an hour to talk to me. He spoke quickly, like a maths teacher on amphetamines.

'Now, listen,' he said. 'I'm going to do you a big favour. Philosophy is the over-arching human enterprise of taking fuzzy concepts and theories and replacing them with *less fuzzy* concepts. Ultimately, even arithmetic depends upon the assumptions of Number Theory, so you never completely avoid the *fuzziness*. But accepting some airy-fairy, religious, spiritual whatever . . .' He cracked a breadstick in two. 'Decision Theory made a hugely important advance in our understanding of the relationship between optimism and uncertainty. Are you ready?'

He flagged down a waiter. 'We'd like menus, American style – rapidly!' I rearranged my napkin on my lap. I would not be intimidated by this mathematician.

'The concepts of pessimism and optimism,' said Woody sternly, 'are at a very deep level scrambled up with concepts of uncertainty. Suppose there was no uncertainty about the future *what*-soever, then the notion of being an optimist or a pessimist almost has *no meaning*, because you already know what's going to happen. Repeat: it has no meaning. You may say, I don't *like* the fact that World War Three will start in four years, but I *know it*.'

Goddamit, I thought. Brock was talking to me like an idiot. Who did he think I was? An American? I stroked my stubble briskly.

'First concept,' he said, 'a lottery. A lottery – in its most basic form – has two outcomes, good outcome and bad outcome. Each outcome has a probability attached to it.' He glanced at my head. 'Seventy per cent you'll be completely bald in three years, 30 per cent you'll be slightly bald.' I glared at him, powerless to argue. 'A lottery is a description of risk, because it says how unsure you are about the outcome. Now this is relevant – life is a series of lotteries.'

The waiter appeared. 'More ice, sir?'

'Lots more . . . American style!' Woody looked at me irritably over his spectacles. 'Second concept. You're given fifty-fifty odds of winning a million dollars, so your lottery ticket has an *expected value* of half a million dollars, that is the *probability weighted pay-off* – its statistical, actuarial, objective value. If you played it a million times and divided by a million. *Not played once* like the lottery of life.'

It was a small restaurant and the other diners started listening quietly in.

'Now in *reality* we face a *sequence* of lotteries,' lectured Woody. 'Like the stock market, for example – sometimes we win, sometimes we lose, but over time there's an average. Let's say the average return on stocks is 7 per cent per year, we call that the *normal pay-off*. We all agree that 7 per cent is the long-run, objective, one-hundred-year average. But in any particular year it could be higher or lower.'

Woody lowered his glasses and asked me to imagine two different outcomes: a high return – 10 per cent – and a low return – 4 per cent.

'Then ask that woman, "What are your odds of each outcome?"'

I looked reluctantly at the corner table where the only female luncher was seated. She was pretending to be occupied with her spaghetti.

'In 1980 – when people had been burnt for fifteen years

by a terrible stock market – she would have given you a high probability of 4 per cent and a low probability of 10 per cent. But in 1999 it would be the other way around – because they were used to above-average returns. Gottit?'

An optimist, he summarised, with a flourish, is someone who guesses a higher than average probability of a good outcome.

'That's an optimist,' he concluded. 'It's as simple as that. Now if the *whole market* is like that, what do you think they do with their money? They buy. When they buy, they push up the valuation of stocks, and suddenly they realise they're getting rich, so they buy more and more. It's called "psychological" but I don't use that word, I don't need it any more. What happens is *the experience of having been an optimist with other optimists means we got richer* so we do it again and again and again. That's the genesis of so-called "bubbles": our optimism was justified. It was not only justified it was *self-fulfilling.*'

'Wait a minute,' I said, a cloud moving across my mind. 'Are you saying that positive thinking changes the probabilities?'

'That's exactly what I am saying. Except that now I no longer need fuzzy psychological concepts like positivity. I can *dispense* with them!'

He took a sip of his Punt e Mes. 'So that's why optimism becomes a *propellent* for major social movements – like why Americans like to borrow, because times have been very good to them in the last twenty years, so they're *optimistic.* Their assessment of odds of success is skewed, but this creates its own reality.'

He picked up his menu. 'That's the main point I wanted to make. Now we must eat our food.' He pointed at my microphone. 'Turn this off.'

I picked at my salad. In Woody's world, there was no

room for hope or vision. His mathematical vision of life had shuttered his eyes to the beautiful and infinite possibilities of true optimism.

Afterwards Woody hailed a taxi. He got in and rolled down the window. 'The problem with you, Laurence, is that you believe you're somehow above the physical rules of the universe. So you accept these airy-fairy notions. Do you need a lift somewhere?'

'No,' I said.

I was hoping that my next optimist might provide a slightly more compassionate view of things. James Montier was a financial psychologist who studied behavioural economics. This was close to my own field of interest, I felt, a unique fusing of spirituality with advanced management theory. Montier worked at an investment bank in the City of London, where he wrote papers for City traders explaining that money does not lead to happiness.

GLOBAL EQUITY STRATEGY
It doesn't pay: materialism and the pursuit of happiness.

Materialistic pursuits are not a path to sustainable happiness. A mass of evidence shows people who have more materialistic goals are less happy than those who focus on intrinsic aims such as relationships or personal growth.

It takes balls, I decided, to write that kind of thing in one of the great financial centres of the world.

I met James at his office.

'Optimism,' he said, leaning back in his chinos. 'It's one of my big interests.'

'Good.'

'Because most people are actually *too* optimistic.'

I laughed, confident that this was a joke.

'Because,' he explained. 'We have two major flaws, and they seem to be universal. Our biggest flaw is chronic miscalculation of the odds. Human beings are terrible judges of outcomes. We almost always overestimate the chances of success.'

'What do you mean?' I asked, nervously.

'We're not good at forecasting events. If you ask someone for a spot forecast and ask for their 98 per cent confidence intervals – i.e. the true answer should lie outside of those bands just 2 per cent of the time – it lies outside 30 to 40 per cent of the time.'

I shook my head, confused. 'And that means that people are too optimistic?'

'Yes,' he said. 'People are immensely too sure about themselves and their answers.' Montier paused, looking at me. 'Are you OK?'

'Yes,' I mumbled. How was this possible? Seligman had told me that there was an epidemic of *depression*. Were we talking about the same species?

'The second flaw is overconfidence. Ask a thousand people. The majority of them will say they're above average drivers. Most men think they're above average lovers. People trust their own judgement.' I looked down at my hands. 'They shouldn't! When you combine this with overoptimism it's lethal. I gave a survey to a bunch of our fund managers recently. Seventy-six per cent of them claimed they were above average at their jobs. They were wrong!'

'But that's not *true* optimism,' I protested. 'Most people don't have true optimism.'

'How are you defining that?'

'It's complicated,' I said. 'True optimism comes from acceptance and facing reality. But it's also self-fulfilling.'

Montier stroked his chin. 'Optimism very often *is* self-fulfilling . . . for a while.'

'And then?'

'In the stock market, once the optimism starts snow-balling, it's unstoppable. Everyone cooperates in it.'

'Because it makes them all rich!' I liked the analogy.

The analyst nodded. 'But only for a while, because then people stop cooperating in the illusion.'

'What happens then?

James allowed himself a smile. 'Then the bubble bursts.'

I had a headache and it was getting worse. The headache had been brought on, I felt sure, by my meeting with Montier – it had hit me almost the moment I stepped out of his office. Montier was exactly the sort of person, I realised, who gives 'optimism' a bad name, even if it is with the best intentions.

I decided to make a transcript of my interview with Woody. Prickly as he was, the professor at least rated optimism as a positive thing. He was an ally, not an enemy, and that seemed to be an increasingly rare thing. What's more, I was worried that if I didn't figure out what he was talking about now, it might slip forever out of my grasp.

As I read through the interview I gradually realised that everything the professor had told me about Decision Theory could be compressed into one basic statement: *Optimism depends on your judgement of probabilities.* Nothing else. This seemed so simple it was almost horrible. I tried to summarise his 'lottery' explanation into a written formula.

Life = (% chance of good outcome x value of good)
      + (% chance of bad outcome x cost of bad)

I looked at it, impressed. What did it mean? If you're an optimist, he had said, you give higher than average chances of good outcomes and lower than average chances of bad outcomes. If you're a pessimist, you do the opposite. So far, so good. You also give higher *value* to positive outcomes and lower value to the costs – which would also make the game more attractive for you to play. Optimists and pessimists are people who consistently get the probabilities wrong. A realist, supposedly, gets it just right.

I should have felt depressed by this, but to my surprise I felt light-headed and high – as if I had drunk a magic potion that suddenly made me all-powerful and made everything manageable and easy. I felt as if I were looking down on existence from above, like a kind of god. Life is nothing personal, it's just a bunch of numbers. And then you move them around. Zara hadn't sent me an email for eight days, but that wasn't even a prime number.

'We all face life as lotteries,' said Woody. It's anything you're taking a chance on. So what if

'lottery' = involvement with Zara

. . . would there be a *formula* for the relationship? My fingers raced ahead of my thoughts.

IF
lottery = fulfilling long-term relationship ('FLOR') vs painful and heart-rending waste of time ('PHWAT')
THEN
likely outcome of relationship = (chance of FLOR x value of FLOR) + (chance of PHWAT x cost of PHWAT)

The walls of my room shook as a truck drove past. What odds was I going to use? Everything came down to the odds.

RELATIONSHIP = (.99 x value of FLOR) + (.01 x cost
of PHWAT)
=> wonderful and fulfilling long-term relationship

Aha! Now I understood: I had given something like a 99 per cent probability to our friendship ending up as a Fulfilling Long-term Relationship (FLOR) or, to put it in English, a wedding, in a pretty church somewhere in Surrey. I looked at my formula again. With odds that high, no wonder I was ready to fight for the relationship. But what about other couples? Zara and I had a highly unusual and enlightened process for working through our problems. What were the odds for ordinary relationships?

RELATIONSHIP = (.50 x value of FLOR) + (.50 x cost
of PHWAT)
=> awkward collision of different wants and needs

That was the depressing reality for most people, and that was only the average. For some people it was much worse. But then a disturbing thought came to my mind: what if I was getting the probabilities wrong for my own relationship? Could this be the overconfidence that James Montier had been telling me about, the optimism? Were all my hopes – visualisation, dreams – no more than a mathematical mistake, a miscalculation of reality? I sat down heavily on a cardboard box. Was it possible I had isolated the mathematics of denial – and I was its first victim?

Was my love affair a FLOR or a PHWAT?

I stumbled downstairs and fixed myself some tea.

No, I thought, *the odds can change*. Woody had said so

himself. Surely this was the antidote to Montier's curse: optimism creates its own reality. It doesn't have to crash. Did Bill Clinton start his political career with 50 per cent odds of being president? Of course not. I wasn't comparing myself with Bill Clinton, but the similarities were striking. Six months ago, the chances of Zara and I staying together must have been lower than 10 per cent. And today we were still going strong – give or take a few misunderstandings. I had stuck by my guns and my optimism had become a reality. *It was a self-fulfilling plan that defied the normal rules of historical probability.*

I opened the door and reeled out into the sunshine, rubbing my eyes. I hadn't felt so genius since learning how to do simultaneous equations in fifth form. I had found the mathematical basis of dumb optimism. Shoppers walked past, doing their morning errands. They looked like people . . . but they were actually numbers. I experienced a moment of almost terrifying megalomania.

If only they knew.

15

The trouble with your mother and me is that we'd exhausted our illusions. As you grow up, and you'll find this, Dwight, you keep getting involved with larger and larger illusions that take longer and longer to fall away. The great hope is eventually to find an illusion that will outlast your life.

Benjamin Kunkel, *Indecision*

'I'm a writer,' I said proudly to the sparkly old lady. We were at a drinks reception for an exhibition about famous explorers. Some of the explorers were there, sipping champagne under giant prints of their own faces. 'I'm searching for the secret of optimism.'

'Why would you do that?' she asked brightly. 'How will you support yourself?'

I gripped the stem of my glass. 'I'm writing a book.'

'I don't suppose anyone will be interested in that,' she said, looking up at me with a wrinkly smile.

'Well, they are, actually.'

'Writers never make any money. Even famous writers. You should get a job in finance. You look terribly thin.'

My face reddened.

'It's odd,' I said, smiling through my teeth. 'We're at a

party about explorers, and yet here you are, discouraging me from taking a risk. I don't think much exploring would get done if everyone had that attitude.' The lady was under-estimating the probabilities of success and overestimating the cost of failure, thus assuming a low value for my lottery ticket and leading her to estimate a high opportunity cost.

optimist project = (1% success) + (99% failure)

'Realism,' I added, twisting my glass, 'consists of accurately seeing the probabilities of a good or a bad outcome, then accepting this reality. But *true optimism* consists of accepting the risks and then *doing it anyway*. You see?' I had come up with this innovation during the night, some time between 4 and 5 a.m. Sleep had been elusive recently.

'Maybe so,' said the lady. A tweeded man appeared at her side and slipped an arm around her waist. I was astounded to note that he was one of the explorers featured in the exhibition. 'But it's not risk I'm talking about,' she smiled. 'It's certainty.'

I excused myself and made for the door. It was getting harder and harder to talk to ordinary people. My beard was getting too long. People were starting to make assumptions about my living conditions. They didn't understand that certain sacrifices are necessary if you want to find the truth. That was the price of optimism, I reminded myself. Once I had touched the void and finalised the Grand Universal Theory I could reconstruct my life on the basis of pure trust. Zaia and I would buy our house together and I could start my lecture tour of the world.

Blocking my way out was the organiser who had invited me to the event. 'Laurence, can I introduce you to Steve Brooks? Steve's a true optimist.'

Steve Brooks was wearing tweed and twirling a

champagne glass. He reminded me of Dastardly from the *Wacky Races*. 'Steve recently crashed his helicopter into the Antarctic Sea,' said my guide.

'Oh, excellent,' I said, still flustered by my encounter with the woman.

'Yes,' grinned the explorer. 'Without optimism I would be dead. It's as simple as that. We survived for eleven hours in freezing water.' He swaggered. 'Life was hanging from a cheap lady's necklace!'

'Do *you* take risks?' I asked him, glancing over at the old lady.

'Not at all. I hate risk. That's why I do so much preparation.' He handed me his card. 'If you want to talk about optimism I'd be happy to meet up. Give me a call sometime.'

The next morning I woke to news of a breakdown in talks between Iran and the United Nations. President Ahmadinejad was threatening the West with 'untold forces of anger and destruction' and Washington was talking openly about regime change. This couldn't be described as good news. However, I now had an opportunity to introduce my theory of spiritual optimism to a much wider audience.

I had already emailed the President of Iran, but I had received no response to date. Although I was superficially attracted to the idea of interviewing him, I knew it would be far more effective to address myself to the real power behind the throne.

President Ahmadinejad's spiritual guru was a man called Ayatollah Mesbah Yazdi. Mesbah Yazdi was obviously the key. If I could open a dialogue with him this would be the first step in the task of bringing advanced spiritual therapy to the world. If all nations, especially those in the Middle East, understood that true optimism is blocked only by

underlying emotions and hidden negative beliefs, which
are then projected outwards onto external situations, they
would no longer be able to blame everything on the
Americans or the Muslims, respectively. For all I knew, the
Palestinians and the Israelis didn't even realise that they
were projecting their repressed inner pain onto each other,
thus creating the whole problem. Once I had got over that
hurdle I could introduce the more delicate topic of Creative
Visualisation.

I could then start communicating these complex and
difficult subjects to a wider public. And this would form
the basis of my unstoppable movement for world peace.

> Dear Ayatollah Mohammad-Taqi Mesbah-Yazdi
>
> I am a writer from England and my subject is opti-
> mism. I am concerned about the state of relations
> between Islam and the West and I would like to ask
> your advice. Please help me.
>
> My question is this:
> Do you consider that a refusal to accept one's
> suppressed inner anger may lead to projection of pain
> onto an imagined 'other' enemy, which then creates
> a situation of conflict?
>
> I look forward to your response.

I wrote it under the name of a friend I hadn't seen for years.
If there was any trouble then they would have to deal with
her first. I scanned it and pressed send. Then I went about
my business. If the Ayatollah answered me, I thought, then
there really was hope. People had misunderstood the
Iranians for far too long.

Two days later I opened my email. My face flushed hot.

In the name of Allah

Dear Madam

Whoever reviews Islamic main sources, will acknowl-
edge that patience, controlling one's anger, and forgiving
others are among the greatest Islamic ethical values,
and retaliation upon enemies is favoured only if forgiveness would make them more arrogant and impudent.
Therefore, temperateness and tolerating others are
fundamental principles in the behaviour and discourse
of a Muslim, and using such feelings as anger is accept-
able only in case of defence and as the last resort.

Good Lord! I thought. I scanned the page with a beating
heart. I had underestimated the psychological maturity of
the opposition.

Taking such teachings into consideration, there
remains no need for projection and the assumption
of an imagined enemy, or other divergent and uneth-
ical defence mechanisms. But a complete realisation
of these values is not easy, as an understanding of
them is hard for those who are lacking them.

I immediately regretted not using my real name. The man
was familiar with projection and other defence mechanisms.
No doubt he knew about creative visualisation, detachment
and the law of attraction. I felt tears welling in my eyes.
What a lack of trust there was in this world! But then I
looked again. If Mesbah Yazdi already knew all this, then
what would become of my plans to spearhead the global

introduction of Level 4 optimism? And how was I supposed to make a name for myself?

Maybe he didn't yet know about Cosmic Ordering.

Dear Ayatollah Mohammad-Taqi Mesbah-Yazdi

May I ask a brief follow-up question? . . . Do you feel sufficient efforts have been made to visualise a world where Iran, Israel, Palestine, and the USA are actually at peace rather than at war? These leaps of imagination can sometimes make all the difference, even in international affairs!

I closed my laptop. Even if that were the end of our correspondence, I reasoned, at least I had achieved something. The Ayatollah and I had touched hands over the net and world peace was thus a step closer.

But it was to be the only good news that week.

The following day I got a letter from Prince Charles explaining that he didn't want to talk to me. The Prince was flattered to be asked, he claimed, but he didn't believe he was actually an optimist.

I stared at the letter. A knock-back from Charles was manageable, but earlier that day American superstar Oprah Winfrey had also turned me down, and within the same hour Paolo Coelho and former Irish premier Mary Robinson had also said no. Al Gore's office had said no thirteen times.

What was happening to my powers of visualisation? What was happening to self-fulfilling optimism? I desperately needed these interviews to get funding for my book, to show the world I was a respected and credible theorist.

The Grand Universal Theory was in danger of becoming internally unstable.

'Do you think,' suggested Xanthe, 'the reason why these

people don't want to meet you is because *you* don't really want to meet *them?*'

Oh, Xanthe. 'Of course I want to meet them.'

'But do you *really* want to meet them, or are you just doing it for your project?'

I rubbed my forehead. 'But I *am* my project.'

I decided to call Zara on her Indian mobile phone. I felt tired and discouraged after my rejection by Prince Charles, and I needed some emotional support. It was now two weeks since Zara had been in touch, and I felt with all the poetry in my heart how much I would like to lay my head in her lap and talk about the day's events. I was sure she would feel the same.

I dialled her number and waited tensely for a response. It rang in an unfamiliar tone. I pictured my girlfriend on the other side of the world, looking down at the number on her display. No doubt she was with friends, or in the middle of meditating. Probably she was wearing something Indian and see-through. There was no reply. I imagined her looking coldly at the handset. *I'm in the moment right now. I can't deal with this.* I could feel the frustration building in my chest. Zara never wanted to talk about anything difficult. Only light stuff. Had I got the formula wrong? Was our relationship actually a PHWAT? No! It didn't have to be that way. As long as we both kept our side of the bargain, to communicate and be honest. The phone rang and rang. Eventually it stopped.

I stomped into my bedroom. I knew how I was supposed to feel. I was supposed to feel loving and relaxed. But I didn't. And the fact I didn't made it worse. I brooded darkly. Zara was simply doing what she had always done – escaping from reality and pretending to be 'free', protecting herself from 'difficult energies' and forgetting the true connection that we had. Yes, I told myself, she was allergic to *real life*.

A moment passed. Was this the 'emotional chatter' that Srikumar had warned me about, the inner monologue that defines reality? Maybe. But I had to express myself! 'It's all very well living in the moment,' I thundered, 'but communication requires a certain amount of effort!'

I opened my email, scouring the inbox for some token of love or affection from the other side of the world. Instead I found a reply from Mesbah Yasdi. *Oh*, I thought. *Him*. The Ayatollah's elegant English greeted me as before.

Dear Madam

. . . Perhaps our understanding of Israel and Palestine is quite different from that of many people who live in some western countries. We believe that whoever recognises the reality of Israel and Palestine would never hope for them to peacefully live together, as it is unrealistic to envisage the cohabitation of *wolf* and the *lamb*.

I read it, depressed. His reply was a clear rebuff of advanced-level optimism. My attempt to introduce visualisation as a tool for peace had hit stony ground. Of course! How could I be expected to do anything properly? I was totally distracted by the situation with Zara.

This time she picked up the phone.

'I'm sorry,' she said. 'I missed your call!'

'Right,' I said tensely. 'Did you get my email? I sent you an email last week. And I . . .' My voice was trembling. I didn't seem able to control it.

'What's going on?' said Zara. 'This feels very heavy. This doesn't feel light at all.'

'Why does it always have to be light?' I pressed the phone to my ear. 'I'm trying to be honest. I'm trying to express myself. If you were here it would be fine. We need to talk about it.'

'I can't get into analysing things right now,' she said. 'Maybe when we meet again, but not now.'

The phone went dead. I looked at it for a moment. Then I hurled it against the sofa.

'Bitch!' I yelled.

Then I threw it again. If I had been French I would have smashed it against a wall, but I'm English, so I made sure to hit the soft furnishings.

I was completely overwhelmed. 'My anger will be heard!' I shouted, waving my fists in the air. *Wait a minute*, I thought. That felt *good*. I picked up an orange and weighed it in my hand. Then, with lightning fury, I hurled it against the kitchen wall. It exploded and bled down to the floor. *Wow!* I picked up another, and then another. One by one I whacked them into the woodwork. An avocado followed, then a banana. *Spectacular!* Soon the fruit bowl was empty.

Gabrielle came back home and saw the mess on her wall.

'I was throwing fruit,' I confessed.

'In my house!'

'I'll clean it up,' I said. I skulked to my room and made an entry on an anonymous bulletin board:

help!
9 November 2007

I'm paralysed!

Despite six months of massage therapy, rebirthing, osteopathy, Chinese medicine, homeopathic remedies, group forums, Tarot cards and interviews with the happiest people on earth, I'm still a hopeless wreck. All it takes is one call and the angry, scared teenager that sleeps permanently inside me like a dormant herpes virus is suddenly awake. Like an enthusiastic Soviet historian, my brain agrees to airbrush all the positive evidence and use carefully selected data to condemn girlfriend as uncaring, unthoughtful and incapable of affection. Like a cunning barrister, it wraps events in a moving and tragic story, the sort that would have you in tears, and soon does . . . Within moments my entire metabolism is worked up; it's firing on all cylinders. I feel like being sick. Or killing a grapefruit. With a pick-axe.

Even Mesbah Yazdi seemed to disapprove of my behaviour:

> . . . using such feelings as anger is acceptable only in case of defence and as the last resort.

I dropped to my knees. What was wrong with me?

Gabrielle knocked on my door. 'Can I come in?'

She sat on my bed. 'I'm not mad at you,' she said, 'if that's why you're hiding.'

She listened quietly as I spilled the story of the last two weeks: the celebrity rejections, the sarcastic explorers, the sudden failure of my powers of visualisation and, finally, the meltdown in my communications with Zara.

'I'm not surprised, you know, Laurence. I've been expecting something like this.'

I looked at her amazed.

'The trouble is,' said Gabrielle, 'once you've started on an emotional journey like this, there's no going back.'

I pulled a hand through my hair. 'I'm not *on* a *journey*. I just want to feel OK.'

She laughed. 'You've chosen the hardest goal of all!'

'I thought I'd already cracked it.'

'Believe me,' she said, 'it's not easy. I've been through this myself. What you're doing is expressing feelings which have been trapped inside you for years. It can be painful. But it's the only way you're going to get there . . .' I slumped back and gazed at the wall. 'Your relationship with Zara has made this journey possible,' she added.

'What? By being a nightmare?'

'You know,' said Gabrielle, 'maybe the two of you just want different things?'

'No,' I said, definitely. 'No. That's not it. We're very similar. We're very, very similar.'

She smiled sadly. 'Sometimes people just have different priorities.'

'No,' I said. 'Not us. This is temporary. Then everything will be OK. Like you said.'

She tilted her head. 'Maybe you should take some time on your own. Go somewhere quiet, anywhere you can get deeper into your feelings. Stay calm. Try to meditate. When you meditate you can let the feelings pass through you much more quickly.'

'I'm *not* meditating.' I said.

I stood up.

I had another plan and it didn't involve further navel gazing.

Seeker

16

*What is this country . . . which is unknown to the rest
of the world, and where nature operates under laws so utterly
different to ours? It is probably the land where all is well, for such
a place has to exist.*

Voltaire, *Candide*

Mary-Jane twisted a fingernail between her perfect white
teeth. My eyes trailed down her arm and across the room.
A silk print of the Buddha shimmered over the fireplace,
smiling across spliff burns and beer stains. Prayer charms
dangled in the window and a yukka celebrated in the
morning sun. I was in San Francisco.

'Why am I an optimist?' considered Mary-Jane, putting
on the kettle. 'That's an *in*-eresting one!'

She grinned. I grinned back. Mary-Jane – a waitress and
psychology student who rented the biggest room in my
brother's house in Haight Ashbury – was so positive and
laughed so loudly that even advanced optimists like myself
had to be careful not to get too close.

I watched the steam rising across jars of lentils and
spirulina, postcards of Hindu deities and a fridge magnet
from a porno magazine. My brother, Alaric, was waiting for

me outside the kitchen, safe from the seismic waves of his housemate's laughter. After six months in the same house he had learned to limit his exposure to very small doses.

'Because I realised some time ago that I have, like, power over my perception?' said Mary-Jane. 'It started when I was about fifteen or sixteen? When I read a book on Powerful Affirmations, and how your Word is Your Wand, and if you're really mindful about how you use your words then you can start transforming your thought patterns?'

I looked up at the fridge. Someone had written the letters: I AM LOVED.

'Like "I am blessed" and "I am fortunate"? I also use "I am grateful" and "I am loved".' She smiled at the fridge. 'Yeah, definitely "I am loved" – all the time.'

I am loved. I formed the shapes with my mouth. I had always assumed that affirmations were strictly for beginner-level optimists, but maybe there was something to it.

'I know it works,' said Mary-Jane, pushing her blonde tresses across her shoulder. 'I have several stories of how my affirmations have worked for me. But I really had *trust*, and that's part of it. You can't just ask and, like, *expect*, you know?'

I watched her, uncertainly. Was Mary-Jane enlightened or just vacuous? It was a tough call. Her comment about trust and expectation seemed majestically wise for a person of her age. And 'Trust' was exactly the question I was now asking myself. Could I trust in some *abstract* way, without expecting any particular outcome? And would that get me what I wanted? How could I develop this facility without losing something vital – like my sense of humour, or my long-term marriage plans?

I was hoping that the next six weeks would supply the answer. A fortnight ago, I had shoved the last of my possessions into plastic bags and stowed them in Gabrielle's attic in South London. It was the moment I had been waiting for all year, the moment when I could finally close up shop and step into the future. This is how a quest was supposed to be: a proper adventure into the unknown. And this was the country I had chosen for it. The Promised Land, the West coast of America – the last place the settlers came in their search for paradise before they fell into the sea: California! Home of Creative Visualisation, Google and hydrogen-fuelled cars – it was the global generator of everything optimistic. It was a high-consciousness energy field. It contained Shakti Gawain. Here, surely, I would find what I was looking for – the word, the definition, the real-life people who were living it: true optimism, and *how to get there*. Trust? Freedom? All I knew was this: If I let go of everything and reduced myself to nothing – no plans, no possessions, no appointments – then wouldn't I meet exactly who I needed to meet, exactly when I needed to meet them? And wouldn't I one day stop worrying about my relationship with Zara and quietly become the impressive man I was always meant to be? If Immaculée was right, then all I had to do was trust, and everything would work out by itself. Somehow this thin strip of land on the edge of America held the key to everything.

'What is it about California?' I asked.

'There's this . . . awakening?' said Mary-Jane thoughtfully. 'I believe we're evolving as a species.'

'You think Californians are more evolved than the rest of us?'

'It's more magnified here, more apparent and, um, easier to see?'

I looked at my brother. 'Don't worry,' I said. 'I'm coming.'

We wandered to a café on Haight Street to get wireless access. I was in a good mood, and the whole world seemed to be in a good mood too, including the Mexicans who were chopping onions and salad for our burritos. They were whistling and singing as if they owned the place. 'Look at those guys!' I said, shaking Alaric's arm. 'You'd never see that in London! It's the perfect flow of self-interest in a context of synchronised mutual cooperation.'

'Please,' he said. 'People can hear.'

'It brings to mind Leibniz's concept of *monads*,' I said. 'The world is made of independently autonomous atoms . . .' I glanced down at my computer. 'What happened here?'

'I don't know, it just turned off.'

The screen was black. I tapped it with my fingers.

'It's dead,' I said. 'Kaput.' I couldn't believe it. I had had the laptop for three years and it contained everything – my emails, my contact numbers, the personal address of Arnold Schwarzenegger. What the hell was I supposed to do without it? I stared at the cool winter light outside. 'It's the quest,' I marvelled under my breath. 'It's commanding me to let go of everything – even my computer.'

I had no choice but to do it properly.

The next morning I sat eating waffles while my brother surfed the internet.

'Have you heard about the *Surfing Rabbi*?' he asked.

I looked up. 'Are you serious?'

'He has a website.'

'And he surfs while . . . rabbying?'

'I dunno.'

I read through Rabbi Shifren's website. It seemed he was for real.

RABBI NACHUM SHIFREN

'The Surfing Rabbi'

His lectures include topics such as:
1) Can I be Jewish and still be a professional surfer?
2) What is the connection between Torah, Mysticism, and Surfing?
3) Where is the best wave in the world?
4) How can diet and physical fitness influence your spirituality?

Check out our outrageous new bumper sticker:
'FORGIVE ME RABBI, FOR I HAVE SURFED.'

A magical encounter for my quest, I thought to myself. A friendly character who will give me vital information for my journey.

Maybe it would be information concerning surfing, I mused. I had often wondered if my destiny were connected with surfing or, perhaps, because it seemed to be the same thing, with just doing nothing – in some genuine professional capacity. Surfers seem to understand something vital about the universe and how pointless it is, and I had always wanted to know what that was. What's more, they didn't seem to get stressed about anything, and they were usually tanned and attractive – 'Maybe the rabbi can show me how to achieve pure optimism,' I considered. 'While becoming deeply attractive and mysterious to women.'

Forty-eight hours later I was in downtown Los Angeles, standing outside a military replica shop with a life-size statue of an American GI pointing his rifle in my face. The soldier was painted green and appeared to be very, very mad about something. I was already feeling nervous due to the closeness of South Central LA – possibly the last place a middle-class white boy wants to be in his Gieves & Hawkes blazer.

I looked up and down the street, blinking in the sun.

'I'm looking for a surfing rabbi?' I said, walking into the store. A giant man in a Fidel Castro cap and fatigues appeared, and nodded lazily across a shelf full of grenades.

I moved back towards the door. 'I think I have the wrong address.'

'Come in,' said the man. He scratched his army hat and pointed to a cluttered office at the side. Inside I caught the unmistakeable outline of a surfboard. A look of shock must have crossed my face.

'You're the Surfing Rabbi?' I asked.

'That's what they say.'

The wall of the office was strewn with post-it notes in Hebrew. 'Do you surf with your yarmulke on?' I asked. Rabbi Shifren shook his head. He looked like the common ancestor of Santa Claus and the Unabomber.

'I want to know if surfers are optimistic,' I explained.

'Cool,' breathed the rabbi, 'cool,' as if he had seen a hundred optimism-seekers in his time and approved of them all. 'One of the most optimistic things that man can do is be a surfer. The reason is, surfing brings out some real character: diligence, never giving up, working hard. Surfers are, by nature, very positive – by and large they're people with one step in society, one step out – which I like.'

I looked around at the icons of self-reliance which stocked the shop: Mountie hats, plastic bullets, gas masks. I had read that the rabbi took inner-city kids out to surf, that he worked with gang members and hopeless cases. On his website there were quotations from the Talmud and the Kaballah – I had pictured some kindly liberal dude with orthodox ringlets and maybe a spliff in his mouth.

What was with the survivalist stuff?

'I don't have too much to do with society,' he said. 'It's just a means for me to go to the beach.'

'But you're a rabbi. You have a synagogue?'

'Of course, of course. It's kind of a contradiction . . . like yin and yang, you know?'

The bell rang to announce a customer and the former life guard sprang slowly to his feet – he used to be a champion paddler and he was still beefy as hell. I sat and listened as the holy man fielded questions about the gauge sizes and escape velocities of his plastic bullet collection.

'Are you a military enthusiast?' I asked, when he came back. The rabbi folded his hands calmly over his belly. 'No interest at all – it's purely economic.'

I narrowed my eyes.

'OK,' I said, glancing at a rack of airguns outside the office door. 'So why do they call you the Surfing Rabbi, not just a rabbi who surfs?'

'Probably because I'm the only one there is? I use surfing to tap into that energy, that spiritual energy which is found in the ocean.'

Shifren fell silent and waited for my next question, leaving me in the unusual position of feeling lost for words. By priestly standards there was definitely something intimidating about the guy.

'Tell me about the kids,' I said, playing for time. I still hadn't figured out exactly what I was doing here. Could it be that I actually wanted the Surfing Rabbi as a role model? For me?

'A lot of them are involved in gangs,' he said. 'Surfing for them is like a new breath of life, it's seeing a new world which can get them away from the immediate influences of their communities. The waves have this . . . it's like a magnetic power. Once people get mesmerised by the waves they focus more on their own spirituality, it reminds them of the hand of God. It's important for kids to know they're not the reason for the creation of the world.' He leant back in his seat.

'Why do more rabbis not surf?' I asked.

'Because they're wusses, basically.' He looked down at his hands, unmarked by the virtuous nobbles of prayer beads. His self-composure was awesome.

'So, what can you teach me . . .' I attempted, '. . . about optimism?'

'Surfers are always optimistic just by virtue of being surfers, 'cause the surf doesn't get good that often. The good times are rare . . . you get my drift?'

I paused. 'But if you're always waiting for the great wave to arrive . . . then surely you must be living in the future – not the present moment?'

'Totally! Surfing is always in the future.'

I scratched my head. 'But a lot of spiritual teachers would say that the trick is, um . . . to live "in the moment".'

'Those are spiritual teachers, not surfers,' he sighed. 'It's obvious. It's like having the perfect girlfriend . . . but she has to go away from you for a while, so you're always wondering, when will I see her again?'

'Ohh . . .' I thought. *That's what this was about.*

The rabbi's hands rested placidly on his lap.

'You're always combat-ready,' he said. 'Surfing is like war, you've got to be ready to go, especially when you're my age. You've got to keep moving, there's no time to sit around. That separates us pretty much from almost *any* other person.'

'And do you think about the past?' I asked. 'Because I think about the past a lot.'

The rabbi smiled dreamily. 'Oh, totally. All the time . . . matter of fact, every day. Every day I dwell on the past . . . the good days, the good surf. That's what keeps you going: dreams, constant dreams about waves.'

'But then you're never content. You're always unhappy.'

'When you're out in the water, then it's all different. Then I'm right there in the moment. It's a very unusual situation – there's nothing to really compare it to. It's very, very difficult to describe – there's a feeling of power, of harnessing power, there's no comparison in the whole world.' He put his hands behind his head.

'How does it feel?' I asked.

'A lot of it's just pure fun?' said the rabbi. 'And ecstasy?'

I was impressed. The rabbi had found a pursuit so absorbing nothing else mattered. Was that the secret? Surely it was. That was freedom. That was being *in control*. I looked admiringly at the mess in his office. If I surfed, I wouldn't have to bother interviewing people, or writing books, or falling in love with unsuitable Dutch people. I wouldn't give a shit!

And all the women would adore me.

'Hang on,' I said. 'Isn't this a kind of escapism?'

'Oh, totally. It's escape from the limitations of our body. There's a passage from the Book of Proverbs which compares the soul to the flickering of a flame, the flame is always trying to leave the wick, that's why it always goes upwards, but the flame cannot leave the wick because then there would be no flame – just as we have a soul basically imprisoned in the physical body – so for the brief moments we can leave our body behind it's definitely worthwhile.'

'Right.'

'Surfing gives you focus and it makes you really appreciate life. Once you have that appreciation of life, you know who you are, and then there's this tremendous self-esteem. Then you can actually give to other people, and you're totally OK with it. Whereas if you don't have this focus you only worry about achieving for your own self. Then you're an asshole.'

The rabbi stopped. For a moment he looked sad.

'What makes you most unhappy?' I asked.

'Nothing,' he said. 'I'm never unhappy.'

'Does anything throw you off?'

'Nothing, not a thing. I'm very focused. As a surfer you have to be. Whatever is superfluous or unnecessary, it's out – you don't deal with it at all.' He paused. 'I know that's impacted my life: I've been married three times.'

'Three times!' I regarded him with awe.

'Yeah, you're always focusing on the surf and it's pretty obsessive . . .' He rubbed his cheek, pensively. 'But I'm optimistic. I've been with my current girlfriend for the last two years. We'll probably get married.'

'It must be hard to be the perfect girlfriend of a surfer.'

He smiled. 'This one's going to be great, I can feel it.'

A couple of days later, I got a call from a woman called Paula. 'I'm Rabbi Shifren's girlfriend,' she said.

'Hey! Hi!' I pulled over and parked my car. I had been expecting Paula to call. At the end of our meeting the rabbi had scratched down a number on his business card and handed it to me. 'Give her a ring,' he said, 'if you want some more stories.'

'You're the rabbi's future wife.'

'Actually, we just broke up.'

'No way!'

I had spent at least half of that week wondering how I could find a pasttime as transporting, absorbing and selfish as surfing – so that I, too, could stop paying any attention to my relationship and thus become gruffly and impressively in control of all emotional situations.

Maybe the rabbi was taking it too far.

'It happened this morning,' Paula said.

'I'm sorry.'

'It's fine. Nothing has changed. I still love the rabbi. But I finally decided that I couldn't convert to Judaism. I told him last night.'

And then, as if to honour their freshly deceased love, Paula delivered a half-hour eulogy on the giant, flawed enigma that was her ex-fiancé.

'Twenty-five years ago Rabbi Shifren was the craziest LA life guard who ever came down the pike. They called him Shifty, and the name really fits. He was crazy, he was a notorious womaniser, he got in trouble all the time. He was out of control. To us life guards he was a legend. He was a champion paddler. He did lots of incredible things. People still talk about him. They've been talking about him for thirty years.'

She paused lovingly. 'Eventually he got fired from LA County for some reason or other. Then he disappeared, and no one heard from him again for fifteen years. Turned out he'd gone to Israel and when he resurfaced he was a rabbi. That's when I met him.'

'You really think he's an optimist?'

'Oh, yeah. One of the things I love about him is his optimism. He's ambitious, he believes he will prevail. I have to tell you, that's very exciting to be around.'

'You find that attractive?'

'It's *very* attractive.'

I leant back against the car. One day, I too would be as stubborn and dysfunctional and irresistible as the rabbi.

'Not an easy man to be in a relationship with,' I said wistfully.

'Oh, no,' she said. 'Definitely not.'

Notes to Pessimists

After a surreal experience in a box – which appeared to propel me through a moving landscape at the cost of no physical expenditure of energy, but an increasingly tense and painful tendon and a speeding ticket – now I find myself in another box, with walls and strangely perfect square-framed windows. Outside, a city I know to be LA appears to be in full summer and cars drive past. After talking with a person who lives in the box and does everything to make me feel welcome, I prepare for bed on the living-room sofa. I feel like my life is lived in full view on stage and I sleep with my face turned to the wall. I wake up feeling frightened and alone. I am very still. I have no plans. I make some calls and people don't call me back. I try to go for a walk but instead I sit on the corner of the street and feel my eyes going cloudy. Maybe there is stuff I need to process. I walk back to the box. I don't know what to do next; I've already decided not to hustle people and arrange meetings but to let stuff happen. I walk to the very large box known as a supermarket to buy some food and they are playing a song which reminds me of a memory of someone I love, and I say to myself, 'I miss her,' and I want to take her hand, but she's not here.

17

The more accidental the phenomenon, the more divine
its nature, for the divine is what has not been envisioned, what cannot be
deduced from general rules, nor irreducible to them.

Mikhail Epstein

I closed my computer and rubbed my eyes. It was time to wake up. A maple tree stood hopefully in the yard, longing to drop its leaves. Permanent summer. *Los Angeles.* Today was my last chance. I had a suitcase and a hire car. I had nothing to hold me back. I would head into the chaos of the city and let synchronicity decide.

Freedom.

First, I took a walk up Runyon Canyon, a rugged patch of parkland in the Hollywood Hills. The perfect blue of the LA dawn broke into daylight as Shih Tzus and collies went bounding down the path. I looked out over the pulsating blanket of Los Angeles, spread across the valley like some prehistoric monster ready to rise up at any moment, shake off the cars and buildings and walk into the Pacific Ocean. What would this look like in a thousand years? Would there be anything here at all?

The Optimist, they would say. It was him. *He changed the way we thought.* I clenched my fists in my pockets and walked down to the organic hypermarket.

The news from Baghdad was getting worse. Another bomb. Fifty citizens dead. I watched the faces of the shoppers as they filed past the newspapers. They didn't seem bothered. Maybe they were right. *Whatever is super-fluous or unnecessary*, I told myself, *it's out.*

I weighed up the day. Before I completely let go I still had time for a quick phone call. Dr Wong was a Chinese psychologist who had developed a radical new approach to optimism. I had found the doctor while scouring for the missing piece in my Grand Universal Theory. I was still hoping for some flash of insight that would make my job of changing the world straightforward and simple – and wouldn't require me to fall back on fuzzy, mystical explanations that people would consider ridiculous. Maybe Wong would show me the way. From what I had read it was clear that the doctor didn't care much for Seligman and the other positive psychologists – they were more popular than him and they had forgotten to consider the majority of the world's population.

> What do we say to those whose lives have been devas-
> tated by war, terrorism, poverty and AIDS? The gospel
> of expecting good outcomes and the mantra that we
> all can achieve our dreams with our own efforts sound
> hollow to those who can neither understand nor
> control the negative forces that are destroying their
> lives.

I paced around my friend's living room, waiting for the doctor to answer.

'Dr Wong!' I said. 'I understand you have identified an advanced form of optimism?'

'I call it tragic optimism,' he said.

'*Tragic* optimism?'

The scientist cleared his throat. He spoke with an almost impossible Chinese accent.

'Americans like Seligman, their basic assumption of optimism is self-confidence: "I can achieve things, and good things will happen most of the time, things are under my control." My starting point is opposite: for the majority of the world bad things happen all the time, and very often you don't have any control over it: corruption, poverty, war. In many parts of the world bad things happen *every day*.'

'Oh, God,' I said.

'Tragic Optimism is an attitude, and its defining characteristic is acceptance of reality.'

'Acceptance?' I sighed.

'It's based on the work of Viktor Frankl,' he continued. 'To develop tragic optimism you need some kind of spiritual belief, a religion, something bigger than yourself.'

'What's different about this and, say, Srikumar Rao's synthesis of modern management theory with ancient Hindu philosophy?' I walked over to the window.

Wong paused. 'The big limitation of existing models is that they treat optimism and pessimism as opposites.'

A breeze rattled the window frame. 'They're not?'

'In the East,' said the doctor firmly, 'we don't feel the need to split everything into opposites. We see things as a whole. For example, people can be both realistic-pessimistic and idealistically-optimistic at the same time.'

I scribbled this down. 'Isn't that a paradox?'

'Chinese philosophy is always paradoxical. Optimism and pessimism are two related but independent dimensions.'

'But how is that possible?'

'Tragic optimism means admitting that life is tragic but still maintaining the hope that tomorrow will be better.'

'Admitting that life is tragic?' I said. 'But I *don't*.'

'I'm a Chinese. Our history is five thousand years of suffering, right? That's why we're still around. Life must go on. We can endure horrible situations: flood, famine, foreign invasion. We've had thousands of years of suffering. We're still strong. Unlike other civilisations,' he added, ominously.

'I don't know,' I said. 'It doesn't sound like optimism to me.'

'It's tragic optimism! We know that bad things happen most of the time, but also life is worth living. I tell you a story.' Dr Wong adopted the tone of an oriental sage. 'Old man in village is trying to remove mountain with shovel. People say, "Old fool, you are seventy years old, how do you think you can you remove whole mountain?" Old fool reply, "When I die, my children keep digging, then my children's children, then their children. Eventually we move mountain. Then we get to next village without walking around it!"'

'You think Americans have something to learn from this,' I said.

'It doesn't matter how bad things get, there's still something worth living for.'

I said goodbye to Wong. I wasn't sure about tragic optimism. Hopefully, everything would turn out OK. Hopefully bad things would *stop* happening.

The day yawned emptily ahead. I decided to drive to Santa Monica to see the beach. That was, after all, the final resting place of positive thinking – geographically speaking. Unfortunately I had locked my keys in the car. I felt a wave of stress.

'Now I won't have time to interact spontaneously with the universe!' I held my head in my hands. A car drove by. *Wait a minute . . .* Wasn't that the whole point of interacting spontaneously with the universe? Surely this was the ideal opportunity to test out my 'trust theory of existence'. After all, I was in California. In California no one cares about plans.

A mechanic came to open the car. Gustavo was a thoughtful, slow-talking Californian from Guatemala.

'Can I interview you?' I asked. 'I'm looking for the perfect optimist.'

'Sure,' said Gustavo. 'I'm an optimist.' He looked at his watch. 'As long as you can do it while I work. I have another job in twenty minutes.'

I leant over the bonnet of my Chevy while Gustavo employed a variety of pumps and levers to jemmy open the window.

'Are you optimistic about my car?' I asked.

'We'll get it open in no time.'

Dropping beads of sweat onto my front window as he manipulated a glorified coat hanger in the door lock, Gustavo told me he had lived in LA since 1968. He was fifty years old and he still worked twelve hours a day. 'I choose to work that many hours. I *like* working that many hours.'

'You've worked that hard since 1968?'

'Just about, yeah. I don't mind working it because I have friends who would like to work more hours but they can't.'

Gustavo wasn't feeling tragic in the least.

'Do you think immigrants who come to this country have a special optimism?'

'Yes, I do,' said Gustavo, cranking on a pump which was slowly wrenching open the front hinge. 'I feel that most of us come with a high level of optimism – I remember being in school and thinking about my whole future and looking at the natives and thinking: how come they don't want to go to college? They already know the language! Hmm, I don't know how I'm going to get into your car . . .'

I thought about the onion choppers in my brother's

diner. I didn't fancy driving a pick-up truck, but life wouldn't be bad if I were an onion chopper. I'd have a wife and kids, I'd have clear goals. Zara wouldn't be in an ashram. She'd be in the kitchen preparing my dinner.

'Do you still have that optimism now?' I asked.

'Yes, I do,' said Gustavo, swinging open the car door. He handed me the keys with a gallant gesture and walked towards his wrecker, glancing at his watch. 'So many people say they can't make a living, can't pay the rent – but I've tried it myself and I think if you're willing to work hard there's plenty of work out there.' He stopped on the pavement and turned to face my microphone. 'I'm willing to drive a truck, I'm willing to do laundry, I can go shopping for you and I'll go walk your dog. You can still make a decent living . . . I'm very optimistic.'

I felt pleased. Gustavo had just redefined optimism in the most simple and enviable way. It was the American dream – the original straightforward one – the one that people used to have before things got complicated by yoga, raw food diets and personal satisfaction. I longed for that simplicity.

'What are you looking forward to?' I asked. 'What are you excited about?'

'Excited?' said Gustavo, slowly. 'My daughter getting married . . . me retiring, when I'm still healthy and with my wife. I'll be celebrating my twenty-fifth wedding anniversary this coming March. So, it's an exciting time for me.'

The courteous mechanic climbed into the front of his lorry and backed up the drive. I chased him into the middle of the palm-lined street. 'Do you feel optimistic about America?' I asked. Gustavo pulled the hand brake and looked thoughtfully into my microphone.

'Yes, I think it's just a few obstacles. If you want to get filthy rich you might have an impediment, but for the average folk who wants to work hard I think the sky's the limit.'

I saluted him and jumped into my vehicle. Gustavo was working hard to get somewhere, I was working hard to get nowhere. We were like climbers passing each other on a mountain.

Three o'clock. Halfway up Fairfax there was a man sitting at the side of the road. He was holding up a sign:

I WILL ONLY WORK FOR MARIJUANA

Time was running out, but I was trying to be spontaneous, so I jammed on my brakes and swerved across the street.

I had to talk to the guy.

'Are you a tragic optimist?' I asked.

'I'm Lostboy,' said the man, smiling. 'I sit out here Monday through Sunday. I hold this sign up, people love me. They give me marijuana sometimes. Sometimes they give me money.'

A man leant out of his car and honked the horn. 'Yeah!' he shouted. Lostboy waved. A queue of vehicles backed up on the road.

'What's your purpose here?' I asked.

'I'm fighting for people's freedom of speech. If they want to lock me up for this they're violating our rights, all of our rights. I won't get off this wall.'

I felt a surge of adrenaline. 'You've got guts!' I said.

'I'm from New Jersey,' he explained.

He told me he was on the run for a variety of misdemeanours. One of them was breaking and entering, and then crapping, in someone's house.

'Wow,' I said.

'I was so high! I didn't realise what was going on.'

'Even so,' I said.

'They found my fingerprints so they put me on three years' probation and as soon as I get out it's my twentieth birthday and I'm with my cousin and we're so wasted? He's driving the car and we crash into a cop car!' He paused. 'It would have been OK if I hadn't run away.'

'You ran away?'

'Yeah, and now I'm stuck. I can't go back home, to my kid and my girl, I can't go back to nothing!' He smiled and waved at a busload of commuters. The driver had slowed down to see what was going on.

'You should just go back,' I said.

'I ain't going to prison. Once you go to prison it's over. Right now I'm not a convicted felon. I'm not really on the run now because there ain't nobody chasing me but if I go to prison I'm a convict.' He nodded. 'I respect myself. I take care of myself. I believe everything happens for a reason. If I end up in New Jersey I'm meant to be there, too.'

'Do you feel optimistic?'

'I don't think about the future too much, I just go day by day. I just get up here and hey, whatever! If I can't go home, I'm up here!'

'You're mad,' I said.

He shrugged.

'Why do you wear a tie? With a T-shirt?' I stared at his Bermudas, shivering in the breeze.

'It's my work tie,' he said. 'Ready for work!'

I walked away from the fugitive, elated, convinced I had just met a saint.

By the time I got to Santa Monica the sun was down. The rollerbladers and surfers had gone home, and only a few dog walkers were left on the beach. I strolled down the boardwalk, feeling melancholy. The sunset was beautiful. It faded in the sky like the final credits of a romantic movie. I climbed back into my car and watched it die. My day of freedom was over. What had changed? I was still me, and I was still alone.

Here I was on the edge of the world, and everyone else had gone home.

More Notes to Pessimists

EXPRESS YOUR NEGATIVE THOUGHTS

I buy a new Mac. For a few hours I am full of excitement as I open this longed-for object of desire and
install the disks. Then I realise it is a different oper-
ating system from my last computer and when I start
using the word processor to write a letter I realise
that the keys and the shortcuts are different from
the ones I know. I get panic and tightness in my
chest as I fumble for the letters. I feel claustrophobic
and stressed thinking about all the work I should be
doing. I mutter insults to myself and the whole world
– I want to kick myself around the room and throw
the stupid computer out of the window. I want to rip
my arms out of their sockets and throw them onto
a rubbish heap. I feel like a defective piece of equipment. A factory reject.

I watch a hair fall earthwards from my head.

Night

4 a.m. The second night in a row, waiting for sleep.
I freeze my body and command it to relax, informing

it that I won't move until I fall asleep. Half an hour later, I thrash around, trying to knock myself unconscious. Eventually I realise nothing is going to work. I give up and turn the light on, then off, then on. It's hopeless. Finally I open my notebook. What is it that I am afraid of? I look up at the dark, unfamiliar ceiling.

I'm afraid of being abandoned.

I'm afraid of being alone.

I'm afraid of dying in a dark empty room.

Yesterday I met a man who suffers from insomnia. When he wakes up in the middle of night, sweating, unable to sleep, dogged by worries about his career or his children, he writes them down and puts them in a jar. Then he screws the lid and places the jar on top of the bookshelf, far out of reach. Once a week he allows himself to schedule a meeting with the worry jar. They get half an hour of his time and that's it. At the end of each year he invites his friends around for a party and he burns the jar.

I wonder how big my fire would be.

18

'Get out!' she shouted. 'You will never come in my café again!'

The manager was standing at the door, pointing in the street. A drunk-looking man rammed his wheelchair up against the door. Everyone turned to look.

'What's your name, bitch?'

'That's my name!' she shouted. 'Now get out.'

The man wheeled himself into the street, cursing. The manager crossed her arms and closed the door. A few people cheered. I sat in stunned silence.

In San Francisco!

'It's the perfect flow of self-interest in a context of mutual cooperation,' said Alaric, wryly.

It was all too much. I needed to write down my negative thoughts before an explosion occurred in my psychic hemisphere. Srikumar had taught me this technique back in the spring, and I had only just remembered. Suddenly it was of pressing importance.

Practically everyone I had met in California, with the exception of the Surfing Rabbi, had told me to be cool and live in the present moment. Living in the 'now' seemed to be the state religion, even if most people – strangely enough – seemed busy working on the technology of the future. As a result I found myself doing mental gymnastics while I tried to master the art of 'going into' my feelings but not letting them bother me at the same time. The key seemed to be not thinking at all. During my long drive back from Los Angeles I had almost swerved off the road while trying to stop myself from thinking. In fact, my brain was turning over the same thoughts – about not thinking – every two to three minutes. I was no longer able to control it. Not only that, I was exhausted from months of living in guest rooms and camping on sofas. I wanted it to end, I wanted to go home, I wanted to settle down and have kids.

Freedom be damned!

My phone rang. It was my friend in Los Angeles.

'I want you to meet Roko,' said Rob. 'He's a filmmaker and a very optimistic person.'

'Well,' I said, still shaking slightly after the wheelchair incident. 'Someone must be.'

Two hours later Roko was standing in my brother's living room, looking like Yul Brynner in *The Magnificent Seven*. He tipped his cowboy hat and grinned.

'What brings you to California?' he asked.

'I'm writing a book about optimism.'

Roko sat down and planted his hat on his knee. 'No way! I'm making a film about happiness.' He handed me his business card

THE HAPPINESS DOCUMENTARY

and I handed him mine

THE OPTIMIST PROJECT.

'That's very funny,' I said.

'Are you optimistic about optimism?'

'More or less.' I glanced dolefully at my mobile phone: I had left it on all night in the hopes of getting a message from India. 'I'm trying to let the universe happen to me.'

'Right on,' said Roko.

A Yank making a film about happiness and a Brit writing a book about optimism? It was like *Band of Brothers*. I pictured myself wading next to Roko through the muddy fields of Normandy, liberating the oppressed pessimists of France.

We drove down through Golden Gate Park in his battered old convertible, while Roko told me about happiness.

'I've been talking with hospice nurses in terminal wards,' he said. 'They deal with death every day – but they're among the happiest people I've met.' Roko tipped his hat to prevent it from flying off his head. 'It's mysterious, but there's something about being close to death that makes people very happy.'

I watched the traffic listlessly. I didn't want to offend Roko, but happiness was really a bit passé. The subject had already been debated for over 4,000 years. Optimism was unique. It had never been done before. It was *mine*.

'What's the difference between optimism and happiness?' he asked. 'Have you thought about that?'

'Well,' I said. 'They're completely different. They may be related,' I conceded, 'but they're not the same.'

'So what *is* optimism?'

'Real optimism,' I said, gazing out across the houses, 'is when you let go of everything. You're totally free and underneath all that there's a kind of natural spark, underneath your thoughts.'

'Sounds like happiness,' said Roko.

'It's not the same.'

'You should meet Akira,' he said. 'Akira Kastan. She lives in Santa Cruz and apparently she's always happy.'

'Ah,' I said, 'I've heard that one before.'

'A friend of mine knows her.' The ocean suddenly came into view at the end of the block. 'Hey,' said Roko. 'Here's my house.' We jumped out into the watery sunshine.

'What's that?' I asked. There was a yellow thing on bricks in front of his garage.

'It's a rowing boat,' said Roko.

'It's a funny-looking boat,' I said. It looked like a submarine.

'It is,' he said.

'What's it doing in your drive?'

'It's a long story. I'll tell you sometime.' He stepped up onto his porch. 'Wanna have some pancakes?'

That weekend I drove to Santa Cruz. Akira Kastan had agreed to meet me at a café in the centre of town. I spotted her standing outside in a raincoat and sunglasses. Despite her exotic name, she looked like an American housewife from the 1980s, the type who might whip a hipflask out of her jacket pocket if things got too boring down at the country club. She shook my hand with a smile.

'Apparently you're happy all the time,' I said.

'I'm happy *now*,' she replied.

'Is it permanent?'

'I don't know!'

Her eyelashes pointed brightly upwards.

'Are you ever *not* happy?'

'I prefer to call it "uncaused joy",' she said. 'Happiness is a loaded word. People always have a reason that they want to be *met* in order for them to be happy, and I just figured out a way to go straight for it.' Akira scrunched up her nose like the good witch in *The Wizard of Oz*. 'That's why I call it "uncaused", because if something has the power to make you happy then not having it has the power to make you unhappy – I wasn't interested in that rollercoaster.'

'Hmm . . .' I rubbed my chin. 'But you do need reasons. There are definitely things that make me happy and other things that don't.'

'Well, that's your choice,' said Akira. 'I just "got" that, personally, I like being happy. I could just choose it. I just realised – why would I want happiness later? I want to be happy now!'

How could anyone be happy *all the time*? Even Doctor Seligman required certain conditions to be met. Weren't there chemicals involved? Didn't certain activities make us happier than others? I recalled the professor's formula.

Life Satisfaction = Positive Engagement + Flow + Meaning

That formula required a certain amount of box-ticking.

'I always used to think,' said Akira, 'it was about positive thinking, or something with the mind, but it has nothing to do with that. You don't have to do anything! It's already there.'

'So do you jump out of bed every morning feeling wonderful? Because sometimes I wake up,' I admitted, 'and I'm not really excited about anything.'

She looked at me as if I had just questioned some elementary law of the universe. 'I like *being* happy, I don't like *doing* happy. How can you *do* happy? Happy is what you are.'

'How did this happen to you?' I asked, perplexed. '*When* did it happen?'

'One day it just happened. I was always a spiritual seeker, you know, looking for God, and Happiness. And at one moment it was clearly, *this is it*. If it's not now, it's never. I guess the constant seeking just stopped and I dropped into it: right here, right now.'

'You dropped into what?'

'Who I am – pure happiness. When you're actually with what *is*, then the uncaused joy is right there.'

I looked at myself. Where was this happiness? Was it located in some part of my brain, some under-performing gland? Maybe I just needed more sunlight.

'Wait,' I said. 'There are times when life is just depressing. Let's say you're on a boring, shitty, eight-hour drive – it's raining, it's dark, you're tired . . .'

'I'm listening to show tunes and singing!' she said.

I flinched. 'What if something terrible happened to you? What if you were in jail? Let's say you were in a medieval jail, in solitary confinement? How would that be for you? You're in a box, it's dripping, it's dark, there's no air . . .'

'That's so abstract and, you know, it won't happen!'

'OK, then. What if Santa Cruz got nuked? That could happen!'

Akira became serious. 'You just deal with what shows up when it shows up. That's why I don't play with the concepts of "what if?". Why would I deal with something which isn't here? Optimism to me is about the future, and I don't think the future exists.'

Now I was annoyed. 'You say the future doesn't exist, but you make plans. Even you must make plans!'

'Yes, of course you make plans. But when do you make

plans? In the present moment! I've always felt there's nothing I can't handle in the moment. So I'm going to keep staying there.'

I looked into my coffee. 'Don't you ever get down?'

'No. And I don't *worry.*'

'You don't worry?'

'I used to worry, and I made a conscious effort to stop worrying twenty-five years ago. I thought, what a ridiculous emotion!'

'Hmm.' I had spent most of the week worrying about why Zara wasn't emailing me, and then worrying about why it worried me so much. If not worrying was one of Akira's ingredients of happiness then maybe optimism and happiness were closer than I thought.

'Maybe you just have less baggage than most people?' I thought woefully about *my* baggage. It would take me years to get rid of it and finally arrive at this so-called 'present moment'. That morning in the car I had suddenly, for no apparent reason, started shouting violently at my windshield.

I was beginning to wonder if I was deranged.

Akira looked at me and laughed. 'Oh, stop it,' she said. 'You've just been conditioned with the idea that you have to do some process, or something's got to happen before you can be happy. It's not true. I never went through any of that stuff . . . I never even did therapy.'

A gust of rain blew off the trees outside.

'I just started *watching thought,*' she said. 'And any time I was worried I'd say to my Thinking, thank you for sharing, I'm not interested in going there.'

I thought about Seligman again. 'What you're doing, I suppose, is replacing one thought with another?'

Akira pulled a face. 'You can't *think* your way to uncaused joy. If you have certain *ideas* about being happy, about being peaceful and stuff, like "you have to present" or "replace your thoughts", it's just going to get in the way. Eventually you have to drop those concepts.'

I almost hit the table. 'Then how?'

Her eyes glittered. 'Discover what it is you really, really want – and what you'll discover is . . . you want to be happy. But you're still waiting for other things to happen before you can be happy. Just be happy now! And stop looking for it.'

19

That thing the nature of which is totally unknown to you is usually what you need to find, and finding it is a matter of getting lost.

Rebecca Solnit

I decided it would be cool to meet an anarchist – an optimistic anarchist, ideally, who believed in a future where human beings would no longer need armies or policemen, because everyone would just behave without being told to.

By now I felt somewhat disillusioned by California – the people were not so different from people everywhere else – but in my mind there was still an ultimate optimist out there I hadn't yet found. This perfect being wouldn't be demented like Lostboy, but he would have the same kind of insane courage. He would be laid back like the rabbi, but less selfish. Akira might have qualified too, but I found her talk of instant happiness mystifying and frustrating. What's more, Akira wasn't proposing radical structural changes to the entire human race.

The optimist I was looking for would definitely be doing that.

I wandered into the Anarchist Bookshop on Haight Street and approached the man at the counter. He was wearing a pair of broken spectacles repaired with a Band-Aid. That seemed like a good start.

'Are you optimistic about anarchy?' I asked.

'Not really,' he said.

'You don't believe that anarchism will one day transform the world and liberate the people from the shackles of their own mental slavery?'

'I dunno,' he said, unhappily. 'I've never really thought about it. I think human beings are too greedy.'

'But you're an anarchist, you work in an anarchist bookstore. You don't believe that it actually . . . works?'

He laughed uncomfortably. 'We try to live in an anarchistic way, ourselves.'

I left him my card in case any real anarchists should pass by. What was wrong with people these days? All they did was complain about George Bush, agree with each other, then go back to their jobs and email all day. Whatever happened to the barricades? Whatever happened to the Utopians and the sexy revolutionaries in bandanas? People weren't idealistic any more. Even in California!

My last hope was technology. The true anarchists, I figured, had gone to work for dot-com companies. The internet, after all, was bringing about massive social change without any help from revolutionaries. Maybe that's where idealism had taken up residence. I had been fantasising about meeting one of these techno-lunatics for months. One of them, surely, would turn out to be my perfect Californian optimist. Then I could go home.

My first call was Craig Newmark. Craig was the founder of craigslist, a cult website which started in the mid-1990s as a modest local event service for the residents of San Francisco and then grew into one of the largest free communities in the world. You can now go to craigslist Korea or craigslist Hungary and search for someone selling a bust of the late President – or just request a liftshare to Warsaw.

casual encounters >>>>> w4m m4m m4w w4w t4m m4t
mw4mw mw4w mw4m w4mw m4mw w4ww m4mm mm4m ww4w mm4w m4ww w4mm t4mw mw4t

This – obviously! – was the perfect jumping-off point for a new era of peace on earth and natural, spontaneous co-operation between human beings.

I found the café Craig had specified and waited for him to show up, chewing nervously on a bagel. I had a good idea how he would look: laidback, tanned, possibly in tennis clothes – exactly how I would look if I had started an iconic, visionary internet service and then refused to make any money from it. I positioned myself at a table and waited, watching the door for his arrival. After a minute, one of the men at the bar came over and asked if he could take a seat.

'Sure,' I said.

'Are you Laurence?'

'Craig!' I sat up. I had assumed the man leaning against the counter was a waiter, or a photocopy repair man on his coffee break.

'I thought you were . . .' I waved at the door. 'You're smaller than I expected.' Craig registered my surprise with the battered dignity of the last kid on the basketball team.

'I have about fifteen minutes,' he said, 'if that's OK?'

I stuffed my bagel into my mouth. Looks could be deceptive. 'I'm searching for a new kind of optimism,' I explained, by way of background. 'Do you think we're seeing a paradigm shift? Is technology going to change the way human beings behave?'

Craig considered this. 'I think it's happening already. I see people helping each other out on a day-to-day basis.' He looked into his coffee. 'But it's nothing radical. It's just people giving each other a break.'

'But isn't this humanity evolving? Isn't this the start of something new? A new way of being?'

Craig spoke carefully, as if a word out of line might unleash a volcano of chaos. The cappuccino machine behind us kept making small explosions of steam right next to his head.

'I don't know. I don't really have a vision of the future. Remember, I had no vision at all when I started this, it just happened.'

'Aha,' I said. 'It "just happened".' The universe was organically unfolding its will via the ego-less persona of Craig. Still, I thought, a bit of ego could go a long way.

'You never sold out,' I said. 'You ran craigslist through the dotcom bubble and you refused to sell the shares. That's pretty idealistic.'

Craig took this in. It was a compliment he had clearly heard before. 'Sometimes I look at how much money people are making and I think, should I do that? What would I do with all that money? And I don't have good answers.' He frowned. 'I could have dogs. And pay someone to look after them full-time. That would be good.'

I scratched my neck. Craig was refusing to be exciting. 'But do you think . . . do you think companies like craigslist can actually change the world?'

He aligned the edges of his napkin with the corner of the table.

'It does remind people overseas that the American people are still OK, that we are still the people we were ten years ago . . . people of good will . . . But I'm not an idealist. I'm an optimist, not an idealist.'

I looked at him. If this was the legendary Craig Newmark then what would the others be like?

'I'd just like to say something else,' he said. 'What makes me optimistic in a big way – by following through with our principles, giving people a break and treating others well, somehow we've created a culture of trust with the community.' Craig adjusted his coffee spoon. 'And that's really big.'

'Right,' I said. 'Thanks Craig!'

It wasn't over for anarchy. I had one more visit to make before I conceded defeat: Google, the world headquarters of democratic, non-hierarchical information management. I had a friend who worked in their London office. He loved it. 'Structureless structure,' he called it. 'Organised chaos.'

'That's exactly what I'm looking for,' I cried. 'It's the next stage in our evolution!'

Two hours later I was in Palo Alto, the home of the fastest growing verb in the English language. What Lenin couldn't achieve with the Soviet Union, Google was pulling off by means of hypertext mark-up code. At Google, they would know exactly what I was talking about. No doubt the people who ran this company would show evidence of the highest levels of optimism. They may even possess qualities I had never heard of before. Would the senior executives have open-source bank accounts, or networked schedules that anyone could access, based totally on trust? One of these giants of techno-anarchy, surely, would understand the spiritual implications of their work and agree to be my mentor.

I drove up to the campus, staring at the legendary logo – a symbol I saw nearly every day of my life – in noble font against the yawning blue sky. I sighed, taking in the finely cut lawns, the volleyball court and the software engineers walking from building to building. How right that Google should call its HQ a campus. How I missed it – university! The ideal structure for the flowering of network-driven utopia. No wonder the anarchist bookshop wasn't happening. The action was all here, in Palo Alto.

An official approached me in the car park. 'Are you a visitor?' he asked.

'Excuse me,' I said, stepping around him. 'This is Google?'

'Yes.'

'Famed for making the world's content available to people of all creeds and beliefs, at no charge?'

'That's correct.'

'Why would you need security?'

'Who are you here to see, sir?'

'Marissa Meyer,' I said. 'Senior executive.'

'You need to go to Block D, sir. That way.'

I was met at reception by a PR girl who looked like Uma Thurman, only thinner. 'Welcome,' she said, smiling tightly. 'I'm Eve. Can I take you through?'

I followed Eve through the security doors. She led me through the lobby, past shimmering video presentations and a life-size model of a spacecraft. All around me Google people were coming and going: kids under thirty in chinos and T-shirts, laughing and telling jokes. I had finally reached my technology paradise. It was slightly too clean. 'We have seven cafés,' she explained. 'All with different themes.'

'Seven . . .' I was distracted by a cluster of staff who seemed to be discussing something important. I wandered over to listen. Maybe I could learn something about the structural application of Level 4 optimism? Eve performed an elegant blocking manoeuvre. 'Smoothie?' she asked.

Marissa Meyer was an attractive blonde woman with precisely symmetrical eyes. She didn't look much older than Eve, but then, age has no bearing on your position in Google land. Marissa had joined the start-up in 1999 when no one else had heard of them and now she was a board director. She was Employee Number 7, a software coder and officially part of the Google legend. I shook her hand and sat down. Somehow in the last decade, while I had been busy destroying shareholder value – at least my own – this young woman had materialised the assets of a medium-sized country.

'Do you think technology will change the way human beings relate to each other?' I asked. 'Will the internet free us from the shackles of mental slavery?'

'I'm very optimistic around technology,' said Marissa. 'When you see how quickly people can problem-solve, how much more efficiently people can use their time . . . It frees you up to do more things, shave down the administrative trivia . . .' Her eyes swivelled towards me. 'You know – laundry, sleeping, eating – all of that.'

'*Sleeping*?' I laughed. 'You make it sound like our brains are evolving into super-efficient search engines.'

Marissa allowed herself a chuckle. 'It gives you more time on what you really care about. To do what you really love.'

'Tell me about Larry and Sergey,' I said. L & S were the Russian-American founders of Google, the unlikely dream team who invented the whole thing, whose friendly personality had blossomed into the famous, laidback culture of the company, with its exercise balls, non-hierarchical management and free drinks cabinets. To me, Google was like MTV in the 1980s – it encapsulated the values of the decade. So decent and straightforward! So creative and funny! That's why I was here. That's why there was still hope for the world.

'If you walk around Google, it's such a happy place,' said Marissa. 'It's not just all the bright colours and the toys and the creativity, but also a sense of comfort, psychological comfort and respect. I think optimism stems from that.'

'And you have this sense of purpose?'

'Yes, there was always this *mission*,' Marissa smiled. 'When I came for my interview Larry and Sergey were in this tiny little office, they couldn't even afford to get the floors vacuumed. There were little schnibbles all over the floor, they were all running around barefoot, bouncing balls, and bragging about how the soda was free. They were amazingly and delightfully hopeful.'

'And it's a communal purpose, higher than any single individual?'

'Exactly! I remember thinking it was awfully grandiose for a web search engine company. But it has been there right from the start: this sense of entrepreneurship, purpose and hopefulness for the world. It's really inspiring. For example, my current project is to digitise every single book in the world and make it available online.' Marissa gurgled, happily. 'Imagine how different the world would be if all books were online!'

'And yet you don't seem emotionally attached to any particular outcome.'

'No . . .' she said. 'We don't hang onto projects if they don't work. We test everything out. If they don't work, we drop them. It's very scientific.'

I leant forward. 'What if Google were a person?' I asked.

'I'm sorry?'

'If Google were a person? Would they be the perfect optimist?'

'I'm not sure what you mean.'

I toyed with my wheatgrass and echinacea smoothie. If the perfect optimist wasn't a Californian then maybe it was a Californian company.

'What would happen if *everywhere* was like Google? I mean, it has a sense of purpose. It's totally meritocratic. It sets huge goals but doesn't get attached to the outcome. It's an advanced-level optimist! Couldn't everywhere in the world become like that?'

Marissa reflected momentarily. 'I think it depends on the industry you're in.' She walked over to the whiteboard.

'In the old days manufacturing companies were organised on assembly lines, you had people doing specific jobs so you needed managers to oversee them, and more managers to oversee those managers.'

'But now you have companies like Google – internet, service companies, this kind of thing, with big data centres – and our process is completely different. Google actually works like a network, with lots of nodes, so when you have an idea, like, say, Google News, you grab people from all over the organisation to work on it. It's like a neural net firing, like when a search enters a data centre and there's thousands of computers there, and some five or seven hundred randomly selected machines work in harmony to answer your request.'

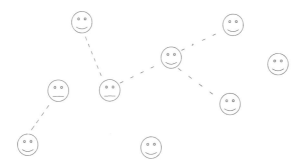

'If you think of us like computers, that's how it is when a new project turns up.'

I chewed my pen. I wasn't a computer, but that wasn't the point.

'Could this model work in the outside world? Do you think the whole of society might become more like Google?'

Marissa's face flickered as she ran a quick simulation of the entire Western world running itself like her company.

'Yes, but you have to manage your organisation entirely on data and metrics, so that everything is based on merit, rather than favouritism. And you need to have commonality of purpose. We definitely have commonality of purpose.'

'Are we close to a perfect world? Is it within reach?'

'I don't think so,' she said. 'What would a perfect state be? The perfect state is a moment frozen in time.' She shook her head. 'It's that quote from Doctor Faust: "Linger moment, thou art fair." It's not feasible.'

I checked my nails. Marissa was obviously an interesting human being. But there was something missing. I needed something more.

'Larry and Sergey,' I said. 'They must be very optimistic people?'

'Actually they're not,' she chortled. 'Especially Larry. He often says, what makes me a great entrepreneur is that I'm always hungry, I'm always trying to figure out how to spend my time better. There's this relentless sense of lack of fulfilment.'

'Lack of fulfilment!'

Marissa frowned. 'They're very future-oriented . . . I think they're very concerned about the state of the world.'

After our meeting I wandered around the campus. I read the notice boards and watched the workers lunching in the café. I passed them in the corridors and eavesdropped on their conversations. None of them looked like the perfect optimist either. They all just seemed . . . normal. I stumbled out to my car, demoralised. Maybe there was no one. Maybe I was alone.

I drove south. I kept driving until the lights of the city disappeared. If it wasn't a person I wanted, then what was it? A place? A feeling? No. What I wanted was *it*. It. The only trouble was, I didn't know what it was. But I wanted it. Even more than I wanted a good night's sleep.

For some reason, I had a clear idea of what I had to do next. I felt sure that It was somewhere in South California, in the desert. Where I got this idea from I don't know. But I could see a picture of it in my head, a map. When I got there I would be free, when I got there I would find . . . I don't know. The end of my quest.

I spent the next few days in Joshua Tree, a desert between LA and Las Vegas. I slept in a trailer on a plot of land surrounded by yucca trees and empty scrub, and spent all night on a leather sofa in a sand dune watching meteors roll across the sky. I had the idea that if I went far enough into the wilderness and stopped talking to anyone I would finally hit rock bottom and meet the living core of my soul. Nothingness, I realised, *that* was it – that was what I had been looking for all this time – the place where trust and freedom meet. That's what I needed.

I wasn't sure how to get to Nothingness but I was hoping it might be located somewhere in the National Park. I decided to stay in the RV for a few days and then set off into the hills without a map or a rucksack. Unfortunately, I was sharing the van with a hyperactive film director called Alex. I couldn't ask him to leave because it was his trailer and I had only known him for three days. He had brought with him his equally wired friend, Dave, who suffered from

depression and looked like the natural brother of Simon Le
Bon. Every time I tried to get silent or stare into the ultimate emptiness, Alex and Dave would offer me a drink, or
play some interesting piece of music, or get into an argument about John Lennon.

Dave was in the middle of an emotional legal battle for
custody of his not-yet-born son. He kept taking calls from
his lawyer while puffing on a giant spliff.

'Optimism!' he sneered. I dropped the subject. There
was a dangerous glint in his eyes – and I had nowhere to
run to if something went wrong. I lapsed into a doughy
stupor on the fold-down bed and watched Alex busying
around the van. The wind from the hills was rocking the
vehicle backwards and forwards like a small boat in a storm.

Alex looked over and said: 'Shall we drive around, or
just chill here and make some food? Let's go for a walk. I
think we need to relax. Why don't you tell us about optimism, Laurence? Dave, put down the whisky.'

What am I doing here? It was like being a kid again, on
summer camp. Sleeping in a strange, uncomfortable bed;
well-meaning strangers talking nonsense. Was my quest for
optimism just a search to get back home?

'I've got to go,' I said.

The boys looked at me with confusion. 'But it's eleven
o'clock.'

'I've got a meeting,' I said, 'in San Francisco.'

I drove all night and finally made it to Roko's house in
the suburbs of San Francisco. I stayed in his mother's living
room and I slept for ten hours.

The next morning Roko told me the story of the boat
in his drive. I had been thinking about this boat ever since
I first saw it. It fascinated me – I didn't know why.

'I'll tell you as we drive to the airport,' he said.

It was my last day in America.

'My dad had this thing about rowing across the Atlantic,' explained Roko, pulling out of his drive. I watched the yellow submarine disappearing from the rear-view mirror. 'He was always talking about it, how he was going to do it one day. But he was busy with his work, and he kept putting it off and the years passed by. Then one day he said: "Now I'm going to do it. I can't put it off any longer." So he designed a boat and had it built and he took it for a few test runs on Lake Michigan. But then his wife – my step-mom – told him, if you do this I'll divorce you. And she meant it. And my little sisters begged him not to go. So he abandoned the project.'

Roko turned the vehicle. 'Eight years went by. Dad took retirement, and he tried filling his time with various activities, but one day he couldn't resist any more. He decided: That's it. I'm going to do it. Now I'm going to do it. I have to. But his wife said, I'll divorce you, this time I really will.' Roko looked at me. 'I'm not sure what they decided. All I know is – he went.'

'He did it!'

'Yup, in that yellow boat that's now in my driveway. He equipped it with everything necessary. And he trained. And he went.'

'He went!'

'He almost made it all the way to Ireland.' I waited, silently. 'They received an emergency signal from his boat about 200 miles off the coast. There was a huge storm with forty-foot waves.' Roko glanced up at the traffic lights. 'The boat was found by a fisherman a few weeks later. One of the hatches was broken. Everything was gone from the inside of the boat – apparently washed out by the storm.' He took the exit onto the freeway. 'They never found my dad, either.'

'My God,' I said, 'that's . . . amazing.'

Roko drove on in silence.

'It's a great story!' I said.

Roko smiled. 'I know, I know. Crazy and awesome.'

'He did it.' I shook my head. 'He really did it.'

Fool

20

MAGIC THEATRE

ENTRANCE NOT FOR EVERYBODY

Herman Hesse, *Steppenwolf*

I stopped and looked up the mountain. Tourists were making their way reverently along the path, most of them in bare feet, to a sacred cave where a guru was said to have attained Enlightenment. I couldn't decide whether to carry on up to this cave, which was bound to be full of meditators, or return to the noisy city below. Both places had drawbacks. Noise and lack of noise, with no obvious middle ground. That was India for you.

I looked along the path. There was always the chance that I might meet an attractive European if I stayed somewhere near the cave and looked seriously detached and spiritual. This much I had learned; pursuing Enlightenment is a great way of meeting women. What is more, I had been told that the mountain was an incarnation of the god Shiva and that if I stayed long enough on it, my ego would burn away leaving only the living core of my soul. If my ego burned away I wouldn't have to think about women at all. There in the middle of my soul, I was convinced, lay true optimism – the sort of optimism that generates happiness and confidence without help from anyone, least of all ladies in sandals.

A blond man strolled past, in the gowns of a wandering sadhu. He had shoulder-length hair and a necklace of sandalwood beads. 'You are a god!' he said, suddenly. Then he gazed into my eyes, as if to say, *I am not afraid to stare into your soul without blinking*, and carried on down the path. I frowned and sat on a stone. This fellow, who was obviously American, clearly considered himself to be more spiritually advanced than me.

Later I caught sight of him at my guesthouse. 'We met on the mountain!' I said, amazed by the coincidence. 'I know,' he said, calmly, pushing a lock of hair behind his ear. 'Want to join us?' He pulled up a seat and turned to his female companion – a beautiful woman in her forties – 'Leeza, get our friend a plate, please.'

I watched, astonished, as Leeza left her seat and went to fetch me some lunch. The American leant back and put his hands behind his head.

'I'm Narayana,' he said.

'Narayana?'

'It means Supreme Goal.' He yawned and stretched, his necklace bunching up on his bare chest. 'What's your name?'

'I'm . . . uh, Saladin,' I said, improvising quickly. 'It means medieval Islamic warrior. From the twelfth century.'

'Saladin, huh?' He sized me up, like a seasoned sportsman checking out a rookie. 'I like it. Saladin the Crusader.'

A long silence followed. Narayana's eyes were half closed, as if he were trying to absorb my aura with his presence. It was the same look he had given me on the mountain.

'So, tell me,' I said, clearing my throat. 'What are you doing in India?'

'We're just kind of *being*,' he said. 'Leeza and I are travelling together.'

I turned to look at his companion. 'Holy men have girlfriends?'

'Sure,' he said. 'My father always taught me that if I wanted to attain the highest levels of Enlightenment I should never spill my seed. That changed when I met Leeza.'

I blushed as she returned with a tray full of curry.

'We actually met in a previous life,' continued Narayana. 'I was a black magician during the reign of the fifth Caliph of Egypt. And Leeza was my fifth wife.'

'Wow.' I thanked her for the food. 'What's your job this time?'

'Leeza's path,' said Narayana indulgently, 'is to serve me.'

Leeza picked a leaf off her boyfriend's hair. 'Eventually I'll have to leave her,' he explained, 'but for now I have a clear intuition that I'm supposed to have a family and lead a relatively normal life.'

I glanced at Leeza. She didn't seem bothered by this.

'Yeah,' said Narayana. 'If nothing happens to deter me, when I'm seventy-five I'll leave everything – my wife, my family – and go to the Himalayas to wait for the immortalisation of my body.'

He nodded flatly and carried on with his lunch.

'Are you serious?' I said.

Narayana folded his hands on his tummy. 'When I am seventy-five I will exchange this body for a perfect and immortal one, through a secret process that will be shown to me by my guru Mahabatar Babaji, sometimes called the Immortal Yogi. The new body is not born of nature,' he added, 'it's born of yogic power. So it's not affected by nature. It's immortal, it never ages.'

I swirled my water diplomatically. Now that I was

burning away the last fragments of my ego on the holy mountain of Arunachala I was authorised to ask certain questions. After all, I was a god. Narayana himself had seen that.

'Don't you think,' I suggested, 'that this goal of yours might be a distraction from the real task of living in the present moment and awakening to the vast illusion of life that is all around us?' I didn't want to be presumptuous but it was clear my new friend was on the wrong track.

Narayana reflected for a moment. He was obviously familiar with the local emphasis on 'non-duality': the idea that all objects are illusory and the only reality is the supreme consciousness of the self. That's what Arunachala was all about. 'Maybe,' he said. 'But it's my purpose. If I didn't follow it I'd be miserable.'

'Oh.' I took a mouthful of dhal. My path to awakening was clearly superior to Narayana's path to awakening. Even so, I mused, it was nice to be sitting here with him and his girlfriend, under a sumac tree next to a paddy field. It was exactly what you were supposed to be doing in India – hanging out with yogis and beautiful women in saris. On the other hand, the longer I spent with Narayana the more I suspected he was just an ordinary guy who, through a quirk of birth, just happened to be pursuing immortality.

Immortality! I couldn't help smirking.

Leeza sliced a mango delicately with her fork. 'What about you?' she asked. 'What are you doing here?'

The question took me by surprise. 'Oh, well, nothing much. I'm writing a book about optimism. I'm looking for inner happiness. And I'm trying to let go of all attachments and achieve a state of total trust. So I'm travelling around India and just kind of . . . seeing what happens.'

Narayana gave me a look of mesmerising approval. 'That's cool, man.'

'Are you alone?' asked Leeza.

'Not really. I came here to travel with my girlfriend but . . .'

Leeza nodded discreetly.

I hated telling people about Zara. It sounded so incomplete. Why was my girlfriend 400 miles away in Goa, anyway? I lit a beedie and stared into the rice field. Narayana and Leeza excused themselves and left me with my thoughts.

My reason for coming to India had been straightforward: put an end to the spiral of miscommunication that had developed between us, confront Zara with the wrongness of her attitude and renegotiate our relationship on more favourable terms. This was the absolute next step in my journey towards optimism: get the relationship sorted, then move on. Or to put it in therapeutic terms, release my trapped emotions in a controlled environment and therefore end the cosmic malfunction that was stopping my life from being perfect. It should have been easy. So long as I could keep my cool.

Unfortunately, as the plane winged my body towards the Indian subcontinent, the 'process' which had started that autumn with the destruction of a bowl of fruit against Gabrielle's wall was still unfolding somewhere inside my solar plexus. It rumbled, anxiously, as the aircraft tilted sideways through the clouds. Waves of angry panic, made worse by six weeks in America without radio contact, were pushing their way up my thorax and causing my body to vibrate like a toddler after an overdose of wine gums and caffeine pills.

The undercarriage quivered as we started our descent towards Goa. I had tried everything – affirmations, self-disputation, even beating my car windshield repeatedly with my hand. I still couldn't get myself feeling optimistic. It was just as Gabrielle had told me. The fears I had held inside for so long were coming out, and now they needed to be heard. Enough was enough! No longer would I put a brave face on things and pretend that everything was OK.

I walked into the arrival lounge. She was standing by the conveyor belt. How beautiful she looked. How separate! I felt shy and terrified. I forced a smile. In the taxi I tried to take her hand. She told me she had arranged separate rooms for us. I trembled and agreed. What, not even touch? Not even hold each other?

'Things are very different here,' said Zara quietly. 'It'll take you a few days to relax. Then you'll be fine.'

The next morning we had breakfast on the veranda, looking out over the ocean.

'Look, Zara . . .' I said, 'we have to talk.' I was determined to keep my head.

'No,' she said. 'I won't tolerate the projection of your resentment and anger.'

'But I haven't even started!' I felt my lips trembling. 'Anyway, why *shouldn't* I be angry? You didn't call me for six weeks!'

'Look at me,' she said, sternly. 'This anger you're feeling. Is it real?'

'What?'

'*Is it real?*'

'I . . . I don't know.' I looked in her eyes and spluttered. 'Yes! No!'

I burst into tears.

The sea heaved patiently as I sobbed in her lap.

I had not cried in the arms of a woman for over thirty years. It felt amazing. As I cried I imagined to myself how deeply this show of emotion would touch my lover's heart.

'I've missed you so much!' I wept. 'Please don't leave me!'

My cries subsided into a low groan. *Amazing*, I thought, observing myself from afar. I'm finally releasing my trapped emotions. And underneath the anger, there's nothing – just tears! Yeah! I felt like a man who had been dragged up from the sea at the point of drowning.

I started to blubber through my nose.

'I'm going to leave you for a while,' said Zara.

'What?' I looked up through tear-stained eyes. 'Where are you going?'

Zara gave me the measured look of a professional anaesthetist. 'You need to be with yourself for a while. I'll come back later.'

I wiped my eyes. 'But wait.' Something was wrong. This was supposed to be our moment of tender and perfect reunion.

An hour later my girlfriend returned with a cup of tea. She had a distant look in her eyes. What had happened? Where was the Zara I knew? The Zara who used to love me?

'Laurence,' she said, 'if you can let go of this idea that we're going somewhere, then we'll be fine. Remember – we're not in a relationship. And we're not together.'

I felt danger course through every cell of my body. 'Do you mean not-together in a real sense, or not-together in a conceptual sense?'

Zara gave me a sad look. 'If you can just be with that and understand that, then we'll be fine. Then it can unfold as it should.'

'But I *don't* understand,' I said. 'I was just expressing my emotions so we could work through them. And now you're rejecting them! Relationships require work. You can't just live in the *moment* all the time!'

Zara sighed and put down her teacup. 'I think you need to spend some time on your own now, Laurence.'

'But, babe,' I pleaded. 'What about last summer?'

'Laurence. The past is gone. Let's just be who we are.'

She hesitated and twisted her spoon in her fingers. 'And don't call me babe. I'm not your *babe*.'

That night I lay on the doorstep and stared at the light-bulb above my door. Zara had gone out for the evening and she hadn't told me where. The inconceivable was happening. I listened to the sea roaring mercilessly on the cliffs. 'Let go,' I whispered to myself. 'Let go. *Let go*.'

The next day I wrote her a poem explaining my feelings. She listened coldly as I read it out.

'Why don't you write a poem to yourself?' she suggested. 'In the end, I'm only a figment of your imagination. Anything you believe exists outside yourself is an illusion. Including me.'

I looked at her face in disbelief.

'If you can remember that,' she said, softening, 'it will help to free you from this anguish you're feeling.'

'Free . . .' I muttered. '*Yes*.'

I decided to leave Goa. It was the only way I could think of to regain the initiative. I had to let go of my girlfriend, put her out of my mind. Then – when I had completely forgotten about her – we could get back together again. That, surely, was the plan. The formula . . .

RELATIONSHIP = FLOR x %

might look close to zero, but that was only the short-term picture. The odds would come back up.

In the meantime my mission was clear – to become the advanced spiritual being that I was always meant to be. I would walk through India, trusting in the goodness of the universe. I would sail into the ocean of nothingness – like Roko's dad – and wait to be swallowed whole. I would be completely free. Then, once I had achieved a state of pure detachment, I would finally have attained the highest level of optimism, and Zara would return to my arms. My quest would be complete!

The next day I asked Narayana if I could interview him for my book.

'We can do it on my porch,' he said, 'where there's a proper chair. I get joint pain from sitting in the lotus position all day.'

I met him on the veranda of his bungalow, a pretty plaster house which he had hired for the season.

'We stay here as often as we can. I love it, close to the mountain. I go into deep bliss.' He poured me a cup of tea and we gazed out at the late afternoon sun. By now I was used to Narayana's strange way of talking. I had almost forgotten his intention to leave the physical realm and become an immortal man-god. If he were to hand me a can of Bud Light and invite me to do a shotgun I wouldn't have blinked. He had the laidback manner of a frat boy on a camping holiday.

'So, you're aiming for physical immortality in your life time?'

'Yeah,' said Narayana, slinging his arm over the back of his chair.

'That's pretty optimistic.'

'Well, I had never actually thought about that possibility for myself,' he explained. 'But then the Immortal Yogi, Babaji, came to me in a dream, when I was twenty-three.'

'What did he say?'

'He said, "I'm going to teach you how to make your body like my body." Behind him was a line of masters going off into infinity. So it became a very real subject in my mind. The highest human attainment: Immortality.'

'But you already knew about Babaji?' I asked.

'Yeah, well, I'd been meditating all my life. My dad initiated me into Transcendental Meditation was I was five. I started getting really interested in it when I was twelve and I started meditating every day from the age of thirteen, because I wanted to go for Enlightenment. I figured that was the most worthy aim in life.'

'Because your dad said so?'

'I guess so. I was getting up at four in the morning, facing the East, meditating on a deerskin rug, reading the *Bhagavad-Gita*, reading yogi books, going to school, doing homework, then reading the *Bhagavad-Gita* again, meditating again in the full lotus position for another hour, facing the East . . . and that was my high school life! It was very dry. But then after ten years I had an audience with Lord Krishna.'

'The god, Krishna?'

'Yeah . . . the god Krishna merged into me and I went into pure ecstasy for more than two hours. And then I had a kind of visitation from an angel, and the angel was an eight-foot tall, golden angel with long beautiful flowing hair.'

Narayana talked about mystical powers and his attainment of them in the same way a tennis champion might talk about his backhand.

'Was this some kind of dream?'

'No, no,' said Narayana. 'It was real . . . the angel was standing right in front of me. It was a physical experience.'

'Maybe it was a projection of your subconscious?' I said. 'A figment of your imagination?'

'I thought that might be true in the beginning,' said Narayana, matter-of-factly, 'but then I kept having experiences that showed me that it was a real, valid experience. There's plenty I've seen to prove the validity of these things that nobody can explain.' I waited for him to provide details. 'Like meeting yogis who can teleport.'

'You've seen that?'

'Sure.'

I thought about this. If there really were yogis who could teleport, then there might be other magic powers available too. Maybe Level 1 spiritual optimism was something I hadn't properly explored. 'Can you transcend the boundaries of space and time, magnetically attract people into your life, this kind of thing?' I tried to sound casual. It was a hypothetical question.

'Possibly,' said Narayana. 'I don't know. I had lots of things I wanted to find out. So I went to India and became a wandering sadhu. I spent three years walking around the Himalayas as a penniless monk, living in ice caves and living on God's grace.'

I looked at his robe, which he had thrown raffishly over his shoulder in the style of a Roman consul. It was kind of cool to carry off such garments and keep a straight face.

'It must have been amazing.'

'It was difficult,' he said. 'And dangerous. Climbing mountains I almost fell off to my death, barefoot, spending the night in freezing cold ice caves. I didn't really sleep because it was so uncomfortable, and also I became very, very sick from dysentery and parasites. But in itself being a sadhu is a very spiritual experience, living this very austere life, wandering around, being in beautiful places, living in caves – to not have any money, going from meal to meal, place to place, just trusting . . .'

'Trusting,' I said. 'Yeah.'

'You develop total trust. I never lacked for food or shelter, not once.'

He broke a cookie in two and handed me a piece. Leeza appeared and sat down next to us. 'Was this before you met?' I asked.

'Yes,' said Narayana. 'I was already back by that time. I

was giving a lecture in upstate New York and Leeza was one of my students. She fell at my feet and said, "You are my master!"' He laughed and stroked her hair. 'Didn't you?' Leeza smiled shyly. 'I did,' she admitted.

I turned to her. 'Isn't it a bit . . . *insecure* living with a man who is completely focused on immortality?'

'Sometimes I do feel anxious,' she agreed, 'but that's the path I have chosen.'

'Can you teach me some of this stuff?' I asked, turning back to Narayana. 'Some of this . . . what do you call it?'

'Kriya yoga,' he said. '. . . I don't know. Let me think about it. It takes a long while to wear down your habits and consciousness, your belief system and so on. You have to take it slowly. If you go into a higher state too fast you usually go crazy. That's why yoga takes years. It trains your body to do this one step at a time.'

'Oh.'

'It's a lifetime commitment. The path of yoga is about overcoming all of your limitations as a human being. Kriya is a combination of *mudras* and *asanas*, and breath control and going through the *chakras*, controlling the breath, controlling the life force, controlling the mind. It's a lot of work.'

'You do that every day?' I asked.

'Yeah. Though after a while your breath stops naturally and you go into an effortless state of bliss.'

I looked at my cookie. I was beginning to understand why I had chosen the path of non-duality. It was just so much easier. Akira would never have bothered with all this meditation effort. She was happy already.

'Some days it's easier than others,' conceded Narayana. 'Some days I find if I'm able to do my whole programme in the morning, then after lunch, bliss will take over by itself and the rest of the day will be in bliss.'

Narayana was beginning to remind me of the Surfing Rabbi: the same pleasant affability; the same hardened addiction to natural highs; the lengths they went to were just as extreme.

'Are you in bliss now?'

Narayana shook his head. 'Not so much,' he said. 'I'm talking to you. If I was in bliss I would sound totally incoherent.'

I laughed.

'I'd be like a drunk man,' he said.

I watched my toes wiggling in my sandals. A bird swooped down and snatched a piece of biscuit from my plate. I had nothing more to learn. 'How confident are you that you'll get there?' I asked. 'To immortality?'

Narayana shrugged. 'I'd say 100 per cent?'

'In your lifetime?'

'Yeah. Definitely. Because Babaji wouldn't lie. Why would Babaji lie?'

That afternoon I went up the mountain again. I had just got an email from my father. To my amazement, he seemed to approve of what I was doing.

Makes me want to hit the road too. Maybe once I've finished all this I can disappear for good up some holy mountain.

I felt pride and happiness fill my heart. Maybe it was worth going up that mountain one more time.

I set off for the cave. I would meditate until sundown. How else was I going to achieve perfection and magnetically attract Zara? I started up the path. Every now and then a meditator from America or Denmark passed me on the way down with a distant, dreamy look. Then, halfway up, I stopped, exactly where I had stopped the first time. The cave was only a hundred metres on but my legs didn't seem interested. I sat down on a rock. What was I doing anyway, walking to a cave? A cave full of cross-legged Europeans. Wait a second, I thought, scratching my beard. Where am I going? I had a feeling of clarity. A young woman strolled past.

'Where are you going?' I asked her.

'I'm going down to the town,' she said. 'To have some tea.'

'No,' I said. 'Where are you *going*?'

'What?' she said.

'Where are you *going*?'

Her eyes sparkled. 'Say it again!'

I smiled. She was really very attractive. *'Where are you going!'* I said.

'Thank you!' she cried. 'Yes! Where am I going?!'

'That's it!'

'Yes! Yes!' She staggered away, staring at her hands.

I ran up the path. 'Where are you going?' I announced, to the next person I saw. 'Where are you going?' I said, to the trees and the monkeys. 'Wait!' I thought, remembering the girl. I ran back down the hill.

The next day I went around to Leeza and Narayana's to say goodbye.

'I'm leaving,' I said. 'I'm heading up North.'

Narayana nodded wisely. He seemed to have forgotten about my request for initiation into the path of Kriya yoga.

'Yeah, man,' he said. 'You've got your own thing. Keep it going.'

'It was fun to meet you,' I said.

'It was fun to meet you too, Saladin.' I hugged them and climbed into my rickshaw.

'I love you man,' called Narayana, as the taxi pulled away. I watched him put his arm around Leeza.

'I love you, too,' I said.

Notes To Anyone, Pessimists Included

Central Bangalore

I watch ladies do earnest laps of the park in their brightly coloured saris and leggings. One in particular keeps coming around and around, a serious, almost fanatical look on her face, in her pink traditional costume and Nikes – studiously ignoring us as we sit talking on the bench, laughing. She must have come around seven times.

I'm now the helpless recipient of hospitality – breakfast pressed on me at 8 a.m. when I am still half asleep, my host brings me things and stands in front of me as I eat, asking how it is. They eat breakfast later; have a proper brunch. I sit helplessly while the family goes about its business, the Brahmin mother ignoring me, the father quaking back and forth from his study, his head covered in chalky paint.

Tamil Nadu

The ashram. Outnumbered by women being calm, talking about spiritual stuff. It's driving me crazy. Savita (original name Jude Butler) is talking about Pranayama. What is it? I ask. She can't believe I haven't heard of it. She's been practising it for months – breathing practice she explains. I'm being polite, soft-spoken. Suddenly I feel claustrophobic, trapped: the notion of an endless succession of retreats, therapies and practices – without end.

Give me a simple life, where my imperfections can dissolve at their own pace! Enough of the constant voyage, the spiritual seekers, the insecurity of travel and not-belonging which brings out all my fears and anxieties. Am I to be perfect?

When will I feel happy and secure, and things always flowing? I keep thinking, haven't I got there yet? Must this go on for ever?

I start to do breathing exercises myself. Savita teaches me some Pranayama to try out in my own time.

I decide not to join the others as they start a meditation retreat. I am alone in the ashram. I lie on my bed and watch the fan go around through the mosquito net. There's nothing particular I want to do, I'm just sort of listless. I let some ideas play in my head, then let them drop. It's only 7.30 and I have the whole evening ahead of me. Not so long ago I would have felt tormented by the time-passing-and-life-slipping-past thought, or the feeling-left-out thought, or the I-made-a-mistake torment. But not now. Still, I could by no stretch be described as joyful. I play with a few ideas. I could walk up to the main road and buy a cigarette but I know it wouldn't do much for me. I could run into town and look for friends, but I'm too lazy.

So I walk to the tiny hamlet behind the ashram and a little naked girl guides me through paddy fields and flower plantations to the internet village place which I had heard about. I find myself in a magical Indian farmstead under the hill and meet an English woman who built a house there facing the mountains after twenty-two years travelling and working at Mother Teresa's House of the Dying in Calcutta and studying with a guru who taught her how to use mantras. He was staying with her today, she said, and his return was imminent. However, after a fresh glass of lemon and jaggery, a broken cigarette and the story of her life, I was off.

Still I reach for snacks and consolations, eating from a jar of peanut butter and Danish plum preserve. These small crutches, I have still to let go.

It's pretty clear my way is not spectacular yoga, supernatural powers, perfection. The idea of spending the next twenty years following gurus, travelling etc., *No! Quicker please.*

No big Enlightenment. Enough already.

I am finally learning the trick – to observe my thoughts, feelings, and leave it at that. I don't give them a second thought, and I don't believe them. I leave them on the jungle floor and I soar above the trees.

Metaphorically speaking.

21

In psychiatry there is a certain condition known as
'delusion of reprieve'. The condemned man, immediately before his execu-
tion, gets the illusion that he might be reprieved at the very last minute.
We, too, clung to shreds of hope and believed to the last moment that it
would not be so bad . . . Nearly everyone in our transport lived under the
illusion that he would be reprieved, that everything would yet be well.

Viktor Frankl

'Most people tend to be nostalgic about the past,' said Murthy, tapping his pencil neatly on the table. 'They think the past was better; people had better values and so on. But my belief is the opposite.'

We were sitting in the coolness of Mr Murthy's air-conditioned empire, one of the biggest technology companies in the world. Murthy – now among the richest men in India – was a small man in milk-bottle glasses who smiled modestly and answered my questions with precise consideration. He was renowned for his idealism and kindness, as well as for transforming the fortunes of the Indian software industry single-handedly. What impressed me, though, was the coffee. It was freshly ground and came in proper china mugs. After six weeks in India, this was an emotional moment.

I had just finished a tour of Murthy's headquarters,

in a dazzlingly clean golf caddy. The carless, tree-lined avenues of the Infosys complex were dotted with twenty-something, clean-cut, executives. I took in the volleyball court and the free canteens and the saplings planted by Bill Gates and Tony Blair. This was all as it should be, I reflected. It was as if a section of North California had been cut and pasted right into the middle of India, except without the casual atmosphere. The gardens and the sports facilities were empty. The sound of Bangalore's demented traffic echoed softly over the walls.

'My belief is the opposite,' repeated Murthy, in his small, sober office. 'Yes, and I'll tell you why. I see that younger people are more idealistic, have better values, are ready to make more sacrifices than we were in our time. Each generation is better than the last one.'

'That's what I believe, too.'

'When I was a student,' he continued, 'I rarely came across youngsters doing social work – I'm talking about the 1960s, 1970s. But today at Infosys we have literally hundreds, in some cases thousands of employees, who want to contribute to the work of our charitable foundation. Even in the West, it's the same. I have spoken at business schools all over the world: Stanford, Harvard, Wharton, Kellogg. There is a great desire to make a difference.'

I settled back in my chair. Murthy was right. Even if the universe was entirely illusory, society was evolving, getting better all the time. Although India happened to be going through a particularly annoying phase of capitalism right now – piles of discarded plastic bottles, concrete hotels and yuppies in SUVs playing Kylie Minogue at full volume – eventually the whole world, including the open sewers of Bangalore and the illiterate rickshaw drivers queuing up outside, would reach the same level of air-conditioned clarity as Murthy and myself.

As long as I didn't have to get too close to them in the meantime.

'In my opinion,' said Murthy, 'relating to society is extremely important if you want to succeed. I don't know any business that has lasted long without the goodwill of society.'

'Yes,' I said, 'although companies with traditional organisational structures may not be able to replicate these attributes.' I was about to explain Google's model of non-hierarchical management when Murthy shook his head.

'I think it is possible,' he said, gently touching his frosted water glass. 'I'll tell you why. If we respect each other; if we smile at each other, if we shake hands with each other, then the lowest-level employee will feel as enthusiastic about the company as the highest-level employee. And when the lowest-level employee is as enthusiastic as the highest then there is a sense of owner-ship, a sense of hope, a sense of optimism. It doesn't matter what kind of business you run.'

I returned to the commotion of Bangalore, encour-aged by Murthy's optimistic view of the world. Illusion or not, it was good to know that it was an illusion with a future. The anti-globalisers might complain about pollu-tion, sweatshops and abuse of the environment; what they didn't realise was how many Indians could now afford Ray-Bans.

A lorry roared past me without warning, almost severing my arm. A family of six on a moped whistled into the gap, two centimetres between a ditch and the juggernaut. Chicken feathers exploded off the back of a bus. I cursed and tried to keep my balance. All this humanity – it was actually quite horrible when you saw it up close. Luckily, the natural progress of free market capitalism would soon empty these streets of uninsured

truck drivers and dangerous rickshaws and Bangalore
might start to resemble modern San Francisco.

Until then I didn't want to be anywhere near it.

I passed the open sewer of a river, channelled between
two concrete banks. A hellish pong of shit rose to meet
me. *Sweet Jesus!* I thought. *There are people there.* Children,
picking through the rubbish on the banks of the canal. I
could hardly stand the smell a hundred metres away. I
thought about Ashley Judd in the slums of Mumbai. 'The
day I went there was the best day of my life,' she said.

'Go away!' I shouted. 'Get out of there!' I stumbled
towards them, along the concrete bank, gagging as I
covered my mouth. The kids stared. There was industrial
waste all over the ground. 'You shouldn't be here,' I barked.
I made frantic gestures with my arms. A volley of honks
raked my ear. A 4x4, blasting its horn, almost shouldered
me off the bank. I turned in time to catch the drivers in
freeze-frame, staring at me – a look of shock on their faces.
Something slipped. I thrashed the air. I went shirt-first
into the shit.

I was shoulder-deep in slime.

That was the end between me and modern India. Ignoring
Narayana's advice that the mountains were lonely and
dangerous, I travelled to the Himalayas to find a house to
rent. If it weren't for Zara I wouldn't be in India at all, but
so long as we were both here I needed to find somewhere
safe where I could work. It was time to draw my search
for optimism to a close.

I found a guesthouse in a hill station called
Dharamshala, the home in exile of the Dalai Lama. It was
bitterly cold, empty of tourists and the perfect place to

hide. With Buddhists everywhere I would have no temptation to leave my room.

Above us the gold-tinted sunshine glided timelessly across the peaks. Below, a small village full of empty hotels. Up here, among the boulders, I could work on my book without further interruption.

I locked the door of my room and spread my papers out on the desk. After a year of meeting optimists I had hundreds of pages of notes, fifty or sixty interviews, seven notebooks and twenty-three mini-disks full of thoughts and ideas to synthesise into a perfect argument against pessimism. It was vital I get the book written before returning to England. I had no money left, no home to return to and a CV which had expired in the late 1990s. If I didn't come back to London with something to show for my year of travelling then I was as good as ruined.

What I needed now was proof.

I closed the curtains and lit a candle on the windowsill. On one hand, I realised, optimism was a thing almost impossible to prove. On the other hand – whether the mechanism was psychological, mystical or governed by unknown laws of the universe – I was quite sure I had figured out how it worked. After all my complicated theories, it turned out to be simple: as long as you are truly confident and trusting, you can make anything happen. But you can only be confident and trusting when you don't care. And you can't pretend you don't care when you do. It was a Catch-22. As Dr Wong might put it, it was paradoxical. The Holy Grail was to figure out how to trick the system – how to care without caring. In other words, how to really wish for something while pretending not to mind if you didn't get it. None of the books had an answer for that. It really stumped me, because if you don't care about the outcome, then why would you bother wanting it in the first place? Was it even possible? I wasn't sure.

That night I filled another scrap of paper with biro.

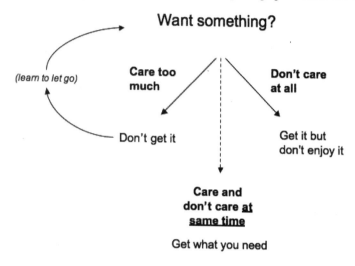

Want something?

(learn to let go)

Care too much — **Don't get it**

Don't care at all — Get it but don't enjoy it

Care and don't care <u>at same time</u>

Get what you need

Scraps of paper were now my only hope.

Then, slowly, as I thought about it, something dawned on me: everything I had done over the last two years had been done to test this question out. The book, the meetings, the whole story with Zara. It had all been an experiment. And the results were still unknown. Either Zara would come back to me and Bill Clinton would agree to meet – or they wouldn't. Optimism would stand or fall on that alone. And so would my career.

The lady who ran the guesthouse brought me a cup of tea. I thanked her, closed the door and carried on with my work. In the morning, before it got light, I crept outside and went for a walk along the ridge of the lower hill. I thought about my report, and my state of mind, and Bill Clinton. These days I thought a lot about Bill Clinton. Of course, there was no question of my *not* meeting him. It was just a question of when. And *how*.

Over the course of the next few days I tried the whole range of techniques. I tried thinking about him, I tried not thinking about him, I tried sending emails, I tried not sending emails. I took to planning our interview as if it were about to take place. I pictured myself in a room with the President, reading my questions out from a notebook. I copied a photo of him onto my website. Weeks passed. I worked on my book and tried to forget about him. Nothing happened. Spring passed into summer. The mountains started to shed their coat of ice and blossom into life. Travellers arrived from the South to set up bars and yoga workshops. Rhododendrons bloomed across the hillside and villagers walked past the guesthouse, their voices echoing off the boulders as they advertised mangoes from baskets on their heads. I was starting to feel hopeful. Then, four weeks after sending my last email, I finally got a reply.

Dear Mr Shorter

On behalf of President Bill Clinton, I would like to thank you for your interest in requesting his partici-pation in your forthcoming book.

Unfortunately, due to the high volume of worthy inquiries that he receives, as well as the tremendous demands on his time, President Clinton is unable to con-tribute to as many of these requests as he would like.

President Clinton and I wish you all the best and success in this work and your future endeavors. We appreciate your understanding.

I looked at it for a long time. Nowhere did the email actually say that the President wouldn't contribute to my book. It was simply a general statement about how busy he was. It was a test, I thought, another test of my persistence and courage.

That night a storm came down off the mountains, dumping blankets of ice into the garden, cutting the flowers in half. I sat in candlelight, watching the hailstones bounce off the roof in wild arcs, like bullets shot by madmen. It was incredibly beautiful.

Next morning, thick beds of clover had filled the footpaths of the mountain. *Clover!* I thought. It was a sign. In the watery light of dawn I scanned the ground for four-leaf clovers. If I could find a lucky clover then maybe everything would be OK after all. I searched and searched, until I got hungry. Supposing I *believed* that I would find one? 'If positive thinking works,' I said out loud, 'then let me find a four-leaf clover.' The rest of that morning I scoured the garden and the paths around the house. Nothing. I wasn't playing by the rules. The rules were to forget about the outcome. If I could care about the clover and also not care about it at the same time, *that* was the point. I put it out of my mind.

I was roused by a knock on my door. It was the Swiss lady from the neighbouring guesthouse. She had borrowed my gas cooker for a few days. Now she was bringing it back.

'Thank you!' she said. She gave me a hug.

'You're welcome,' I smiled.

'Wait.' She opened her wallet and reached inside. 'I have a gift for you.' She pulled out a dark green leaf. 'I found it on the road this morning.'

I regarded it, dumbfounded. 'Thank you,' I mumbled. 'Thank you very much.'

I closed the door, the clover in my hand. 'It works,' I whispered. 'It actually works.' The sun was out, the birds were singing. Suddenly, anything seemed possible.

Outside there was a commotion in the yard. The owner's dog was on heat and all the strays had come to the yard, yelping and biting. I watched with admiration as a bouncy spaniel went for her, running up and down the rocks. She barked him away, and the other dogs joined in. The landlady smiled, approvingly. Apparently he got the same welcome every year. The spaniel kept coming back for more, heroically stalking her from the lawn and then jumping up again to try his luck. He was a good-looking dog, and his hair bounced jauntily as he leapt up, again and again, to her rock garden – like a canine Count of Montecristo. There was no look of dismay on his face, no resentment, anger or discouragement, just a kind of focus . . . enjoyment even.

That's the way.

My mobile rang. It was Zara, her voice distant and sweet. My spine shivered as if it had been expecting this moment all month. Everything was connected. Surely the time had come. I had done my work, been faithful and unflagging, finished my journey, changed utterly – and now the universe was bringing us back together again. All would be forgiven.

I smiled to myself. Everything I had worked for, everything I believed in; it had all been true. Justice would be done! I looked dreamily at the peaks. Zara was coming up North to join me in the mountains . . .

'That's wonderful,' I said tranquilly. 'It will be wonderful to see you.' I listened while she talked. There was something else she wanted to say.

'You're with someone?' I laughed. 'I . . . I don't understand.' Suddenly the ground seemed far away. 'What do you mean, *someone*?' I tried to keep my voice steady. 'You're travelling *together*?' I felt my heart contract. 'Is it a . . . physical thing?' There were icicles in my legs. 'Right. Right. Of course. Well, thanks – thanks for telling me.'

I put down the phone and walked outside. My body felt delicate, tired. I moved cautiously. A rock dislodged under my foot and rolled down into the canyon. It split into fragments and scattered down the slope. I watched it.

'It's over,' I said, at last. 'It's finally over.' The fragments bounded out of sight.

The next morning I woke early and sat down at my desk. It was just me and the book now. Nothing else. I watched some ants disassemble a fly. I had weeks of work ahead of me.

Keep going, Laurence.

I glanced through the window above my desk. Out in the boulders there was a local kid sitting up in the rhododendron tree. He was picking flowers and throwing them down to his sister. They were laughing; the sun was shining on their faces. I watched him for a while, then I looked back down at my computer.

'I don't have to do this,' I said suddenly. 'I don't have to do this any more.'

22

Teach us to care and not to care
Teach us to sit still

T S Eliot

My father met me at the airport. 'Welcome back!' he said.
'How's the masterpiece?'
'It's over,' I said. 'I'm not doing it any more.'
He looked at me, surprised. 'Well, don't give up.'
Giving up was exactly my intention. My proof had failed.
The experiment was over: optimism was not something
you could control. The lesson from India was clear: either
you feel positive and relaxed about something, or you don't.
Either way, you have no choice. All that life requires of you
is to lie down and wait while it strips away your preten-
sions and leaves you with nothing.
Then at least you can relax.
I sat in my father's flat and stared at the ceiling. It looked
like any of the dozen ceilings I had stared at over the last
six months: the Jet Airways departure lounge in Mumbai,
my hotel in Delhi, the ceiling of my room in the mountains. For a moment I wondered if I had got stuck in some
kind of endless loop, a sort of psychic waiting room, where
I was doomed to stay until the end of time. Waiting – that's

what I was doing. Waiting to be rescued. But there was no one coming. It was just me. Me and the ceiling.

'Hello?' I said. 'Hello?'

I turned to look out the window like an invalid with a slipped disc.

It's sunny, I thought. *It's very warm.*

I don't even feel that tired.

I sat up. It was the gratitude exercise. I was doing it by accident.

I scanned my father's room. My clothes, folded neatly on the chair; my suitcase, sitting faithfully in the corner; the window, guarding me from the street – strong enough to keep out noise and wind, but transparent enough to see through! I felt my heart swell with appreciation.

That evening I started doing writing exercises to flush out my negative beliefs. If I was going to spend the next sixty years with myself then I would have to get comfortable with my own mind. I had given up on dissolving my fears, getting to the bottom of them, or otherwise removing them from my life. I figured it was enough to write them down and see them plainly for what they were.

loser . . . failure, reject . . . old
too old!
running out of time, alone, ALONE
DEATH

I panted, satisfied. My inner pessimist was still alive and kicking.

My father would be proud.

I decided it was time to emerge. I had been back for a week and I still hadn't seen a soul. I arranged to meet Mark for a drink. I had been dreading this moment for months. I hadn't seen Mark – or any of my friends – since before leaving for California. He would be expecting a progress report. I walked quickly to the pub. What would he think when I told him I had abandoned my book? Would he even want to speak to me? It was a pitiful thing to admit.

When I got there Mark was already at the bar, looking sturdy and full of life. 'How's it going, Loz!'

'Great!' I said.

He punched me on the arm. 'How's the optimism?'

'It's fine . . .' I looked into my drink. 'Actually,' I stumbled. 'I'm wondering if I might have . . . It's quite possible that I . . .'

'What, Loz?'

I steeled my nerves. 'I think I might have failed.'

'Don't be ridiculous!'

I looked away. 'The thing is, Mark, I was *wrong* about optimism.' I squinted in the sunlight. 'Positive thinking, looking on the bright side . . . they're just strategies – strategies to protect us from reality.'

Mark looked worried. 'Is there something wrong with that?'

'It doesn't even work!' I said. 'We worry about the future and we live in fear, and we spend all our time believing that we're going somewhere. But we're not going anywhere! This is it.' I looked down at my half lager. 'This is as good as it gets.'

'That's not very optimistic, Loz.'

'And that's why I did this whole project! Because I wanted to get somewhere. Well, I've finished. Game over.' I looked out the window. Well. I would lose friends, that was inevitable.

'But optimism can be very healthy,' protested Mark. 'Optimists live longer, they have better sex.'

'*True* optimism,' I said, 'is just the absence of fear. You stop being afraid because you know that nothing can change

you. Even the thing you feared the most in the world . . .'
I looked at my hands. 'It's not that bad. You're still alive.'

'Oh,' said Mark.

'That's true optimism,' I said. 'But it's nothing revolutionary. It's just what you have when everything else is gone;
you know, real life, the present moment, all that stuff.' I
sighed. 'Actually it's what Leibniz originally defined as optimism back in the eighteenth century: everything is already
perfect because it couldn't be any better. He proved it mathematically. And then everyone laughed at him.' I stared,
resigned, at the bubbles in my glass.

Mark looked mystified. 'Why don't you write about that?'

'No one wants to know about that!'

I looked at my watch. Any moment now Mark would
make his excuses, leave early, meet another friend. That was
fine. I was ready for it. I pictured myself in years to come;
sitting in this pub, growing quietly old, the parties and the
action elsewhere.

'You're so funny, Loz.' Mark punched me gleefully. 'It's
great to see you again.'

I looked at him with surprise. 'What do you mean?'

He stood up. 'I mean, let's get some lunch!'

On my way home I collided, head-on, with a man in a
tweed jacket. The man laughed heartily, and apologised.

'Wait a minute . . .' I said. 'Don't I know you?'

'Steve Brooks,' said the man, holding out his hand.

'You're the explorer,' I said. 'We met at that party.'

'Yes,' he said. 'I remember! We were going to talk about
optimism.'

Steve was the man I had met in the autumn whose
helicopter had crashed into the Antarctic. His rugged face

glowed with enthusiasm, as if he were still overwhelmed by the good luck of being alive. 'Well, I'm not in any hurry,' he said. 'Shall we grab a drink?'

Why not? I thought. There was nowhere else I was going.

We found a café.

'So!' He clapped his hands. 'Optimism!'

'Yes,' I said, wearily. 'Well, a lot has changed. Anyway . . . I seem to remember . . . Didn't you tell me that *optimism saved your life?*'

'Absolutely!' said Steve. 'If we had had one negative thought, like *we're not going to be saved*, we would have died. It's as simple as that. We were in freezing water for eleven hours.'

'Eleven hours!' I craned forward. 'You didn't have a *single* negative thought in all that time?'

Steve ordered a drink, grinned at the waiter, and cracked his knuckles. 'The whole adventure would have been impossible without optimism. If you were pessimistic, starting it in the first place would have been a ridiculous idea.'

'Because it's dangerous?'

'Yes, hugely!'

Steve doubled over with laughter, as if he had no say in the matter.

'So, tell me what happened.'

'We're in the Antarctic Sea, in a life raft, we're hundreds of miles from human life, and the water's zero degrees!'

'Are you freezing to death?'

'Yes, but you don't pick up on that. There isn't a feeling that you're about to die. There's a feeling that, in order to survive, *this* has to happen, then *that* has to happen. *We have to get in that life raft. We have to use the satellite phone.* Everything was one step at a time.'

Steve cradled his teacup. 'The first thing was to get a

call in. I tried the rescue services in Chile, but there was no answer. And then a wave came over and the lights went out on the phone. Then they came back on again. And I thought *there's just one person to call*, and that's my wife. She was asleep in Clapham at the time.'

'Clapham!'

'Yes. So I rang and said, have you got a pen? And she said, yes. My wife said, leave it with me, and at that point another wave came over and the phone just went *out*. So we were now out of contact with the outside world. And now I get to the main point . . . .' He splayed his weatherbeaten fingers on the table. '. . . that the only way of living in such ridiculous circumstances is *utter and complete optimism*. Nothing but.'

'Optimism.'

'Yes. *There was never anything else.* There was not one single moment in the entire eleven-hour experience when I remember having a single negative thought. Just the start of a *thread* would have been enough. That's all you need, just the start of a thread and that possibility could have become a reality.'

I left my tea untouched.

'Whatever thread you start,' he said, 'is what reality is going to be. All reality is just something you thought of originally.'

'You're saying your thoughts create reality.'

'Exactly! It made me very aware of my control over my own destiny.'

I circled the table with my hand. I had hoped that the file on positive thinking was closed. But now, here was Steve Brooks, telling me that it worked – a practical man, an entrepreneur, someone who had faced death and was still laughing about it.

'You *knew* you were going to be saved. Right? You had a feeling.'

'Yes,' he exclaimed. 'But that's the thing. We had no basis for knowing it. The odds against us being rescued were tiny. *We decided not to die.*'

I felt the air quiver on my temples. 'You *decided . . .*'

'But I haven't finished the story,' he said. 'The pilot was out looking for us and he couldn't find us, and I could hear the engine, but it was too far away, and I just remember sitting on the edge of the life raft, looking at the sky and talking to the pilot and just saying, *you will, very shortly, fly right over the top of this life raft.* There's no rush, but you are going to fly right over the top of this life raft. I sat for an hour saying this. And about an hour later there was a noise and this plane came towards me, and he was right over the top of us. Some people would say that's ridiculous. Personally, I don't believe, *I know*, that I was involved in making that happen.'

'Optimism,' I said.

'It's everything!' he laughed. 'Everything. First you think something, *then it happens.*'

'But this was an extreme situation,' I said. 'What about ordinary life?'

'The same! There is just more commotion going on in everyday life. There's more noise and it becomes harder to filter out and harder to spot the simplicity of the situation. It's only in moments like this – fighting for survival in ice cold water – that all the noise stops and it becomes absolutely clean. Absolutely clean!'

I watched the sunlight moving across the table. Maybe I had been wrong about optimism. Maybe I *did* have a choice. And if I had a choice, then what did that mean?

'These "threads",' I said, 'you can't *control* them, can you? They just happen.' I thought about my search for the four-leaf clover. I thought about my fears and agonies with Zara. I didn't seem to have any say in these matters at all.

'*You just don't let the negative ones in,*' said Steve. 'That's why it's so vital to keep starting positive ones. So there's no room for the negative ones.' He shook his cup. 'In every single waking moment you have the choice – positive or negative – trust or fear. You always have that choice.'

Or could I choose them both? I thought of Wong's paradox of optimism and pessimism. Was that the key? Accept my thoughts and control them – *at the same time?* I felt my brain starting to spin. *Maybe it was possible.*

Steve waved for the bill. 'The trouble is,' he said, 'in life, you've got to keep going. You've got to keep making new games.'

'What?' I said. 'What about staying still?'

'In this universe nothing stays the same. Plutonium 326 is the most stable thing in this universe and even that has a half life, it's forever getting less. In other words, if you're not getting bigger, you're getting smaller. If it isn't getting better, it is getting worse. You see? The skill is to keep starting new threads. You cannot be resting in life. There is nowhere to rest.' He shook with laughter.

I watched the commuters rushing by outside.

'But we're not going anywhere,' I said. 'There's nowhere to go.'

'Maybe not,' chuckled Steve. 'But you can't be still, either. Everything is moving. I never used to understand it when they said "it's better to travel hopefully than to arrive", but now I totally do – it *is* about the journey. What is impor-tant is that when you reach your destination you must select another one, and then another one.' He paused. 'And that I think is the hard thing.'

'Because you want to have a rest?'

'Ha ha ha! Yes, because you want to rest.' He gripped his knees. 'And the sad fact of life is that there is no such thing!'

23

'Use the force, Luke.'

Star Wars

Tuesday, Greenwich.

A gusty morning. A thousand people waited around the Millennium Dome like the queue for the first Big Mac on the moon. Inside, through another door, stood a line of bankers and lawyers – grown men and women who had paid upwards of a thousand pounds to have their photo taken with the man himself.

I needed to be in that queue.

'I'd like to join the line,' I said, to the lady at the VIP gate. She looked at me and then down at her clipboard. 'You're not with Morgan Stanley,' she said.

'Not exactly.'

'Do you have a letter? You should have a letter like this.' She waved a printed document.

'No,' I said. 'I mean, I left it at home. They told me to come to this queue.'

'Who did?' asked the woman suspiciously.

'The people in the VIP lounge, over there.' I waved vaguely to where I knew there were more bankers, drinking coffee as they waited to be herded into front row seats. The rest of the queue – the plebs – eyed the VIPs with blank curiosity. Fools! They could hardly guess the bun fight that was going on to meet the great man. Taking a seat in the public gallery was my option of absolute last resort – my ticket was row H, upper circle. It was a seventy-five pound, no-lunch-included offer.

I wouldn't even see the whites of Clinton's eyes.

'There's no way, I'm afraid,' said the hostess, as groups of suits pushed past me to the security check, waving their VIP letters. The guards lugged their briefcases onto the conveyor belt. 'I'm sorry,' she said, 'some of these people have paid £3,000 to meet the President. I can't just let you in.' A bouncer loomed behind her, adding emphasis with his eyebrows.

'Can I come later?' I pleaded. 'When the queue's gone down?'

She smiled and shook her head. 'Like I said . . .'

'It's not possible,' said the bouncer.

I stared at the VIP queue – men in suits, many of them younger than me, were standing behind the cordon fiddling with Blackberries. It was a day off for them, a jolly. They looked sleek, padded. Their hair was thick and groomed. I pushed my wayward strands back into place. *Power*, I thought, breathing through my teeth.

I walked away. What would Bill Clinton have done in this situation? By the time he was my age, he had already been governor of Arkansas. Twice.

I had some catching up to do.

Five minutes later I was back. There was a different greeter on the gate.

'Who are you?'

'It's a long story,' I replied. 'Your colleague told me to come back.'

This woman was trying equally hard to be strict, but I

could feel it starting to wobble. Her strictness didn't really believe in itself.

'I'm with the BBC,' I said, glancing down at her name tag. 'And I'm writing a book. About optimism . . . *Rachel.*'

Using people's names was a Bill trick. I didn't know whether it counted as advanced optimism or just desperation. I didn't have time to care.

Rachel smiled, then caught herself. Another official appeared, this time with a list. I leant over to see if I could spot an unused name, but most of them were ticked off. 'This man is hoping for a face-to-face with the President,' said Rachel, 'but I told him there's no space left.' She checked her watch. 'Anyway the lecture will be starting in a few minutes. We're almost out of time.'

It was three minutes to twelve. I watched, helplessly, as another five suits pushed past. I felt my shoulders tense. I was here to hustle; I was here to fight the odds. I could feel the contest clutching at my veins. Panic was hovering near. *Remember why you're here!* I told myself.

I ran back to the other queue, the blood pumping through my heart.

Did I have a chance of meeting the President? Probably not. But that wasn't the point. Something had changed after my encounter with Steve. A penny had dropped: the secret of happiness was simple. You just keep going. You do things for the hell of it – no other reason. And when you know that, anything is possible. Because you know that you have nothing, that you are nothing, that you're going back to nothing – so there's nothing you can lose.

It explained so much – why Cosmic Ordering only worked sometimes (when you were having fun); why Emma Leach and Taddy Blecher and Immaculée all looked so content (because they had nothing to prove); what Akira meant about being Happy Now (because she was); and why the conclusion to my search for optimism was really just . . . what? *You have a choice?*

A choice of what?

The crowd disappeared into the main entrance. Soon the doors would close and I would miss the chance even to take the seat I had bought. I needed to think fast.

If we had had one negative thought, we would have died.

I looked back briefly towards the throng of suits at the VIP gate, then turned on my heel and headed in the opposite direction. This was it, I thought. If I really did have control over my destiny then now was the time to find out. There was a whisper in my memory – was it Immaculée, was it Caroline Myss?

You need to trust. In trusting there is a power to see the future.

Well, I needed to see it now.

I walked out of the building and into the rain.

The forecourt was empty. The air was damp like an old sailor's breath. I stood in the centre of the giant marble piazza and stared up at the cables that harnessed the dome to the marshes of Greenwich. 'Relax,' I told myself. 'Let go.' I thought about Cosmic Ordering.

One day you will know that everything you wish and need comes to you . . . Your order manifests through your belief, your trust, your lack of doubts.

Did I believe? Did I really believe? I stood in the rain and waited for my mind to empty. I would not be defeated. I checked my watch. If Barbel Mohr was right, one minute of 'letting go' was more precious than half an hour of hustling at the gate. The seconds were draining away. It was all or nothing. *No!* I thought. I don't have time for this. 'Hi!' I said. 'It's me again.' I was back at the VIP gate. It was one minute to twelve. 'Could I speak to Rachel?' The bouncer crossed his arms and glanced down at his walkie-talkie. He shook his head. 'They've all gone through now.'

He turned around to pack up the X-ray machine.

'*Last call for Bill Clinton talk,*' said the PA. '*Talk will commence in five minutes.*'

'This is very important,' I said to the security guard's back. 'I need to see Mr Clinton. If I do, it will prove that optimism works. If I don't, the pessimists win. That could be the beginning of the end. Do you have children, sir?'

The bouncer sighed and clicked on his radio. I had decided to treat the door people like human beings rather than obstacles standing in my way. That's what Taddy Blecher would have done. They were intelligent and they deserved an explanation. Rachel emerged from the now empty corridor. 'Rachel!' I cried. 'You're here!'

I told her everything I knew. I told her that Happiness = Positive Emotion + Flow + Meaning; and that Life = 100% x good + 0% x bad. I told her I was an optimist and that I would try until the bitter end. I told her she had a choice, although I wasn't exactly sure what it was yet. I could have gone on. I could have described my cosmic orders, my daily affirmations.

I am now with Bill Clinton/Bill and I are together /Bill is talking about optimism.

I could have told her about the six months I spent harassing business leaders to give me the President's details. I could have told her about my journey to New York to find him in Central Park, and the Democratic fundraiser I took out to dinner, and the cocktail parties I tried to get into. I could have told her how I fell in love with a free spirit because I was determined to be an optimist, and how we split up because I cared too much, and because I wanted to let go, and how I had nothing – *nothing* – left, not even a cent, not a job or a home, and Bill Clinton was my only hope because that was all I had – and if I could just ask him a question then maybe I wouldn't have failed, maybe the world would understand after all – and how I had made a resolution to trust the universe and let it take its course, as the only truly optimistic thing to do, but nothing had happened (nothing!) until . . .

. . . my mobile pinged.

LOZ CLINTON
TALK NXT WEEK!
BE SHARP, XANTHE

. . . and I had decided to trust it and come along and now here I was, and this was it. And how I owed it to everyone, and especially my father, and to the whole line of Shorter grandchildren going off into infinity, for ever, to meet him . . .

But then I stopped. I took a deep breath. I let my shoulders sink. There *was* a choice. And suddenly I knew what it was. I had known it all along.

A businessman rushed past, pushing into the queue. I felt the tension tightening my jaw. I stepped back. I breathed out.

I let it go.

'Just be happy now,' said Akira.

I could worry – or I could relax.
I could keep fighting – or I could let go.
Right . . . now.
It's all I had ever wanted anyway.
'I'll wait here,' I said to Rachel, moving aside.
She turned to deal with a group of lawyers, shaking rain off their coats. 'I can't find you on the list,' she told them. 'You'll have to go to the main entrance.' They argued, waving their arms. 'Can't we pay?' they said. Rachel shook her head. I stood against the wall. I thought about Steve.

I just remember sitting on the edge of the life raft, looking at the sky and talking to the pilot.

You will – I said to myself – *let me in.*
The lawyers gave up and walked off. People were rushing around. Men with walkie-talkies were closing doors. Rachel and I were finally alone. She turned to me. 'Listen, I'd like to help you. The trouble is . . .'
'Yes?' I could feel the tension returning immediately. I could feel the fear. How quickly it came back!
'You're not with any of the companies on our list.'
'Can't you just tell them I'm independently wealthy?'
'They need to send you the photo, they need your company address.'
I bit my nail. 'Wait a minute,' I said. 'I don't need the photo. What would I do with a photo? I just want to ask a question. That's all I need!'
Rachel paused, weighing up the various career-limiting implications of her next move. 'Look,' she said, 'don't tell anyone, OK? And whatever you do, don't give them your name.' She reached into her ziplock bag – it was a bag I

had been watching for over fifteen minutes – and handed me one of the VIP armbands.

'Here,' she said. 'Now go. Quick!'

The guard rushed me through the security gate and I raced up the corridor. I followed the stairs up to a dimly lit bar. *This was it.* I was a VIP. I was finally going to meet Bill Clinton, I was finally going to make it . . . Nothing would ever be the same again.

'Where's the President?' I said. There was an eerie silence. Waiters walked back and forth with empty trays. In the corner a photographer was packing up his equipment.

'Not here,' he said.

'He's gone downstairs,' said a waiter.

There was no line-up, no greeter, no one to tell me where to go.

'But I have a pass!' I said.

'Sir, the talk is starting in two minutes.'

My muscles locked. Adrenaline flowed. It wasn't enough to be optimistic once, I had to *do it again.*

Life = (Possible x .01) + (Impossible x .99)

The odds were flying all over the place.

Hope! I thought. *I am a prisoner of hope.*

I ran to the toilet. Maybe he was there? 'Have you seen the President?' An armed cop turned to me with a dangerous look. I fled the room. The photographer was still there, hauling the camera onto his shoulder. 'They're asking for more shots,' he said into his radio. 'I'll find him downstairs.'

'Who?' I asked.

'No one,' he said.

He ran off through a door and I followed his beetle-like back downstairs. Armed police and bodyguards passed us without comment. No one knew who anybody was or where they were supposed to be.

'I was told there were more photos to take,' said the cameraman, as we emerged into a brightly lit corridor. I stuck to his back and waved my armband. There were people everywhere.

And then there he was. I recognised him immediately, like an old friend. He was wearing a cream suit. Around him a circle of people – admirers, protectors. The photographer readied himself. A banker in his fifties, with the hopeful expression of a puppy, edged forward. Clinton checked his watch and swung his arm around the man's shoulder, a grin of genuine delight on his face. *Snap!* A woman edged into the frame. *Handshake-Snap!* I crept forward.

My breath was starting to go. *Handshake-Snap!* All my hopes, all my dreams, every atom of my being was concentrated towards that light cream suit.

You have a choice, I told myself. *Remember why you're here.*

A man stepped forward. His eyes were bugged with delight and fear. The power! The personality! He was touching it. A thin wash of light glowed off the walls. *Handshake-Snap!*

Clinton grinned. My face flushed hot. I went for it.

'Mr President, I have a question!'

A guard was ushering him towards the stage. I was aware of my heartbeat. Other than that, nothing.

The President glanced back. 'Are you an optimist?!' I shouted. A laugh of surprise. 'You'll find out,' he said, perhaps to me, perhaps to thin air. I watched his back disappear and felt myself being pushed away. Clinton and his cluster swirled down the corridor, like a hungry black hole. The session was over. The stage doors opened.

The President was gone.

★

I strolled down through empty corridors. Everything was quiet. I was the only living being in Greenwich who wasn't in the auditorium, waiting for Bill to talk.

I found a side door and strolled in. The auditorium was smaller than I had expected: a few hundred people, their neat suits silhouetted in the dark, a modest stage. I was the only person standing. The President took the podium. Polite applause rippled through the room. A single American flag stood illuminated at the back.

'What is the fundamental nature of the twenty-first-century world?' asked Clinton, tilting his chin amiably toward the audience. A hush fell across the seats. 'The fundamental nature of the twenty-first-century world is interdependence. Interdependence simply means we cannot escape each other. It means divorce is not an option.'

With the spotlights on his face the President looked older than I expected; his pace slower, more measured. I had a picture of Clinton as an operator, a womaniser – rushing around, drinking coffee, playing poker all night, his red face glowing in the dark. I didn't expect him to have *dignity*.

'But is interdependence a good or a bad thing?'

The orator took off his glasses and waved them over his notes. For the next thirty minutes they remained there, unwanted, as if to say: for you, this is from the heart.

'If you remember one thing I say, remember this.' He raised a relaxed finger, looking out over the crowd. 'Every single problem of the interdependent world is rooted in an imperfect sense of identity. We actually believe that our differences are more important than our common humanity!' He looked up. 'During my presidency the scientists completed their mapping of the human genome. It turns out that we share 99.9 per cent the same DNA as all human beings on this planet. But we stay fixated on the one tenth of one per cent that makes us different! That's what we obsess about. When actually we're the same.'

His hands rested lightly on the podium. 'It's my sixty-first birthday pretty soon. I don't know how I got to be so old.' The audience laughed politely. 'I was always the youngest in everything I did, and now I'm getting to be this old person. But I tell myself, at least I'm not sixty-five. And I wake up and look at myself in the mirror and I wish my hair wasn't so grey. But at least I'm still alive! We organise our minds to obsess about things that don't amount to a hill of beans.' He paused. 'Like that one tenth of one per cent.'

Clinton raised his eyebrows and sighed. 'Think about it. Think how many of you have things to let go of. It's worth thinking about in your life. I think about it every day. You be free,' he said, shaking his head like a preacher. 'You be free now.'

The talk ended. The audience applauded. The compère stepped up and brightly shook his hand. 'Well, thank you, Mr President, and may I say . . .' Clinton raised a palm. 'One last thing,' he said, 'before I go.' He gazed into the audience. 'People always ask me if I am an optimist . . .'

I felt the click of great spheres moving into place.

'I could draw you an ugly picture about climate change,' he said, 'a world without oil, AIDS. I could give you the worst-case scenario. But just recently, I spent a day in Africa, in the Olduvai range, in the Ngorongoro crater where the first human beings in the world are said to have been born. I was standing there, listening to the birds, looking at the sky, and talking to the Masai – reminding myself that I am 99.9 per cent the same as them – that I'm even 99.9 per cent the same as Nelson Mandela, which I find hard to believe. And I realised that all of human history is the story of us coming into contact in wider and wider circles and deciding over time that we are the same; that the other is one of us.'

I sat transfixed.

'If you look at all of human history, that is the story of it.' He gestured into the darkness of the auditorium. 'I wanted to leave you with that thought. I'm pretty sure it's going to be a good twenty-first century, by the way. You've got plenty to be optimistic about. There's a lot of problems, there always have been – but somehow . . .' He gave a boyish smile. '. . . we eventually get it right.'

The lights came on. I whistled softly under my breath. It was so simple. It was all so simple.

Epilogue

Summer, 2008.

I was still in bed.

I turned and stared, bleary-eyed, at the radio. The newscaster was tucking into the morning's spread of happy news: an earthquake in Peru, a massacre in Kurdistan . . . 500 dead, 300 missing. His voice became tense as he delivered the next item: '*Russia has resumed long-range bomber patrols over NATO territory. Russian bombers will be able to attack the US at a moment's notice.*'

I felt the shadow of the Cold War cross my bed, darkening the room. It was just like the old days. World War Three could break out at any moment.

I turned on my side and stared at the wall, willing myself to climb out of bed. I had spent more than two years searching for reasons to feel good about the world, and nothing had really changed. People were still behaving like idiots, in spectacularly dangerous ways.

But something had happened.

My legs swung neatly to the floor. My body stretched and lifted itself to the window. I looked at the radio. 'Enough from you!' I switched it off and walked to the kitchen.

Strange, I thought. *I'm out of bed.*

I shaved and ironed a shirt. I looked through the notes

for my book. I'd have to finish it in my spare time. Tomorrow I was starting a new job. The job was for Virgin Unite, the charitable foundation of Richard Branson. Amazingly, it turned out that Branson worked with Taddy Blecher *and* Desmond Tutu on Virgin Unite. Three of my best optimists in the same place. Did I have any idea this would happen? No, I just answered a call from a recruitment agency. It seemed the universe was even more cunning than I had thought.

That evening I drove round to my father's new flat. He had moved in with his girlfriend, and the old boxes were finally being unpacked. I waited as he tidied the papers in his study. A warm dusk light fell on his desk.

'So, Dad,' I said, as he put on his coat to go out, 'are you still a pessimist?'

'Oh, yes,' he said, 'I'm afraid your attempt has failed!'

I felt a surge of relief. 'Actually, I'm glad.'

'Having said that,' he said, 'something funny happened to me yesterday. I woke up and wrote out a whole screed of just *the* most negative pessimistic stuff. Then I read it and I thought . . . *This is just crap!*'

I giggled involuntarily.

'And it's not even true!' he said.

'I realised, I don't need this! I deleted it all.'

He rolled his eyes and shook himself. 'And you? Are you still an optimist? I suppose you must be.'

'Hmm!' I thought for a moment. 'Not really. But also 100 per cent. Does that make sense?'

'No.'

He laughed, and I followed him into the street. It was a warm evening.

'What about the Jump out of Bed Factor?' he asked. 'Did you find that, at least?'

'The JBF . . .' It hadn't crossed my mind for months.

'Actually, yes. As long as I pay attention to what I eat, avoid coffee, don't drink on an empty stomach, and get enough sleep . . . I usually feel fine.'

'It sounds so simple,' said Dad. 'One wonders what all the fuss was about.'

'One wonders,' I agreed.

'And Zara?' he asked, tentatively.

'Oh, Zara . . .' We passed the shimmering water of a canal. 'She's in Brazil now. She's supposed to come and stay with me over the summer.'

'Are you . . . ?'

'Oh, no . . . oh, definitely not!'

Zara.

'Breaking up with Zara . . .' I started. 'It's hard to explain. That's how I learned, Dad . . . that's how I learned *optimism*. And it's such a relief!'

I looked at the London sky, the cars passing on the High Street. 'I guess I just realised . . . there's always going to be dark and light. We'll always make mistakes. There's *always* going to be bad news. Some things will get better, and some things will get worse. That's OK. It doesn't bother me any more. You just have to keep the plates spinning. Things are OK as they are.'

'We must cultivate our garden,' said my father.

'Yeah,' I said, opening the door to the restaurant.

A menu arrived, together with some worried-looking olives. I picked up a napkin. 'Optimism is a lot of things,' I said. 'The most important thing I've learnt is that none of it matters, at all. Not even a tiny little bit.'

'Aha,' said Dad. 'You've finally figured it out!'

Acknowledgements

Thank you to everyone who gave their time and input to this book, and all who shared their wisdom whether it is printed here or not. For making the book possible I owe special thanks to Myrna van der Zee, without whose time and love the book would never be finished. Also thanks to Malcolm Alexander, Justin and Julia Marozzi, Candida Clark, Robert Norton, Heloise, Xanthe, Alex Hickman, Ned Cranborne, Anne Jenkin, Gordon Wise, and everyone whose house and hospitality I enjoyed on my travels – Thorold and Jenny Barker, Seb Doggart, Ruma and Simon, Pavita and Carter, Antoine Briand, Rachmat and Halima Martin, Crispin and Rachel Jameson, Pierre Thaler and family, George Langworthy, my brothers Matthew and Alaric and my sister-in-law Sarah. I give thanks to my father for his patience and good humour and to my mother for her never-ending confidence and belief. Thanks also to Eliza and Lauren for their friendship and support in India, to my friends Rupert and Stephen, and to all those optimists who agreed to talk to me spontaneously, or whose story was too perfect for this imperfect book – in particular to Jonathan Aitken, Diana Witts, Harold Pinter, Wayne Dyer, Caroline Myss, Andrew Solomon, Lynn Grocott, Melissa Moody, Njorabe, Toyen Fyncountry and Ayatollah Mesbah Yazdi for their time and generosity in answering my questions. Thanks finally to Stephanie and Dan at Canongate for their thorough and perfect finishing, to Nick for his calm and steady hand, and to everyone else along the way who believed that optimism was worth a shot.